Arnaud Lechevalier, Jan Wielgohs (eds.)
Borders and Border Regions in Europe

Political Science | Volume 15

Arnaud Lechevalier, Jan Wielgohs (eds.)
Borders and Border Regions in Europe
Changes, Challenges and Chances

[transcript]

Bibliographic Information published by the Deutsche Nationalbibliothek
The Deutsche Nationalbibliothek lists this publication in the Deutsche Nationalbibliografie; detailed bibliographic data are available in the Internet at http://dnb.d-nb.de

© 2013 transcript Verlag, Bielefeld

All rights reserved. No part of this book may be reprinted or reproduced or utilized in any form or by any electronic, mechanical, or other means, now known or hereafter invented, including photocopying and recording, or in any information storage or retrieval system, without permission in writing from the publisher.

Cover layout: Kordula Röckenhaus, Bielefeld
Proofread by: Scott Stock Gissendanner, Jan Wielgohs
Typeset by: Mark-Sebastian Schneider, Bielefeld
Printed by: Majuskel Medienproduktion GmbH, Wetzlar
ISBN 978-3-8376-2442-7

Content

Introduction
Jan Wielgohs and Arnaud Lechevalier | 9

THEORETICAL PERSPECTIVES ON BORDERS

Border Types and Bordering Processes
A Theoretical Approach to the EU/Polish-Ukrainian Border
as a Multi-dimensional Phenomenon
Bastian Sendhardt | 21

Qualities of Bordering Spaces
A Conceptual Experiment with Reference to
Georg Simmel's Sociology of Space
Sabrina Ellebrecht | 45

EUROPEAN BORDER REGIONS AS "LABORATORIES" FOR CROSS-BORDER COOPERATION

Euroregions
Emerging New Forms of Cross-Border Cooperation
Barbara A. Despiney Zochowska | 71

Territorial Cohesion and Border Areas
Roswitha Ruidisch | 95

IDENTITIES AND STEREOTYPES IN EUROPEAN BORDER REGIONS

Identities and Stereotypes in Cross-Border Regions
Antje Schönwald | 113

Between Borders
France, Germany, and Poland in the Debate on Demarcation and Frontier Crossing in the Context of the Schengen Agreement
Angela Siebold | 129

Cultural Distinction and the Example of the "Third East German Generation"
Jaqueline Flack | 145

VIEWS ON THE HISTORY OF POLISH-GERMAN BORDER REGIONS

Anthropology of Borders and Frontiers
The Case of the Polish-German Borderland (1945-1980)
Agata Ładykowska and Paweł Ładykowski | 159

The Dynamics of Unfamiliarity in the German-Polish Border Region in 1970s, 1980s, and 1990s
Bianca Szytniewski | 183

Historical Culture and Territoriality
Social Appropriation in the German-Polish Border Region in the 19th and 20th Centuries
Thomas Serrier | 201

The View of French Diplomacy on the German-Polish Border Shift, 1940-1950
Eloi Piet | 217

CROSS-BORDER INTERACTION IN EUROPE'S NEIGHBOURHOOD

**Borders, De Facto Borders and
Mobility Policies in Conflict Transformation**
The Cases of Abkhazia and South Ossetia
Giulia Prelz Oltramonti | 237

"Good fences make..."
The Separation Fence in Israel and its Influence on Society
Simon Falke | 255

Authors | 267

Introduction*

Jan Wielgohs and Arnaud Lechevalier

Border studies involve scientific research on the creation, perception, destabilization, relocation, transgression, opening, or dissolution of borders. Since the 1980s, they have advanced to prominence within many academic disciplines and in a broad variety of interdisciplinary endeavors. The rise of border studies during the last twenty to thirty years can be attributed mostly to the acceleration of globalization processes since the 1980s and the end of the Cold War in 1990 (see Sendhardt in this volume). Conventionally, we think of borders as territorial borders between nation states or state-like political entities such as the European Union. However, globalization has made these kinds of borders increasingly permeable for people, goods, capital, social practices, ideas, symbols etc. On the one hand, territorial borders have lost some of their salience as separators and dividers because new spaces for economic, political, administrative, and cultural cooperation have been created (see Albert/Brock 2001: 33). On the other hand, because the increasing permeability of territorial borders has been accompanied by uncertainty about the perceived and real destabilizing effects of economic competition, migration, and multiculturalism, there has been a reactivation of "national 'policies' as well as processes of exclusion based on culture, nation, or ethnicity" (EUV 2012: 9). These ambiguous and puzzling effects of globalization lay behind the current burgeoning of contemporary border studies, first in the USA, where the new

---

* The editors wish to thank the *Deutsch-Französische Hochschule – Université franco-allemande* for its support of the project on French-German cooperation, on which the present volume is based, as well as the *Centre Marc Bloch*, Berlin, for promoting this publication. Our special thanks go also to Scott Stock Gissendanner for his work in proofreading and editing the manuscripts.

dynamics of the US-Mexican border attracted the attention of social scientists and cultural anthropologists. In this context, new conceptual and analytical perspectives on borders were developed and authors eventually went beyond the traditional, static understanding of territorial borders as separators to pay more attention to the social practices that continually create and recreate symbolic borders or the varied spatial dimensions of physical borders (ibid: 10).

The end of the Cold War unexpectedly opened new opportunities for overcoming the territorial borders that separated east from west. These borders insulated Eastern European societies from global developments and clove the European continent. But the borders that had served as barriers before 1989 changed thereafter into zones of contact in which new opportunities for cross-border mobility and cooperation emerged. At the same time, the collapse of the imperial power structure of the Cold War left some geopolitical disorder in the region, which gave rise to "spontaneous" processes of territorial restructuring in Europe as national borders were redrawn either by negotiation as in Czechoslovakia or by violence as in Yugoslavia and some of the post-Soviet territories. The eastern enlargement of the EU (2004/7) and the European Neighborhood Policy (launched in 2004), despite having been driven also by the internal logic of European integration (Vobruba 2008), can be understood as part of a strategy to reduce the disorder and uncertainty created by the end of the old east-west conflict. These policies of integration and stabilization were inevitably accompanied by significant "rebordering" processes as the EU's external border rolled eastward. Moreover, The Russian-Georgian war of 2008 as well as the lingering conflicts in Abkhazia, South Ossetia, Transnistria, and Nagorno Karabakh clearly indicate that territorial restructuring in the wider European context is nowhere near to completion. The belief that a "borderless world" will emerge in the 21st century was widely held just after the end of the Cold War but since proved to be illusory. Border conflicts have in fact increased worldwide during the previous two decades, accompanied by the construction of new border fences and walls (see Falke in this volume).

In the context of globalization, accelerated European integration, and the ongoing territorial and political restructuring of the European continent, border regions have become subject to intense multidisciplinary research by European scholars, too, in recent years. What makes these regions interesting is that they are emerging, dynamic social spaces. Newly created border regimes define the new opportunity structures framing cross-border cooperation, and residents and their representatives decide continually anew how to react to them. In this volume, the problems of different types of European border regions are analyzed. The opening of the internal borders within the EU and within the Schengen space have set off a new dynamism in economic and cultural cross-border cooperation. But a reluctance to fully use the newly available opportunities also has been revealed. This reluctance is perhaps rooted in inherited stereotypes, institutional inertia, or structural legacies. As a result, the EU is experiencing new challenges. In the aftermath of the recent extension of its external borders to the east and southeast, the EU is struggling to balance its internal security needs, economic growth targets, and normative power ambitions. The limited usefulness of its traditional "soft power" approach now seems to have become quite obvious at its periphery.

THEORETICAL PERSPECTIVES ON BORDERS

In the first section of this volume, theoretical approaches commonly used in border studies are discussed. *Bastian Sendhardt* introduces the concept of Debordering/Rebordering. Based on modern systems theory, it has had increasing influence within border studies since the end of the 1990s. The major advantage of this constructivist approach, he argues, is that it helps us to grasp the constantly changing interplay between territorial, functional, and symbolic borders with a single, internally consistent theoretical framework. It helps us interpret the apparent contradictions in the EU's attempts to both tighten its external borders and promote cooperation across them. The same contradictions are also evident in the policies of those member states situated at the external EU border toward their non-EU neighbors.

Interested in the intellectual benefits that could accrue to border studies from the sociology of space, *Sabrina Ellebrecht* experiments with using Georg Simmel's concept of *qualities of space* for analyzing the EU border regime in the Mediterranean Sea. This way of linking border processes to their spatial fulcra, she argues, could help to highlight the particular logics by which border regimes function and by which borderlands develop. Examples include the way in which persons are enabled or allowed to cross the EU border into the protected internal space of EU territory, the diversification of bordering processes, the geographic transfer and externalization of border control functions to third countries, and the asymmetric distribution of resources for moving across borders. The later is, according to Bauman (1998: 86), "the key variable to stratify societies in a globalising world."

Borders as "Laboratories" of Transnational Cooperation

The second part of the book is concerned with recent developments between and within border regions as they emerged after the external EU border was moved eastward amidst much public debate. In this context, Euroregions were created and promoted through European Regional Policy programs. These were intended to enhance economic, cultural, and political cross-border cooperation, to gradually reduce economic gaps among the border regions along which old and new EU member states are adjoined, and to counterbalance the negative effects of restrictive protection measures at the EU's new eastern border. *Barbara Despiney-Zochowska* compares the development of two Euroregions with Polish involvement: the Neisse Euroregion in the Czech-German-Polish triangle and the Carpathian Euroregion, which includes local communities in Hungary, Poland, Romania, Slovakia, and Ukraine. Returning to the concept of the "industrial district" developed by Alfred Marshall (1920), she explores prospects for cross-border economic cluster building through the revitalization of local productive systems. For this purpose, the creation of networks of small and medium-sized companies, supported by cross-border cooperation between local administrative authorities, is thought to be crucial. She identifies some important barriers to the proliferation of clusters in the investigated regions, including local governments that do not appreciate the role they could be playing in economic development and the absence of a tradition of cooperation among competing companies. Her analysis shows that socio-economic structures inherited from the past largely determine the sectoral mix of clusters and their chances of success in any given region. Another approach to cross-border regional cooperation is presented by *Roswitha Ruidisch*, who discusses the concepts of "territorial cohesion" and "territorial capital," both of which are key concepts in recent European Regional Policy. EU documents contain no clear definition of "territorial cohesion," she argues. Using the example of the Czech-German border region, she shows that EU measures to increase territorial cohesion are swayed by competing interests and that these interests are not always compatible with the goal of reducing regional disparities.

THE AMBIGUOUS WORK OF STEREOTYPES

If national borders within the EU are losing relevance for the everyday life of borderland inhabitants, and if prospects for socio-economic development in such areas increasingly depend on cross-border cooperation, the construction of collective identities there will inevitably be affected. The social environment for identity-building is thus becoming more dynamic and more complex and, despite persisting traditional categories of collective identity such as nation, ethnicity, and language, the emergence of multidimensional identities is becoming more likely. In this context, stereotypes, understood as positive or negative images of "the other," play a major but ambivalent role. Stereotypes can, as *Antje Schönwald* argues, enhance cross-border cooperation in that they systemize and simplify complex information and thus help residents deal with cultural boundaries. Using the example of the "Greater Region," comprised of Saarland, Lorraine, Rhineland-Palatinate, the Grand Duchy of Luxembourg, and Wallonia, Schönwald examines factors that encourage the emergence of multidimensional and patchwork identities and presents a typology of sub-identities in this region.

Stereotypes can, of course, impede integration and cooperation, as they block receptiveness to change in the social environment and promote negative discrimination. A case in which stereotypes had rather negative effects is the subject of the analysis of French, German, and Polish media debates on the Schengen agreement presented by *Angela Siebold*. The Schengen Treaty was signed in 1985, long before the fall of the Iron Curtain. When it was implemented in 1995, the circumstances had changed radically. The major reason for the protracted implementation of the treaty, in fact, was the fear of mass immigration from Eastern Europe after German Unification. Thus, the central topic in the French and German print media was the issue of effectively protecting and consolidating the German-Polish border, i.e. the new external border of the EU. Here, it was said, "the poor and the rich part of Europe" meet (Siebold). In Siebold's interesting observation, in the run-up to Poland's accession to the Schengen agreement in 2007, the same fears were raised in regard to the new external border of the EU where Poland meets Ukraine, White Russia, and Russia. In both cases, fears centered on migration and insecurity. She writes that in media assessments, "persistence of Western stereotypes and of the idea of a divided Europe" was manifest. Before 1989, the Schengen project seemed to interest technocrats only. It lacked public resonance. This changed when the new internal EU border was opened in 2007. Reporting became loaded with symbols of the bright future of a united and prosperous Europe. At the same time, however, the print media raised again concerns about mass migration and crime from the East, whereas in Poland unlimited drug trafficking from the Netherlands as well as an expected loss of general national sovereignty became important Schengen issues. These triggered long debates on identity and security.

Stereotypes can persist and reproduce themselves over generations, even long after national territorial borders disappear. From the perspective of the "Third East German Generation," born between 1975 and 1985 and socialized in the 1990s, *Jaqueline Flack* analyzes the emergence and articulation of a common self-perception among this group of young adults as they respond to the images of East Germans constructed by West Germans in the mass media. Whereas the collective identity of young adults from the former East Germany is mainly shaped by the rapid and all-encompassing changes they experienced during the transformation of East German politics, economics, administration, education, and daily life after German unification, the image publicly ascribed to them is largely a reproduction of old West German stereotypes of GDR citizens. These differences and ongoing processes of mutual cultural contra-distinction create a cultural boundary that will continue to impair the formation of a common national identity, at least among this generation.

Views on the History of Polish-German Border Regions

The ongoing dynamics characteristic of the EU's newly configured border regions cannot be fully grasped without exploring the history of the regions involved. Using the example of the region around Szczecin/Stettin, *Agata Ładykowska* and *Paweł Ładykowski* describe the beginnings of a transnational space in which cultural, political, and economic identities not only co-exist but fuse. In contrast to the usual image of the Polish-German border as a persisting "welfare borderline between the poor and the rich part of Europe," streams of mobility in both directions can be observed here. Whereas the rather underdeveloped counties on the German side have become an attractive destination for Poles looking for new housing, unemployed Germans have started to search for new job opportunities on the Polish side. The authors suggest that this specific development has been spurred by resources rooted in the region's post-war history. They reconstruct mobility patterns across the Oder-Neisse border during different periods of regional history between 1945 and 1989 and describe social processes and practices that made the politically demarcated borderline relatively porous. Especially striking is their argument that the new post-war border, which created arbitrary divisions in cities and spaces that had grown "naturally," forced the new settlers (refugees and expulsed Germans as well as Poles) to cooperate informally and formally across the border despite all resentments and mutual unfamiliarity. Cooperation was necessary simply in order to survive economically, they write.

Another experience is described by *Bianca Szytniewski*. The author examines the particular effects of unfamiliarity and familiarity with the "other" side in different historical border situations. In the immediate post-war era, after the redrawing of the Polish-German border along the Oder and Neisse rivers, differences between Poles and Germans were amplified, partly due to the fact that both sides of the new border were settled largely by forced emigrants from the former eastern territories of Poland and Germany, and partly as a result of the Polish government's efforts of nationalizing the new Polish territory. The contrast, however, between the official propaganda of friendship among the two "socialist nations" beginning in 1950 and the fact that the border remained physically closed for another 20 years produced interesting patterns of unfamiliarity that became quite relevant during subsequent open-border periods.

After 1970, Szytniewski argues, unfamiliarity triggered curiosity, which was an important factor motivating cross-border mobility. This, however, ended in feelings of resentment because of shortages in basic goods and inadequate tourism infrastructure. When the border was re-opened in 1990, new opportunities for cooperation were only partially used. In the situation of economic decline and transformation in those years, both borderland Poles and Germans looked westward. European enlargement and cross-border cooperation turned out to be mainly top-down political projects. Among residents, the unfamiliarity inherited from the past manifested itself in a widespread indifference that was especially pronounced on the German side.

However, as we learn from *Thomas Serrier*, it would be superficial and perhaps misleading to look only at the post-war history of the Oder-Neisse region in order to understand current developments. Borders between Poland and Germany had been re-drawn several times during the last two centuries, and this happened in different regions. In his case studies, Serrier presents Eastern Prussia, Danzig, Greater Poland, and Silesia as "geographic systems of historically evolved relations," the social appropriation of which is a multi-state process involving different levels of memory that are at best partially shared by contemporary inhabitants and can display disintegrative effects in times of tension. He thus shifts our attention to the fact that all contemporary advocates of "multicultural" identities in the new Polish-German borderlands should respect the historical experience of destroyed multiculturalism. Thus, despite all institutional validation, cross-border cooperation, including intense de-bordering processes as achieved in recent decades, is vulnerable to unexpected external change. Even from a neo-realistic view point, territorial borders between national states can change their functions within international relations regimes, as *Eloi Piet* illustrates in his analysis of the changing view of French diplomacy on the redrawing of the German-Polish border between 1940 und 1950.

CROSS-BORDER INTERACTION IN EUROPE'S NEIGHBOURHOOD

As mentioned above, the opening of internal borders and the consolidation of external ones are only two of several factors influencing further integration and the development of the EU's external relations. Security and prosperity are also affected by border dynamics in the European neighborhood. As commonly known, the outer periphery of the EU is burdened by frozen or latent territorial conflicts and contested borders. Two such situations are the ongoing Kosovo and Israeli-Palestinian conflicts, and many others haunt the post-Soviet space. "Stability" in such regions – a major concern of EU policies since the end of the Cold War (Lippert 2004) – requires that at least a modicum of "normal life" among the local population be established. Otherwise, mass migration, trafficking in persons, and organized crime will get out of control. All of these problems are perceived by the EU as major security issues. In this context, the permeability of disputed borders or frozen ceasefire lines allow for regional mobility and trade, and they are thus of crucial importance. In her analysis of the political economy of borders and borderlands, *Giulia Prelz Oltramonti* explains the opportunities for residents, private businesses, and political administrations inherent to the logic of such contested borders. Using the example of the post-Soviet de facto states South Ossetia and Abkhasia, she demonstrates how the interplay of actors hardens and softens borders. This process was undertaken by various actors in the interwar period between 1992/1994 and 2008, when the areas oscillated between periods of "normal life" and times of open violence. Whereas the conflicts in South Ossetia and Abkhazia were "re-frozen" at a different level as the result of the Russian-Georgian war of 2008, the territorial conflict between Israel and Palestine promises to be much more protracted and much less predictable, as *Simon Falke* suggests in his analysis of the separation fence Israel has been maintaining since 2002 on the borderline to the West Bank. As this line was never an official territorial border, it is also not accepted as a possible future national border by the majority of Jewish Israeli citizens. Thus the fence, although justified by security concerns, functions first and foremost as a symbolic boundary. As Falke argues, it promoted the process of national unity building in the (Jewish) Israeli society and made Israelis focus for the first time on "normal" internal social conflicts. But it also symbolizes the exclusion of Palestinian Israelis from the rest of Israeli society. As the first real physical and visible demarcation line, the separation fence could, according to Falke, inspire both Israelis and Palestinians to envisage at least the need for a territorial border. How to get to that place from the current starting position in which the borderline between the two societies is represented not by a territorial border but by "the settler" remains, however, vague.

REFERENCES

Albert, Mathias/Brock, Lothar (2001): "What Keeps Westphalia Together? Normative Differentiation in the Modern System of States", in: Mathias Albert/David Jacobson/Yosef Lapid (eds.), Identities, borders, orders. Rethinking international relations theory, Minneapolis: University of Minnesota Press, pp. 29-49.

Baumann, Zygmunt (1998): Globalization. The human consequences, Cambridge: Polity Press.

EUV (European University Viadrina) (2012): B/Orders in Motion. Initial Proposal for a Cluster of Excellence, Coordinated by Werner Schiffauer, Frankfurt (Oder): EUV.

Lippert, Barbara (2004): "Sternstunde oder Stolperstein? Erweiterung und europäische Integration", in: Osteuropa 54 (5-6), pp. 47-60.

Vorbuba, Georg (2008): "Expansion und Integration nach der Osterweiterung", in: Frank Bönker/Jan Wielgohs (eds.), Postsozialistische Transformation und europäische (Des-)Integration, Marburg: Metropolis, pp. 219-230.

Theoretical Perspectives on Borders

Border Types and Bordering Processes
A Theoretical Approach to the EU/Polish-Ukrainian Border as a Multi-dimensional Phenomenon

Bastian Sendhardt

Introduction

Events in 2011 such as the "biblical exodus" of refugees on the Italian island of Lampedusa or the decision of the Danish government to reinstate border controls have underscored the ongoing significance of borders in Europe. To date, however, there has been little agreement in academia on what borders actually are, and border studies remain under-theorized. The objective of this contribution is to augment the ongoing theoretical discussion within border studies by elaborating upon the overarching theoretical approach of "Debordering/Rebordering." This approach interprets borders not as static lines but as multidimensional bordering processes. The empirical situation of the EU/Polish-Ukrainian border[1] is used as a means to illustrate and focus theoretical aspects of border research.

After introducing the history of the Polish and EU border with Ukraine after 1989, this article briefly reviews the state of the art of border studies after the end of the Cold War. For improving on these approaches, the paper then reviews the concept of Debordering/Rebordering, a constructivist approach to border studies. First, the nature of bordering processes is explained and different types of borders are distinguished. Then, territorial borders are explained in their fuller complexity as a form of differentiation separate from the differentiation of functional and symbolic bor-

---

[1] | This neologism refers to both the supranational and the national dimension of this border, which must be thought together.

ders. Finally, the EU/Polish-Ukrainian border is discussed as a complex bordering process involving different types of borders.

The EU/Polish-Ukrainian Border

During the Cold War, the borders between the Soviet Union and other socialist states in Europe's east were almost as impermeable and closely guarded as the Iron Curtain separating the "East" from the "West." The situation changed rapidly after the fall of the Iron Curtain in 1989 and the subsequent collapse of the Soviet Union in 1991. These events set up the conditions for an independent Ukrainian state with full sovereignty over its own territorial borders.

From the 1990s onward, the character of the Polish-Ukrainian border changed dramatically, "from a border of alienation to an 'open' border" (Wolczuk 2002: 246; Kennard 2003: 193f.). While the border mainly served as a barrier before 1989, it now became a zone of contact enabling new forms of political, economic and cultural cooperation across the border. Poland's EU accession in 2004 and the gradual enforcement of the provisions of the Schengen agreement, however, seriously affected cross-border relations between Poland and Ukraine. Having maintained a visa-free travel regime before 2004, Poland now had to introduce visas for Ukrainian citizens, a measure that had a negative impact "on trade, labor market dynamics, and cross-border cooperation" between the two countries (Scott 2005: 442). This was one of the events that caused many authors to decry the European Union as a hermetically sealed "Fortress Europe" (Anderson 1996; Busch/Krzyżanowski 2007; Dimitrovova 2010).

However, as eastern enlargement proceeded in 2004, the EU attempted to counter the alienation of its eastern neighbors with the new European Neighbourhood Policy (ENP). The primary goal of the policy was "to prevent the emergence of new dividing lines between the enlarged EU and its neighbours" (European Commission 2004a: 3), to be achieved by supporting political, economic, and cultural cooperation initiatives in neighboring countries. According to the ENP Country Report on Ukraine, the ENP aims "to allow partners on both sides of the EU's external border to work jointly to address common challenges such as economic and social development of the border areas, the environment and communicable diseases, illegal immigration and trafficking, efficient border management and people-to-people contacts" (European Commission 2004b: 5). Also, the Eastern Partnership, established in 2009, aims specifically at extending cross-border cooperation between the EU and its eastern neighbors (European Commission 2008: 8).

From this perspective, it seems that the EU's policy aims at creating a shared "borderland" with its neighbors, not a "Fortress Europe" (see Comelli et al. 2007). Moreover, Poland established a bilateral agreement with Ukraine, voluntarily instating policies conform to EU policy, to give visa-free passage across the border to all residents living within 30 to 50 kilometers on either side of the border. Encouraged especially by President Aleksander Kwaśniewski, Poland also has advocated Ukrainian interests within the EU and has promoted the goal of Ukrainian accession.

Thus, the policies of the EU are not strictly consistent. They aim to seal off the EU to the east but also to enable cross-border cooperation with Ukraine. Some authors conclude that the EU's neighborhood policy is manifestly self-contradictory (Scott/Matzeit 2006: 4; see also Anderson 2001; Apap/Tchorbadjiyska 2004; Vermeersch 2007). Moreover, Poland's Ukrainian border policy facilitates local border traffic and helps to maintain a rather open border. Thus, Polish and EU border policies vis-à-vis Ukraine also seem to contradict each other.

This apparent contradiction in border policies parallels the contradicting theoretical positions in EU border studies: "Fortress Europe" versus "borderless Europe." Below, a brief review of the state of current approaches in border studies is provided together with a critical view of their limitations. It is followed by an elaboration of the better suited theoretical framework of Debordering/Rebordering.

Border Studies After 1989

When looking back at the recent history of border studies, one is immediately struck by its interdisciplinarity. Following the collapse of socialism in central and eastern Europe, interest in borders increased markedly in various academic disciplines, including political science, international relations, sociology, anthropology, history, and geography (Newman/Paasi 1998: 186). To this day, however, border studies remains a composite of many disciplines and has yet to yield a unified theoretical framework generally accepted by the diverse community of border scholars (Newman 2006b: 145; Kolossov 2005: 612). However, there has been no paucity of attempts (see, for example, Anderson 2001; Brunet-Jailly 2005; Delanty

2006; Kolossov 2005; Martinez 1994; Newman 2003b; Paasi 1996; Rumford 2006).

Driving the renaissance of border studies were the effects of globalization and the end "of the static West-East dichotomy" after 1989 (Paasi 1999b: 14). From the perspective of globalization, what is particularly interesting is the increasing permeability of borders. Ideas, goods, people, and capital move across borders more easily than ever before. An extreme interpretation of these phenomena is Ohmae's "borderless world," where state borders and the state itself have become meaningless, having withdrawn to make room for a world dominated by marketplaces (Ohmae 1994). On the other hand, the 1990s also saw an increase in states and, with them, state borders. Developments in the former eastern bloc exemplify these changes in an especially vivid manner. Here, multiethnic and multiregional states broke up, and ethnic conflicts led to violent wars in Yugoslavia. The European map became dotted with many new states, and it seemed as if the importance of state borders had been reasserted.

Writing on the EU and its new borders, different authors come to different and often contradictory conclusions. Some scholars emphasize the decreasing significance of borders in the EU context. They focus on European integration, the abolition of border controls within the European Union, and the perception of the EU's eastern border as a "traveling" border (Popescu 2008: 424) that will gradually travel eastward to encompass the whole neighborhood and finally create an EU without borders, "the 'borderless Europe' represented by the single market and the Euro-zone" (Delanty/Rumford 2005: 120).

A second group of scholars focuses on the attempts of the European Union to tighten its external borders, emphasizing their "barrier function." More precisely, the EU's external borders are seen as a barrier that keeps out illegal migrants, criminals, unwanted goods, and people who cannot afford the costs of visas. This group of authors refers to the European Union's external borders as a means to create a "Fortress Europe," shutting itself off from its neighbors (see, for example, Scott 2005, 2009; van Houtum/Pijpers 2007; Grabbe 2000).

In the wake of the EU's European Neighborhood Policy, several authors stressed the "bridge function" of borders by referring to cross-border cooperation (CBC) initiatives by the EU and Poland (see, for example, Dandiş 2009; Perkmann 2003). Here, cross-border cooperation is seen as a means to lessen the separating effect of the external border and to implement the EU's regional policy.

Quite clearly, contradictory processes have been set in motion. On the one hand, movement has been made towards "increased protection of the external borders of the EU," but "a new trend has become perceptible within the EU towards increased political, security, economic, and cultural cooperation" with its eastern neighbors (Vermeersch 2007: 475). To date, none of the aforementioned authors has been able to make sense of this basic contradiction in border policies within a single, coherent theoretical framework.

THE CONCEPT OF DEBORDERING/REBORDERING

Borders as Processes

For a long time, the study of borders was focused on state borders as static ontological entities with predominantly physical features, but the past two decades have seen a sea change in the study of borders. During the recent history of border studies, there has been a shift from the consideration of borders as mere geographical demarcations to a perspective that emphasizes the changing meaning of borders, different types of borders with different functions, and the social construction of borders.[2]

The new perspective shifted the focus onto process-like and socially constructed qualities of borders. The ontological question of *what* a border is became gradually replaced by the question of *how* borders are socially constructed, thus shifting the focus from the border to the process of bordering. As Newman pointed out, "it is the process of bordering, rather than the border line per se, that has universal significance in the ordering of society" (Newman 2003c: 15). In this way, the traditional view of borders as static structures made room for a new theoretical understanding of borders as "historically contingent processes" (Newman/Paasi 1998: 201),

---

2 | See, for examples, Anderson (1996); Anderson/O'Dowd (1999); Donnan/Wilson (1999); Newman (2003c, 2006a, 2006b); Newman/Paasi (1998); Paasi (1996, 1999a, 1999b, 2001, 2005); van Houtum et al. (2005); van Houtum/van Naerssen (2002); Wilson/Donnan (1998); Zielonka (2002).

an understanding that includes in the definition of borders their ready potential to change.

This constructivist strand of border studies looks beyond the visible, material, and seemingly objective manifestations of borders such as fences, walls, rivers, or mountains and focuses on the "social practices and discourses in which boundaries are produced and reproduced" (Paasi 2005: 18). It understands borders as "dynamic cultural processes" (Paasi 2003: 464). State borders can now be analyzed as "social practice[s] of spatial differentiation" (van Houtum/van Naerssen 2002: 126) and as institutions "established by political decisions and regulated by legal texts" (Anderson 1996: 1).

In other words, this strand of theory no longer views borders as something given or natural. Borders are always (potentially) "subject to political contestation and change." They "do not exist prior to political action but acquire their societal relevance only as a result of [...] political processes and the accompanying legitimization strategies that produce these borders." Consequently, from this point of view, borders must be considered as "historically and politically contingent"; they "are continuously remade on the basis of concrete political, cultural, and economic practices" (Stetter 2008a). Borders are understood as manifestations of "social practices and discourses that may be simultaneous and overlapping" (Paasi 1999a: 670). From a social constructivist perspective, the focus shifts from the entity to the process itself: from borders to bordering.

Types of Borders

The constructivist perspective in border studies emerged concomitantly with approaches that distinguish different functions and types of borders.[3] However, authors often do not explain why they chose particular types of borders (e.g. cultural, political, language) as their unit of analysis or how each of these kinds of borders interrelate. Bonacker (2006) and Stetter (2005b), however, provided a more systematic approach by proposing the general distinction between territorial, functional, and symbolic borders.

---

[3] | See, for example, Anderson (2001); Anderson/O'Dowd (1999); Donnan/Wilson (1999); Anderson et al. (2003); Delanty (2006); Gropas (2004); Kolossov (2005); Newman/Paasi (1998).

We often think of territorial borders as state borders, meaning "the lines that enclose state territories" (Newman 2003a: 123). Accordingly, territorial borders are those that separate states or regions and serve first and foremost as a means of control, of ascribing areas of competence and demarcating jurisdictions (Bonacker 2006: 81). This view and the focus on nation-states have prevailed in most border studies (Newman 2003a: 124). Following this understanding, borders are by definition more closed than open, and their main function is to separate different entities, mostly states. This is also reflected in much of the existing literature on borders (Anderson et al. 2003: 2), which seems to follow a tacit agreement that borders are self-evidently territorial borders. The assumption of borders' territorial "boundedness" is unquestioned and often the term "border" is equated with territorial borders without further explanation.

The conventional perception of borders has come under criticism because of a significant increase in the variety of transnational cross-border activities such as migration and trade and because of the emergence of supra- and transnational actors such as the EU. These changes are commonly understood as outcomes of globalization, although in central and eastern Europe (CEE), they emerged clearly only after the collapse of socialism.[4] More precisely, one of the consequences of globalization is an increasing permeability of territorial borders. According to Albert and Brock, these transformations "point to a change in the function of [territorial] borders." In order to adapt to the new circumstances, territorial borders must "cease to act as separators and [...] change from transit zones into spaces of economic cooperation, political-cum-institutional innovation, and transnational communication" (Albert/Brock 2001: 33).

This means that borders "are not merely physical, empirical lines or zones that can be frozen on maps and atlases as naturalized entities" but must be conceived of as multidimensional social constructs (Paasi 2001: 22). Some border scholars, therefore, began distinguishing different types of borders in contrast to previous approaches, which took for granted the priority of territorial over other types of borders. Territorial borders (such as state borders) are then but one type of border. Other types include

---

4 | Of course, cross-border activities in Europe took place long before 1989, especially in the context of European Integration in western Europe. In terms of the EU border with Poland and Ukraine border, however, the collapse of socialism was the watershed event.

functional and symbolic borders (Stetter 2005b; see also Ferrer-Gallardo 2008). "Functional borders separate different functional systems, such as politics, law, science, economy, sports, love or the health system" (Stetter 2005b: 5), whereas symbolic borders "constitute collective identities" and allow us to "differentiate between the 'self' and the 'other.' Through the marking of symbolic borders forms of political, ethnic or religious identity emerge" (Bonacker as cited in Stetter 2005b: 5).

These three types of borders, however, do not necessarily coincide. Therefore, territorial borders are in a "complex relationship with cross-cutting functional (and, at times symbolic) borders" (Stetter 2005b: 5). In a nutshell, one can say that instead of clear-cut lines separating different (state) territories, borders have a rather "fuzzy" character as a consequence of the interplay of the three aforementioned border types (Christiansen et al. 2000).[5]

Debordering/Rebordering

In the wake of globalization, borders do not become obsolete. Globalization processes continuously change the relation of the different types of borders to one another and thus require "a constant process of adjustment" (Stetter 2005b: 6) to these changes. A concept that does justice to this "fuzziness" in a theoretically adequate way is the concept of Debordering/Rebordering (Albert/Brock 1996).[6] Based on a constructivist understanding, Debordering/Rebordering conceives of borders as processes and distinguishes between different types of borders. By drawing on modern

---

5 | Detailed descriptions of territorial, functional, and symbolic borders are provided below.

6 | Although other border scholars point to an increasing differentiation of borders as a reaction to globalization processes (see, for example, Anderson et al. [2003]; Rumford [2007]), to date, only few border scholars have taken up the concept of debordering and rebordering (e.g. Stetter [2005b]; Bonacker [2006], [2007]). Moreover, the concept of debordering and rebordering is a good example of the lack of exchange among border scholars. In their otherwise theoretically well-crafted and empirically rich EXLINEA project report, James Scott and Silke Matzeit (2006: 21) claim that the terms "bordering" and "de-bordering" were coined by the EXLINEA Nijmegen research team when in fact, Albert and Brock (1996) had introduced the concept ten years earlier.

systems theory, all of these types of borders are conceived of as societal borders constituted by communication. Albert and Brock established the basis of Debordering/Rebordering, and subsequent applications of the concept placed greater emphasis on distinguishing different types of borders (Stetter 2005b; Bonacker 2006).

Within this concept, debordering "is understood as an increasing permeability of [territorial] borders together with a decreasing ability of states to shut themselves off" against all kinds of cross-border activities (Albert/Brock 2000: 20). In other words, debordering refers to the transgression of territorial borders, for example by functional systems (such as "the economy") or symbolic systems (such as cross-border identities). Debordering and can thus be described as "the dissolution of the territorial congruence of state, economy, and society" (Brock 2004: 89). Debordering can be defined as "the functional change of borders, the loss of importance of their territorial anchoring and – as a consequence – the decoupling of (functional) system borders and territorial borders" (Bonacker 2007: 24).

The affected political entities – mostly states but also other political entities such as the European Union – have to react to the challenges posed by debordering processes. One possible "response to this increasing permeability of borders" is the "adaptation of statehood" and the adjustment of policies to debordering processes. Adaptation can result "in the emergence of new political spaces that transcend territorially defined spaces" like state borders, for example "in the emergence of multilevel systems of governance in transstate contexts" such as the European Union (Albert/Brock 2000: 20).

At the same time, however, processes of debordering are accompanied (and seemingly contradicted) by rebordering processes, such as a tightening of (new) borders, an increase in border controls and the re-territorialization of space (Albert/Brock 2000: 39-40; Rumford 2006: 157). But the simultaneity of debordering and rebordering processes does not necessarily have to be considered a contradiction. Instead, processes of rebordering can be described

as social phenomena within the framework of an overall debordering of the world of states, [...] as a specific reaction to the debordering processes that are actually taking their course within the framework of globalization. Viewed in this light, demarcation (rebordering) would be, first and foremost, a way of *regulating* the process of transformation, not of *arresting* it (Albert/Brock 2000: 42f.).

Reconsidering Debordering/Rebordering

Subsequent applications of Albert and Brock's concept attach greater significance to the distinction of different types of borders (Bonacker 2006; Stetter 2005b). This slight shift of emphasis makes sense, because not only does debordering point to the increasing permeability of territorial borders but also to the decreasing significance of the nation-state. Debordering can then be considered a decoupling of functional and symbolic borders that were formerly coupled in the form of nation-state and other territorial borders (Bonacker 2006: 80).

This intention of this contribution is to add to the concept of Debordering/Rebordering by looking more closely at the interrelations of different border types. In particular, this contribution challenges previous usages of Debordering/Rebordering that adhere to the conception of territorial borders as a type of border sui generis (see, for example, Bonacker 2006; Stetter 2005a, 2005b, 2007). According to these approaches, territorial borders possess an inherent quality that makes them distinguishable from other kinds of borders such as functional and symbolic ones. While recognizing that territorial borders are of relevance especially for the functional systems of "politics" and "law," both Bonacker and Stetter continue to treat territorial borders as a unique type of border. Against this approach, the argument is presented below that territoriality is a strategy of bordering applied in different functional and symbolic bordering processes. Consequently, this study suggests understanding territorial borders as but one possible form of internal differentiation of functional and symbolic systems. Therefore, it is necessary to take a closer look first at functional and then at symbolic borders. In a third step, it is possible to analyze how functional and symbolic borders relate to the principle of territoriality.

Functional Borders in World Society

The theory of world society as employed in this study stems in large part from modern systems theory (MST) as developed by the sociologist Nikolas Luhmann.[7] MST understands society as the "comprehensive social

---

7 | For other, non-system theoretical approaches to world society see for example Burton 1972, Meyer et al. 2009.

system that includes all other social systems" (Luhmann 1998: 78). Thus, society does not consist of human beings or their actions (Luhmann 1998: 24); it is created by communication alone (Luhmann 1991: 249). Only that which is communicated is of societal relevance (Luhmann 2002: 40).

Starting with the printing press in the fourteenth century and gaining momentum with the emergence of modern telecommunication, each and every communication is (potentially) global today. With society being communicatively constituted, society can then only be conceived of as one single social system: world society (Luhmann 1998: 145). This means that society can no longer be identified with a system of political rule (Luhmann 1998: 147). Thus, the world does not consist of territorially defined societies (such as the German, the Polish, the Ukrainian society, and so on) but of one single world society (see Stichweh 2000: 245).

With functional differentiation being the primary form of differentiation in world society, territorial borders can no longer be viewed as the limits of social processes. Instead, the theory of world society holds the view that world society is internally differentiated into functional systems such as the economic, the legal, the political, or the scientific system. Each of these subsystems fulfils one specific function within society. This particular function is then "of priority for this (and only for this) system and precedes all other functions." In the case of the political system, for instance, this means that the "political [...] is more important than anything else, and a successful economy is important only as a condition for political success" (Luhmann 1998: 747). Hence, the different functional systems communicatively demarcate their own functional system borders according to their individual systemic needs.

Functional systems establish borders of communication that separate them from their environment. Functional systems constantly produce and reproduce themselves by drawing a border between system and environment. Conceiving of borders as communications, therefore, not only means that borders can be constitutive (as content) of particular acts of communication, but also that the very process of creating borders is an act of communication. Bordering is communicating by drawing borders, that is, communicating by making a distinction.

Therefore, these functional systems must not be understood as a priori entities. Just like the larger society, functional systems are themselves constituted by communication. Functional borders are constantly being negotiated and drawn, thus revealing their procedural character and their tendency to change (Stetter 2009: 105). Thus, functional systems should not be understood as fixed functional containers in which social processes take place. Instead, these very functional bordering processes constitute the various functional systems and spaces.

IDENTITY AS DIFFERENCE: SYMBOLIC BORDERS IN WORLD SOCIETY

During the past two decades, social science scholars have paid increasing attention to symbolic borders (Lamont/Molnár 2002). Symbolic borders can be thought of as an expression of collective identities based on the distinction between "self" and "other." The constitutive role that "symbolic borders [play] in the construction of contested social identities" (Paasi 2005: 17) is widely accepted among scholars of borders (see, for example, Lapid 2001; Paasi 2005). Collective identities are not taken to be exogenously given essentialist categories. Rather, they are understood as socially constructed.

Of particular interest are collective identities that have a spatial point of reference: nations, regions, cities, and so on. Other reference points for identification such as gender, class, and race do exist but will not be explored further here. The understanding of collective identities used below follows Benedict Anderson's concept of "imagined communities"; for him, symbolic borders are "finite, if elastic, boundaries" that separate different imagined communities from one another (Anderson 2006: 7). Although Anderson primarily deals with but one kind of collective identity, the nation, his concept is applicable to other imagined communities. "All communities larger than primordial villages [...] are imagined" (Anderson 2006: 7).

Luhmann's modern systems theory informs the approach to borders used here in two respects. First, not only territorial and functional borders but also symbolic borders are constituted by communication and thus are constantly subject to change (Stetter 2009: 106). Collective identities gain societal relevance only via communication. Consequently, authors using this approach are less concerned with the "bearers of identity" (Weller 2000: 52) and more concerned with how collective identities are constituted by communicatively established symbolic borders. Second, the starting point of an analysis of symbolic borders is not identity but difference.

According to this understanding, difference is constitutive of identity, and identity emerges only as a product of differentiation (Luhmann 1991: 27 fn. 11): "identity is possible only by difference" (Luhmann 1991: 243). Consequently, collective identities are devoid of essentialist roots and have nothing to do with quasi-natural a priori givens. Instead, collective identities are constituted via symbolic bordering processes.

Symbolic bordering processes in the form of "self/other distinctions" involve the simultaneous construction of the self and "other" ("othering") which "is itself part of the construction of the self." Therefore, the construction of identities necessarily includes the construction of a self "against the difference of an other" (Diez 2004: 321).

Thus, paradoxically, difference has to be created first. Identity emerges in a second step. The construction of the "self" always entails the creation of the "other." More precisely, the construction of the "self" is the very same process as the construction of the "other." However, the distinction between two identities, that is the symbolic bordering process itself, must not be equated with the attribution of certain values to these identities. It is the particular "character of [some] symbolic bordering" processes that may value one side as a "positive" and the other as a "negative" (Stetter 2005a: 343-4).

In regard to value ascriptions, what matters is not so much the "self/other distinction" but rather "the question as to which discursive field the Self/Other coding of collective identities is embedded" (Stetter 2005a: 336). In other words, the "other" can have positive or negative connotations and is thus perceived neutrally, as a foe, or as a friend to the self's collective identity. In this way, "value attributions become intermingled with Self/Other distinctions" (Stetter 2005a: 336). Consequently, these kinds of symbolic bordering processes lead to different perceptions of the "other." The relations with the "other" are then either potentially conflictual (negative "other") or based on the idea of cooperation (positive "other"). Either way, these value-laden constructions of an "other" tend to be one-sided because they turn a blind eye to the multi-facetedness of the relations with the "other" (Stetter 2005a: 336f.).

Deconstructing Territoriality

As suggested above, territorial borders are not considered as a type of border sui generis but merely as secondary form of differentiation of some functional (and at times symbolic) systems. The remainder of this section, therefore, aims at showing which function territoriality serves for functional and symbolic systems.

Robert D. Sack defines territoriality as "the attempt by an individual or a group to affect, influence, or control people, phenomena, and relationships, by delimiting and asserting control over a geographic area" (Sack 1986: 19). One of the major advantages of territoriality is the fact that what is under control does not have to be defined beforehand (Sack 1986: 27). Therefore, territorial control fundamentally differs from earlier attempts at controlling people and things, for example by enumeration. Only now, through "classification by area" (Sack 1986: 21), has it become possible to control and govern vast tracts of land, inhabitants, and resources. As a consequence, in order to prevent misunderstandings, territorial borders must be demarcated exactly. On the other hand, this precision is more theoretical than practical and does not reflect bordering practices on the ground. Even clearly defined territorial borders have "fuzzy edges" (Sack 1986: 21).

As clear-cut, "razorlike" lines (Schlögel 2009: 137), territorial borders exist only on maps. Since territorial borders are a pre-condition for the modern territorial state it comes as no surprise that both the modern territorial state and modern maps emerged as a consequence of progress in cartography since the sixteenth century (Biggs 1999: 380). In this way, cartography helped create "a new kind of space" in which "boundaries were made congruent with the cartographic ideal" (Biggs 1999: 387). Thus, rather than maps being a representation of borders in reality, map lines are actually predecessors of borders on the ground.

Among the most striking examples of the social constructedness of borders are the straight-line territorial borders running for hundreds and even thousands of kilometers in North America and on the African continent. However, borders that follow river courses and mountain ranges are no less socially constructed. What matters most is the fact that territories are created by drawing borders on maps, regardless of whether the point of reference is seemingly natural like a river, a mountain, or a language border or is rather seemingly arbitrary like a wall, a fence, or a pre-existing administrative unit. The decisive point is that both reference points are communicatively constructed and thus historically contingent. The point of reference always could have been different.

The obvious fact that many territorial borders are materially and physically fortified does not support the argument that territorial borders have an essentialist character. Rather it is precisely evidence against such an argument. Territorial borders are in need of physical representations precisely because they are neither essential nor natural. "The necessity of re-narrating and constantly patrolling boundaries is evidence of their incompleteness" (Jones 2008: 183).

The question is, then, What function does territoriality fulfill in a world society differentiated into different functional systems? As indicated above, political systems, in close coupling with legal systems, still rely heavily on territorial borders as a form of internal differentiation (see Luhmann 1998: 166; Bolz 2001: 11). The core advantage of territoriality, that one need not define what one has control over, must then be considered as a basic requirement for the emergence of the modern territorial state. Thus, functional systems such as "politics" and "law" are among those most challenged by the debordering effects of globalization. However, the emergence of new polities such as the European Union and a global human rights regime demonstrate that even "politics" and "law" are able to adapt to debordering processes and transcend, at least in part, the borders of the territorial state.

Symbolic systems representing different collective identities also refer at times to clear-cut territorial borders. The most obvious case is nationalism. One reason why states demanded a precise cartography of their territory in the nineteenth century was to enable the visualization of the nation (Osterhammel 2010: 150). From the standpoint of nationalism, territorial borders neatly separate one nation from the other. Often, the demarcation of the borders was paralleled by a process of homogenization in the newly created territory (Biggs 1999: 388). The territorialization of space and the representation of the state as territory were prerequisites for the emergence of nationalism, despite the fact that national identity discourses usually claimed the opposite: that the nation was a prerequisite for the territorial nation-state. Thus, "through the process of mapping, a new kind of territory and hence a new kind of state came into being" (Biggs 1999: 399). This territorial coupling of different functional and symbolic borders forms the basis of the modern nation-state. Globalization and processes of debordering can thus be understood as a decoupling of borders formerly coupled in the nation-state.

The territorialization of political rule through cartography also had ramifications for the representation of the state. Before its geographical depiction on maps, the state was never the *territorial* state. And this new political entity was then represented in an entirely new way. While realms and kingdoms were represented first and foremost by images and symbols such as coats of arms, modern cartography came to symbolize the "state as territory" (Biggs 1999: 390). Thus, the modern territorial state is not only the result of a functional fusion of political rule and geographical area but simultaneously a fusion of the symbolic representation of state and its geographical extent. Through maps, this representation of the state as territory was preserved and reproduced so that, as a result, maps "[e]ngraved the distinctive shape of a particular territory on the imagination" (Biggs 1999: 390).

Conclusion

This contribution sought to enhance the theoretical depth of the Debordering/Rebordering concept. Instead of interpreting Debordering/Rebordering merely as a crossing or reaffirmation of pre-existing territorial divides by functional and symbolic systems, this contribution understands Debordering/Rebordering to be an application of the principle of territoriality as a special mode of spatial differentiation within various functional and symbolic systems. Territorial borders, particularly in the form of state borders, are thus best understood as territorially converging borders of different functional and symbolic systems.

With this complex concept of Debordering/Rebordering, it is possible to embed the development and changing permeability of the EU/Polish-Ukrainian border in a theoretical framework and describe these developments as processes of debordering and rebordering. In this way, one can attempt to go beyond perceptions that either emphasize the debordering character of European integration (Barbé and Johansson-Nogués 2008) or concentrate on the exclusionary effects of EU bordering policies (Scott 2009; van Houtum/Pijpers 2007).

Instead, this contribution has offered an approach that conceives the EU/Polish-Ukrainian border as a process whereby the borders of the various functional and symbolic spaces are constantly being drawn and redrawn. Consequently, the EU/Polish-Ukrainian border must be viewed as a fluid social construct and as a result of ongoing communications at different functional and symbolic levels, communications that do not necessarily have to be congruent with the territorial border on the map that separates the EU and Poland from Ukraine. It is now possible to analyze the rationale behind EU and Polish policies towards Ukraine in the light of this concept. One can ask whether their policies can be seen as reactions to the challenges posed by debordering (and rebordering) processes. Do EU and Polish border policies vis-à-vis Ukraine illustrate the Debordering/Rebordering processes outlined above? The concept laid out in this contribution leads us to expect that various actors will attempt to adapt to debordering, for example by furthering cross-border activities, but also that new attempts of rebordering will create new spaces. From this point of view, it becomes clear that neither Poland nor the EU are in "the driver's seat" as they set Ukrainian border policy (Stetter 2005b: 8), but rather that they are reacting to complex debordering dynamics occurring in a wider global context.

Debordering/Rebordering promises to be an advance in the study of borders but also in the study of wider globalization processes and related debates. Although the EU border to Ukraine may be regarded as a special case insofar as this one particular nation-state border is embedded within the wider border regime of the EU's external borders, the concept of Debordering/Rebordering promises to be useful for border studies in general. It directly addresses one of the central problems of globalization processes: the increasing permeability of territorial borders. However, instead of leading to oversimplified diagnoses like the "end of the nation-state" or "Fortress Europe," Debordering/Rebordering allows us to analyze from a normatively neutral position the complex bordering processes that occur wherever the territorial anchoring of borders is called into question or actively reaffirmed by social practices.

REFERENCES

Albert, Mathias/Brock, Lothar (1996): "Debordering the world of states: New spaces in international relations", in: New Political Science 18(1), pp. 69-106.

Albert, Mathias/Brock, Lothar (2000): "De-bordering the world of states. New spaces in international relations", in: Mathias Albert/Lothar Brock/Klaus D. Wolf (Eds,), Civilizing world politics. Society and community beyond the state, Lanham, Md.: Rowman & Littlefield, pp. 19-43l.

Albert, Mathias/Brock, Lothar (2001): "What Keeps Westphalia Together? Normative Differentiation in the Modern System of States", in: Mathias Albert/David Jacobson/Yosef Lapid (eds.), Identities, borders, orders. Rethinking international relations theory, Minneapolis: University of Minnesota Press, pp. 29-49.

Anderson, Benedict (2006): Imagined Communities. Reflections on the origin and spread of nationalism, London: Verso.

Anderson, James (2001): Theorizing State Borders: 'Politics/Economics' and Democracy in Capitalism. CIBR Working Papers in Border Studies (2).

Anderson, James/O'Dowd, Liam (1999): "Borders, border regions and territoriality: Contradictory meanings, changing significance", in: Regional Studies 33 (7), pp. 593-604.

Anderson, James/O'Dowd, Liam/Wilson, Thomas M. (2003): "Why Study Borders Now?", in: Anderson/O'Dowd/Wilson (eds.), New borders for a changing Europe, pp. 1-12.

Anderson, James/O'Dowd, Liam/Wilson, Thomas M. (eds.) (2003): New borders for a changing Europe. Cross-border cooperation and governance. London: F. Cass.

Anderson, Malcolm (1996): Frontiers. Territory and state formation in the modern world, Cambridge: Polity Press.

Apap, Joanna/Tchorbadjiyska, Angelina (2004): What about the neighbours? The impact of Schengen along the EU's external borders, Brussels: CEPS.

Biggs, Michael (1999): "Putting the State on the Map: Cartography, Territory, and European State Formation", in: Comparative Studies in Society and History 41 (2), pp. 374-405.

Bolz, Norbert (2001): Weltkommunikation, München: Fink.

Bonacker, Thorsten (2006): "Krieg und die Theorie der Weltgesellschaft. Zur makrosoziologischen Erklärung neuerer Ergebnisse der empirischen Kriegsforschung", in Anna Geis (Ed.), Den Krieg überdenken. Kriegsbegriffe und Kriegstheorien in der Kontroverse. Baden-Baden: Nomos, pp. 75-93.

Bonacker, Thorsten (2007): "Debordering by human rights: The challenge of postterritorial conflicts in world society", in Stephan Stetter (Ed.), Territorial conflicts in world society. Modern systems theory, international relations and conflict studies, London: Routledge, pp. 19-32.

Brock, Lothar (2004): "World society from the bottom up", in Mathias Albert/Lena Hilkermeier (eds.), Observing international relations. Niklas Luhmann and world politics. London: Routledge, pp. 86-102.

Brunet-Jailly, Emmanuel (2005): "Theorizing Borders: An Interdisciplinary Perspective", Geopolitics 10 (4), pp. 633-649.

Burton, John W. (1972): World society. Cambridge: Cambridge UP.

Busch, Brigitta/Krzyżanowski, Michal (2007): "Inside/outside the European Union. Enlargement, migration policy and the search for Europe's identity", in: Warwick Armstrong/James Anderson (eds.), Geopolitics of European Union enlargement. The fortress empire. London: Routledge, pp. 107-24.

Christiansen, Thomas/Petito, Fabio/Tonra, Ben (2000): "Fuzzy Politics Around Fuzzy Borders: The European Union's 'Near Abroad'", in: Cooperation and Conflict 35 (4): pp. 389-415.

Comelli, Michele/Greco, Ettore/Tocci, Nathalie (2007): "From Boundary to Borderland: Transforming the Meaning of Borders through the European Neighbourhood Policy", in: European Foreign Affairs Review 12 (2), pp. 203-18.

Dandiş, Nicolae (2009): "Cross-border cooperation – a strategic dimension of European Neighborhood Policy at the Eastern frontier of the EU", in: Eurolimes (7), pp. 35-48.

Delanty, Gerard (2006): "Borders in a Changing Europe: Dynamics of Openness and Closure", in: Comparative European Politics (4), pp. 183-202.

Delanty, Gerard/Rumford, Chris (2005): Rethinking Europe. Social theory and the implications of Europeanization, London: Routledge.

Diez, Thomas (2004): "Europe's others and the return of geopolitics", in: Cambridge Review of International Affairs 17 (2), pp. 319-35.

Dimitrovova, Bohdana (2010): Remaking Europe's Borders through the European Neighbourhood Policy. Brussels: CEPS.

Donnan, Hastings/Wilson, Thomas M. (1999): Borders. Frontiers of identity, nation and state, Oxford: Berg.

European Commission (2004a): European Neighbourhood Policy. Strategy Paper, Communication from the Commission. COM (2004) 373 final, Brussels 12 May.

European Commission (2004b): European Neighbourhood Policy. Country Report Ukraine, Commission Staff Working Paper. COM (2004) 373 final, Brussels 12 May.

European Commission (2008): Eastern Partnership, Communication from the Commission to the European Parliament and the Council. COM (2008) 823 final, Brussels, 3 December.

Ferrer-Gallardo, Xavier (2008): "The Spanish-Moroccan border complex: Processes of geopolitical, functional and symbolic rebordering", in: Political Geography 27 (3), pp. 301-21.

Grabbe, Heather (2000): "The sharp edges of Europe: extending Schengen eastwards", in: International Affairs 76 (3), pp. 497-514.

Gropas, Ruby (2004): "Functional Borders, Sustainable Security and EU-Balkan Relations", in: Journal of Southeast European & Black Sea Studies 4 (1), pp. 49-76.

Jones, Reece (2008): "Categories, borders and boundaries", in: Progress in Human Geography 33 (2), pp. 174-89.

Kennard, Ann (2003): 'The Institutionalization of Borders in Central and Eastern Europe: A Means to What End?", in: Eiki Berg/Henk van Houtum (eds.), Routing borders between territories, discourses and practices, Aldershot: Ashgate, pp. 193-210.

Kolossov, Vladimir (2005): "Border Studies: Changing Perspectives and Theoretical Approaches", in: Geopolitics 10 (4), pp. 606-32.

Lamont, Michele/Molnár, Virág (2002): "The Study of Boundaries in the Social Sciences", in: Annual Review of Sociology 28 (1), pp. 167-95.

Lapid, Yosef (2001): "Introduction. Identities, Borders, Orders: Nudging International Relations Theory in a New Direction", in: Albert/Jacobson/Lapid (eds.), Identities, borders, orders, pp. 1-20.

Luhmann, Niklas (1991): Soziale Systeme, Frankfurt a.M.: Suhrkamp.

Luhmann, Niklas (1998): Die Gesellschaft der Gesellschaft. Frankfurt a.M.: Suhrkamp.

Luhmann, Niklas (2002): Die Politik der Gesellschaft, Frankfurt a.M.: Suhrkamp.
Martinez, Oscar J. (1994): "The Dynamics of Border Interaction. New approaches to border analysis", in: Clive H. Schofield (Ed.), Global boundaries, London/New York: Routledge, pp. 1-15.
Meyer, John. W./Krücken, Georg/Drori, Gili S. (2009): World society. The writings of John W. Meyer, Oxford: Oxford UP.
Newman, David (2003a): "Boundaries", in: John A. Agnew/Katharyne Mitchell/Gearóid Ó Tuathail (eds.), A companion to political geography, Malden, Mass.: Blackwell, pp. 123-37.
Newman, David (2003b): "Boundary Geopolitics: Towards a Theory of Territorial Lines?", in: Berg/van Houtum (eds.), Routing borders between territories, discourses and practices, pp. 277-291.
Newman, David (2003c): "On Borders and Power. A Theoretical Framework", in: Journal of Borderland Studies 18 (1), pp. 13-25.
Newman, David (2006a): "Borders and Bordering: Towards an Interdisciplinary Dialogue", in: European Journal of Social Theory 9 (2), pp. 171-86.
Newman, David (2006b): "The lines that continue to separate us: borders in our 'borderless' world", in: Progress in Human Geography 30 (2), pp. 143-61.
Newman, David/Paasi, Anssi (1998): "Fences and neighbours in the postmodern world: boundary narratives in political geography", in: Progress in Human Geography 22 (2), pp. 186-207.
Ohmae, Kenichi (1994): The borderless world. Power and strategy in the global marketplace, London: HarperCollins.
Osterhammel, Jürgen (2010): Die Verwandlung der Welt. Eine Geschichte des 19. Jahrhunderts, Bonn: Bundeszentrale für Politische Bildung.
Paasi, Anssi (1996): Territories, boundaries, and consciousness. The changing geographies of the Finnish-Russian border, Chichester: Wiley.
Paasi, Anssi (1999a): "Boundaries as social practice and discourse: The Finnish-Russian border", in: Regional Studies 33 (7), pp 669-80.
Paasi, Anssi (1999b): "The Political Geography of Boundaries at the End of the Millenium: Challenges of the De-territorializing World", in: Heikki Eskelinen/Ilkka Liikanen/Jukka Oksa (eds.), Curtains of iron and gold. Reconstructing borders and scales of interaction, Aldershot: Ashgate, pp. 9-24.

Paasi, Anssi (2001): "Europe as a Social Process and Discourse", in: European Urban and Regional Studies 8 (1), pp. 7-28.

Paasi, Anssi (2003): "Boundaries in a Globalizing World", in: Kay Anderson/Mona Domosh/Steve Pile/Nigel Thrift (eds.): Handbook of cultural geography, London: Sage, pp. 462-472.

Paasi, Anssi (2005) "The Changing Discourses on Political Boundaries. Mapping the Backgrounds, Contexts and Contents", in: Henk van Houtum/Olivier T. Kramsch/Wolfgang Zierhofer (eds.), B/ordering space, Aldershot: Ashgate, pp. 17-31.

Perkmann, Markus (2003): "Cross-Border Regions in Europe: Significance and Drivers of Regional Cross-Border Co-Operation", in: European Urban and Regional Studies 10 (2), pp. 153-171.

Popescu, Gabriel (2008): "The conflicting logics of cross-border reterritorialization: Geopolitics of Euroregions in Eastern Europe", in: Political Geography 27 (4), pp. 418-38.

Rumford, Chris (2006): "Theorizing Borders", in: European Journal of Social Theory 9 (2), pp. 155-169.

Rumford, Chris (2007): "Does Europe Have Cosmopolitan Borders?", in: Globalizations 4 (3), pp. 327-339.

Sack, Robert D. (1986): Human territoriality. Its theory and history, Cambridge/New York: Cambridge UP.

Schlögel, Karl (2009): Im Raume lesen wir die Zeit. Über Zivilisationsgeschichte und Geopolitik, Frankfurt a.M.: Fischer-Taschenbuch.

Scott, James/Matzeit, Silke (eds.) (2006): EXLINEA "Lines of Exclusion as Arenas of Co-operation: Reconfiguring the External Boundaries of Europe – Policies, Practices, Perceptions", Final Project Report.

Scott, James W. (2005): "The EU and 'Wider Europe': Toward an Alternative Geopolitics of Regional Cooperation?", in: Geopolitics 10 (3), pp. 429-454.

Scott, James W. (2009): "Bordering and Ordering the European Neighbourhood: A Critical Perspective on EU Territoriality and Geopolitics", in: TRAMES: A Journal of the Humanities & Social Sciences 13 (3), pp. 232-247.

Stetter, Steohan (2005a): "The Politics of De-Paradoxification in Euro-Mediterranean Relations: Semantics and Structures of 'Cultural Dialogue'", in: Mediterranean Politics 10 (3), pp. 331-348.

Stetter, Stephan (2005b): Theorising the European Neighbourhood Policy: Debordering and Rebordering in the Mediterranean. EUI Working

Papers, RSCAS (34), Florence: European University Institute, Robert Schuman Centre for Advanced Studies.

Stetter, Stephan (2007): "Regions of conflict in world society: The place of the Middle East and Sub-Saharan Africa", in: Stephan Stetter (Ed.), Territorial conflicts in world society. Modern systems theory, international relations and conflict studies, London: Routledge, pp. 33-47.

Stetter, Stephan (2008a): "Territories We Make and Unmake. The Social Construction of Borders in the Age of Globalization", in: Harvard International Review, September.

Stetter, Stephan (2008b): World society and the Middle East. Reconstructions in regional politics, Basingstoke: Palgrave Macmillan.

Stetter, Stephan (2009): "Entgrenzungen in der Weltgesellschaft. Eine Bedrohung für die Demokratie?", in: André Brodocz/Marcus Llanque/ Gary S. Schaal (eds.), Bedrohungen der Demokratie, Wiesbaden: VS, pp. 99-118.

Stichweh, Rudolf (2000): Die Weltgesellschaft. Soziologische Analysen, Frankfurt a.M.: Suhrkamp.

van Houtum, Henk/Pijpers, Roos (2007): "The European Union as a Gated Community: The Two-faced Border and Immigration Regime of the EU", in: Antipode 39 (2), pp. 291-309.

van Houtum, Henk/van Naerssen, Ton (2002): "Bordering, Ordering and Othering", in: Tijdschrift voor Economische en Sociale Geografie 93 (2), pp. 125-136.

van Houtum, Henk/Kramsch, Olivier T./Zierhofer, Wolfgang (eds.) (2005): B/ordering space, Aldershot: Ashgate.

Vermeersch, Peter (2007): "A Minority at the Border: EU Enlargement and the Ukrainian Minority in Poland", in: East European Politics and Societies 21 (3), pp. 475-502.

Weller, Christoph (2000): "Collective Identities in World Society", in: Albert/Brock/Wolf (eds.), Civilizing world politics, pp. 45-68.

Wilson, Thomas M./Donnan, Hastings (eds.) (1998): Border identities. Nation and state at international frontiers, Cambridge: Cambridge UP.

Wolczuk, Kataryna (2002): "The Polish-Ukrainian Border: On the Receiving End of EU Enlargement", in: Perspectives on European Politics & Society 3 (2), pp. 245-270.

Zielonka, Jan (Ed.) (2002): Europe unbound. Enlarging and reshaping the boundaries of the European Union, London: Routledge.

Qualities of Bordering Spaces
A Conceptual Experiment with Reference to Georg Simmel's Sociology of Space

Sabrina Ellebrecht

Introduction

Inspired by the spatial turn and with the consequent impetus of deessentialising borders in general, this contribution is interested in the qualities of bordering spaces (*Grenz-Räume*). Assuming that borders can be conceived of as spaces of their own right, some of their general qualities are inquired. For that purpose, this contribution applies Georg Simmel's sociology of space, set out in his 1908 essay on "Space and the Spatial Order of Society," to the empirical example of the external border of the European Union (EU) in the Mediterranean Sea. In the conceptual experiment below, each of Simmel's qualities of space (*Raumqualitäten*) are briefly explained. The experiment then consists of applying these qualities of space to selected analysis of the EU border management in the Mediterranean region. From this, some proposed general qualities of bordering spaces are extrapolated.[1]

---

[1] | Passages in German or French texts have been translated by the author when not available in English. With regard to quotations from Simmel, I have decided to provide them in the respective footnote.

Applying Simmel's Qualities of Space to Bordering Processes

Several authors refer to Simmel's sociology of space and discuss its potential analytical value.[2] Some of the more controversial aspects of Simmel's approach are, firstly, his use of the euclidic, and with it the idea of an absolute space, frequently subsumed under the metaphor of the container. Second, his purported support for the thesis that social ties are becoming emancipated from space. Finally, his analytical framework for a sociology of space in general. It is argued that his analytical frame, constructed on the building blocks of the "qualities of spaces" (*Raumqualitäten*) and of "spatial formations" (*Raumgebilde*), is not systematic. Moreover, Simmel's approach is criticized as illustrative rather than conceptual.

Andrea Glauser explicitly addresses the first two critiques in her essay, "Pioneering Work with Paradoxical Consequences". Glauser shows that Simmel refers to Euclidean space as an "ideal-typical auxiliary construct" (Glauser 2006: 254). However, Simmel does not offer a mere analysis of space as an abstract concept, but of space as perceived by and employed by societal groups. This is the context in which Simmel makes reference to Euclidean space.[3] By emphasizing the relevance of human percipience, Simmel presents the antithesis to the thesis of mechanical causation as promoted by the early natural sciences and as idealized by social scientists of his time. To Simmel, space is conceivable, perceptible, producible, designable; but it is not a fixed, a priori constant. The sociologist analyzes social projections into space – from imagined, to architectural to institutions – and the way these projections turn back and affect the lives and forms of social groups (Schroer 2006: 63). This emphasis on socio-spatial interactions (*Wechselwirkungen*) is not compatible with the second criticism which has reproached Simmel for his assertion that the social can be delinked and

---

2 | See Konau 1973; Strassoldo 1992; Ziemann 2000; Löw 2001; Schroer 2006; Glauser 2006; Canto Milà 2006; Eigmüller 2006; Cuttitta 2006, 2007.

3 | Similarly, Vilém Flusser in his 1991 essay, "Räume," describes humans as organic tubes, as worms that crawl up and down, left and right and which thus live in three-dimensional space. With regard to contemporary spatial perceptions, however, Flusser sees abstract and imaged forms of virtual space and outer space as challenging the "worm's" perception from the ground and enabling topological understanding and experiencing.

emancipated from space (Läpple 1991; Löw 2001). Addressing the imputed unsystematic nature of Simmel's analytical framework, Glauser argues that Simmel's qualities of space "can be used as a kind of observer's horizon, against which selectivity can be revealed and questioned" (Glauser 2006: 265). Simmel's framework does seem to lack a clear taxonomy. However, considering that Simmel's program for the study of space was intended to be a counter-proposal to the emerging field of anthropogeography[4], his choice to employ qualities of space can also be attributed to a more sophisticated conceptual strategy. With regard to sociation, Simmel stresses the relevance of the qualities of space in contrast to the quantities of geometry. Moreover, he is interested in the analysis of historical and cultural manifestations of societal relations onto space, rejecting causal and geo-deterministic analyses. In this spirit, he writes that "for nature, any demarcation of borders is arbitrary"[5] (Simmel 1992: 695). Likewise, Simmel considers the social reception of "merely" political borders stronger than those of the so-called natural borders along rivers, seas, or mountains (Simmel 1992: 694). His analytical frame of using qualities of space turns out to be a methodological tool when aiming at strengthening the historic and cultural dimension of space, which, in essence, can be seen as an early premise of the spatial turn. Therefore, each of Simmel's five qualities of space – exclusivity; decomposability and delimitation; proximity and distance; fixity; and movement – is

---

4 | Werner Köster (2002) describes how the scientific dealing with space at the turn of the 19th to the 20th century had been shaped by the historical context of two emerging disciplines in the humanities – sociology and geography – competing for institutional viability. In this context, Georg Simmel and Friedrich Ratzel are often contrasted. Interestingly, both Simmel and Ratzel drew on Immanuel Kant's concept of space as pure form of intuition. While Simmel sociologizes the Kantian concept (Glauser 2006: 258), Ratzel turns it into a "naiv-empirical" spatial concept (Köster 2002: 62). However, a coeval review of Simmels On the Spatial Expressions of Social Forms by Émile Durkheim (1904) considered the Simmelian approach less comprehensive and less sophisticated than Ratzel's thoughts on space. Yet, Durkheim pointed to a certain ambiguity within Ratzel's works. Ratzel, he wrote, would vacillate between two premises: the logic of the social and a certain geo-determinism (Köster 2002: 93).

5 | "Der Natur gegenüber ist jede Grenzsetzung Willkür, selbst im Falle einer insularen Lage, da doch prinzipiell auch das Meer "in Besitz genommen" werden kann."

explained below and applied to contemporary analysis of EU migration and border control policies in the Mediterranean.

Exclusivity

In his first lines on exclusivity (*Ausschließlichkeit des Raumes*), Simmel points to the uniqueness of every part of space. "Just as there is only one universal space, of which all single spaces are pieces, so is each part of space unique in a way for which there hardly exists any analogy" (Simmel 1992: 690)[6.] According to Simmel, several objects of the same kind might be found in different places, yet positing a plurality of the same space seems absurd. This apparently banal but crucial characteristic is best understood through its linkage to territory (*Grund und Boden*). "To the extent to which a societal formation is linked or is 'loyal,' so to speak, to a specific stretch of territory, it has a uniqueness and exclusivity that cannot be achieved otherwise"[7] (ibid.). In this sense, territory renders the uniqueness of any part of space palpable. The state is the only example of a spatial formation fully characterized by exclusivity, as it is "so strictly linked to territory that it is impossible to think of the co-existence of another state on the same territory" (Cuttitta 2006: 31 referring to Simmel). Due to its limited scope and reach, the modern national state provides an unambiguous point of orientation. It should also be mentioned that Simmel distinguishes between local manifestations and territorial appropriation or bonds. While the latter produces identity, or rather 'territorial belonging' in the sense of exclusivity, the first refers to the manifestation of particular, social relations in buildings, architecture, and spatial arrangements. Exclusivity thus alludes to membership and its significance for the spatial organization of social structure, amongst which territory is but one mode. While territory evokes the uniqueness of each part of space, it is crucial not to confuse this with the social mechanisms of exclusion,

---

6 | "Wie es nur einen einzigen allgemeinen Raum gibt, von dem alle einzelnen Räume Stücke sind, so hat jeder Raumteil eine Art von Einzigkeit, für die es kaum eine Analogie gibt."

7 | "In dem Maß, in dem ein gesellschaftliches Gebilde mit einer bestimmten Bodenausdehnung verschmolzen oder sozusagen solidarisch ist, hat es einen Charakter von Einzigkeit oder Ausschließlichkeit, der auf andre Weise nicht ebenso erreichbar ist."

which are often organized and justified with reference to territory.[8] With Simmel it is thus possible to obviate the "territorial trap" (Agnew 1994), as he sees exclusivity as one element of the construction of territory, rather than as one of its effects.[9]

Exclusivity as a Quality of Bordering Spaces?

Territorial (state) borders define the inside and outside by drawing a line. They demonstrate and materialize exclusivity by creating the space where membership is regulated. They allow for the operationalization of distinction and exclusion. The definition of inside and outside is manifested in fences and walls, as well as in the metaphor of 'Fortress Europe'. Alluding to Simmel's essay *Brücke und Tür* (1909), Paolo Cuttitta writes that "the EU, as all fortresses, does, however, have a gate and a drawbridge, which occasionally can be opened or lowered" (Cuttitta 2010: 29). Through the metaphors of the gate and the drawbridge, selection is posited as a bordering process. In his article, "Das europäische Grenzregime: Dynamiken und Wechselwirkungen," Cuttitta illustrates the extent to which exclusion and selection are conflated within the framework of EU migration and border-control management. Transit zones or detention centers, he argues, do not function as a means to ultimately exclude third-country members who arrive by boat on EU territory. Rather they are meant to decelerate (Panagiotidis/Tsianos 2007) the project of migration. According to Cuttitta (2010: 31ff.), the status of illegality has become an intermediary stage in the migration process. But where do these (biographical) stages occur? And

---

8 | Simmel further distinguishes between supra-territorial formations (überräumliche Gebilde) and territorial formations (räumliche Gebilde). Territorial formations are characterized by the liaison between territory and social ties while supra-territorial formations go beyond territorial definitions or belonging. The latter might correspond to what has recently been described as transnational formations (Pries 2008; Wimmer/Glick-Schiller 2002).

9 | The fact that borders and territory are defined in reference to one another has been explored by Stuart Elden (2010). According to Elden, borders are a second-order phenomenon and depend on the historical meaning of territory as a dimension of space. The question whether border studies are territorially trapped has been of interest for David Newmann (2010), Fiona McConnell (2010) and John Agnew (2007, 2008, 2010).

where would they come to an end? Locked in the status and the places of illegality, third country members can only get access to selection processes which operate along bordering questions: money enough to pay the facilitator?, fit enough to make the trip?, castaway enough to be rescued on the high-seas?, victimized enough to apply for asylum?, patient enough to wait in a detention centre?, strong enough to survive in the irregular economy of European labor markets? A topology of illegalized border-crossings would reflect different sites along the 'way', such as the refugee boat, the slums in Tripoli, the detention centers, or asylum offices.[10] In so doing, a spatial sociology would link bordering processes to their spatial fulcra.

Whereas inside and outside are about physical access and are decided 'on site,' the tension between open and closed is about access to a legal sphere. In the negotiation of membership, the tensions between open and closed[11] as well as between inside and outside are conflated. With regard to third-country nationals migrating by boat, the selection process seems to be affected by an exclusionary logic.[12] Analytically, however, these two dimensions need to be divided into distinct qualities of bordering spaces, precisely for the reason of disentangling the container-like connotation of an inside-outside binary, which might be at work along a border, from the idea of selection.

---

10 | An outstanding example for such a topology is Silja Klepp's (2011) ethnography of the sea border in the Mediterranean. With reference to Georg Marcus call for a multi-sided ethnography, Klepp follows the people in Tripoli, on arrival in European shores, in the detention center, in court.

11 | Having examined Simmel's qualities of space, Schroer states they can, in fact, be applied to contemporary examples. He states that additional qualities or tensions might well exist and proposes the dichotomies of inside-outside as well as open versus closed (Schroer 2006: 77f.). My argument is that these tensions are already part of the quality of "exclusivity."

12 | In their ongoing research project, "State Project Europe," Sonja Buckel, John Kannankulam, and Jens Wissel analyze the re-grouping of the European population into zones of stratified legal titles, one zone being illegalized migration. A first account is provided in the essay "State Project Europe: The Transformation of the European Border Regime and the Production of Bare Life" (Buckel/Wissel 2010).

Decomposability and Delimitation

When Simmel is quoted on borders, the context from which the quotations have been drawn is seldom mentioned. Under the second quality of space, namely 'decomposability and delimitation' (*Zerlegbarkeit und Begrenzung*), Simmel elaborates on borders between individuals and groups, which in a first step, are defined as 'functional compartments'. He writes: "Another quality of space that significantly influences societal interactions consists in the fact that for the purpose of utilization, space is divided into pieces that are considered discrete units and that are – as both cause and a result of this – framed by borders" (Simmel 1992: 694).[13]

According to Simmel, social differentiation is spatially marked by borders and boundaries. However, and this is important, social differentiation is not necessarily exclusive. In this sense, Simmel defines border in the following way: "The border is not a spatial fact with sociological effects, but a sociological fact that forms itself in space" (Simmel 1992: 697).[14] This definition is frequently quoted by way of stressing the socially constructed character of political borders and other boundaries between individuals and groups. Although Simmel does point to the constructed character of boundaries with this remark, he equally acknowledges the social repercussions of a materialized border, its "physical power," and its "lively energy" (Simmel 1992: 697f.).[15] Once it is materialized or repre-

---

13 | "Eine weitere Qualität des Raumes, die auf die gesellschaftlichen Wechselwirkungen wesentlich einwirkt, liegt darin, dass sich der Raum für unsere praktische Ausnützung in Stücke zerlegt, die als Einheiten gelten und – als Ursache wie als Wirkung hiervon – von Grenzen eingerahmt sind."

14 | "Die Grenze ist nicht eine räumliche Tatsache mit soziologischen Wirkungen, sondern eine soziologische Tatsache, die sich räumlich formt."

15 | "Ist sie freilich erst zu einem räumlichen-sinnlichen Gebilde geworden, das wir unabhängig von seinem soziologisch praktischen Sinne in die Natur einzeichnen, so übt dies starke Rückwirkungen auf das Bewußtsein von dem Verhältnis der Parteien. Während diese Linie nur die Verschiedenheit des Verhältnisses zwischen den Elementen einer Sphäre untereinander und zwischen diesen und den Elementen einer andren markiert, wird sie doch zu einer lebendigen Energie, die jene aneinanderdrängt und sie nicht aus ihrer Einheit herausläßt und sich wie eine physische Gewalt, die nach beiden Seiten hin Repulsionen ausstrahlt, zwischen beide schiebt."

sented by a physical or geographical border line, the border becomes a part of the interaction. This is congruent with his conceptualization of space as both the projection of societal relations and source of effects on the lives and forms of groups (Schroer 2006: 61ff.; Ziemann 2000: 250ff.). The principle of interaction (*Wechselwirkung*) – prominent throughout Simmel's œuvre – is at the heart of his assessment. Drawing on Simmel, Natalià Cantó Milà describes borders as the phenomenon in which social relations, including power relations, crystallize. She writes that "the projection of demarcation onto space strengthens the border and perpetuates it" (Cantó Milà 2006: 192).

At the same time, Simmel emphasizes the ordering and relieving function of borders, pointing to the "security" and "clarity" they provide (Simmel 1992: 699). Lastly, it is worth mentioning that Simmel thinks of darkness as a distorting circumstance for social and spatial arrangements. Darkness transforms social borders, it brings about "a completely unique augmentation and combination of encompassing and expansion in the confinement of space" (Simmel 1992: 705).[16]

These remarks will be considered in the following passage when analyzing contemporary EU migration and border control policies against the background of the spatial quality of decomposability and delimitation.

Decomposability and Delimitation as a Quality of Bordering Spaces?

An application of the second quality of space, "decomposability and delimitation," to borders might not seem necessary at first glance. Yet, Simmel writes about the "line of definition" and the "moment of decision" with regard to societal membership. In his view, physical boundaries facilitate and perpetuate social differentiation. Conceptualizing borders as spaces

---

16 | "Andererseits läßt eben dies auch die wirklich vorhandenen Grenzen verschwinden, die Phantasie erweitert das Dunkel zu übertriebenen Möglichkeiten, man fühlt sich von einem phantastisch-unbestimmten und unbeschränkten Raum umgeben. Indem nun die im Dunkeln natürliche Ängstlichkeit und Unsicherheit hier durch jenes enge Zusammengedrängtsein und Aufeinander-Angewiesensein Vieler behoben wird, entsteht jene gefürchtete Erregung und Unberechenbarkeit des Zusammenlaufes im Dunkeln, als eine ganz einzige Steigerung und Kombination der einschließenden und der sich expandierenden räumlichen Begrenzung."

in their own right allows one to probe further into the decomposability of borders (its practices, institutions, and processes) and into the rationale for geographic demarcations of a given border.

Turning first to the decomposability of borders, the work of the French philosopher Etienne Balibar (Balibar 2002a, 2002b, 2004a, 2004b) is significant "for the priority he accords borders in the study of democracy, citizenship and the question of European identity" (Rumford 2011: 37). Balibar argues that the term 'border'

> is profoundly changing in meaning. The borders of new politico-economic entities, in which an attempt is being made to preserve the functions of the sovereignty of the state, are no longer at all situated at the outer limit of territories: they are dispersed a little everywhere, wherever the movement of information, people, and things is happening and is controlled (Balibar 2002a: 71).

The (cross-border) movement of goods, information, money, and people challenges the ambition of public institutions to establish and maintain order, argues Balibar with much of the globalization literature. Just as the deconstruction of the territorial nation-state resulted in a diversification and multiplication of spatial matters, bordering processes, too, have been diversified. They are becoming fragmented administratively, legally, and practically and they have become increasingly specialized. The transformation of borders over the past 20 years has often been described as the reconfiguration of territorial borders – defining the territorial nation-state – to a networked system of control and surveillance that reproduces the border both inside and outside the respective state. In this context, the metaphor of the network has attracted attention.[17] Moreover, borders have been described as flexible: "The different kinds of frontier, far from dis-

---

17 | Doris Schweitzer's (2011) analysis of Manuel Castells' concept of a network-society as it relates to the topography of borders shows that the topography of a networked society allows for a radicalization of bordering processes. Athanasios Karafillidis (2009) even argues that the network itself is a border. Stefan Kaufmann (2006) describes the transformation of borders as three topographical transformations of the border-line: forward relocation, tightening, an in-folding. He shows that the societal conceptualisation of a network-society has found its manifestation in the reconfiguration of the EU migration and border control regime.

appearing, reproduce and diversify themselves. Therefore, they become potentially omnipresent, and their number and types are potentially infinite" (Cuttitta 2007: 2). With regard to the European external border in the Mediterranean Sea, the phenomena described above are "localizable" as in the case of ex-territorial detention camps in Libya (Nosh 2008) or in the vessels and advising officers provided by the European Agency for the Management of Operational Coordination at the External Borders of the Member States of the European Union (Frontex) to patrols in Senegalese territorial waters – notably meant to secure the external borders of the Member States of the EU. The decomposition of borders has also been described as de-localization, meaning a geographic transfer of border control into the territorial waters of a third country or onto the high seas, and as externalization, which refers to the outsourcing of tasks and responsibilities to third countries (Cuttitta 2010: 26; Buckel 2011). A certain distributedness, in parallel to a specialisation, merge in the example of Frontex whose mandate is 'pioneering' in the field of a supranational border management (Kasparek 2010: 116ff.; Neal 2009; Fischer-Lescano/Tohidipur 2007)[18]. In general, the spatial distribution of bordering practices corresponds to a distribution of competencies and to an overlapping and consequent blurring of legal spheres. The border-land appears as decomposable as it becomes reorganized in the process of Europeanization[19]. Bordering practices no longer run along a fixed geographic borderline. Moreover, the means and practices of border control and surveillance are continually renegotiated and relocated. In keeping with this, the question of *where?* does not merely refer to a geographic coordinate. *Where?* also asks for the legal framework, the policy context, and the position. It asks for the topology of bordering practices, processes, institutions, and sites. This *where?* not only challenges the concept of territory. It challenges the visibility of borders. Similarly, the technologies deployed for border control and border

---

18 | The latest amendment concerning Frontex's competencies has been formulated in Regulation (EU) No 1168/2011 of 25th October 2011. Three aspects point to a strengthening of the Agency's capacities: the possibility to acquire or lease equipment, the task to set up European Border Guard Teams which can be deployed during Joint Operations (JOs), and the fact that Frontex may initiate JOs.

19 | Georg Vobruba (2010) provides a comprehensive discussion on the impact of the European integration on the formation and shaping of common external border policies.

surveillance alter the visibility of borders and produce clandestine and invisible figures, such as the stowaway (Walters 2008). Divers surveillance technologies, such as radar, satellite, sensors, cameras as well as information and communication technologies (ICT), contribute to the production of bordering spaces and determine their qualities. In any decomposition of space to produce a border, there is tension between (being) visible and (making) invisible (or vice versa). The tension between visible and invisible can thus be considered a quality of bordering spaces. While the border, as a contract between states, has hitherto limited the scope and visibility of sovereigns, the border now appears as the mandate for border-related surveillance and intelligence. This way state borders are not only blurred on the high seas where proactive patrolling and surveillance are untied from territorial limitations codified in geographic distances.

The tension between visible and invisible further plays out in the cat-and-mouse game of unauthorized border-crossing vis-à-vis mandated border control and surveillance. In this context, Simmel's remarks on darkness add an astute aspect: under the distorting condition of darkness, the proportionality between means and ends are both on the side of law enforcement authorities while the potential trespassers enter a win or loose scenario. Night-watch cameras, radar and intelligence-driven operations on the one side counter the maybe strategic, maybe frightened attempts to cross the blue sea in dark hours.

Regarding issues of border delimitation and border qualities, these can be simplified into the question of *where should we make the demarcation?* This question raises concerns about the legitimization and the techniques of demarcation, of measuring, and of political decision making. If borders cannot be drawn arbitrarily, the question of demarcation touches upon the criteria which legitimize them, which render them considered "good," "natural," "necessary," etc. This brings to the fore the tension between natural and cultural as relevant to bordering spaces. This tension often appears in border studies as "the enduring geographical myth of natural borders" (Fall 2010).

Proximity and Distance

With the advent of globalization theories, Georg Simmel's sociology of space frequently has been cited to shed light on the relations between proximity and distance (*Nähe und Distanz*), his fourth quality of space, and on movement and migration (*Bewegung, Wanderung*), his fifth quality of space. Both qualities are used to describe the effects of modernity on social relations and to assess the ambivalence of urban life (Allen 2001). According to Simmel, proximity encourages intimacy and social cohesion. Social relations at a distance allow for individualization and freedom; yet they require the capacity to abstract (Simmel 1992: 717). How does the modern ambivalence between proximity and distance apply to bordering spaces?

Proximity and Distance with Regard to Bordering Spaces?

If the border is a point of crystallization, as Cantó Mila suggests, tensions appear at the border more pronounced and more drastically. Asymmetric power relations thus seem to be traceable both along a demarcation line and throughout unequal mobility policies. For the case of migration, distance implies that more than just geographic space is overcome. From the perspective of a person migrating to Europe from a place in Senegal, for instance, distance could rather be described as the amount of capital and resources required to arrive in the Schengen Area. The way in which asymmetric power relations play out in bordering processes is bitterly illustrated by the fact that the route of repatriation (for most routes less then ten hours by air) obliterates resources that may have taken the migrant months or years to accumulate. The tension between proximity and distance, which Simmel rather unsystematically introduced as a quality of space, has been noted in arguments about how social relations are becoming emancipated from their spatial limits. However, resources for overcoming geographic distance are unevenly distributed (Baumann 1998). This alone bestows yet another quality to the tension between proximity and distance on a global scale.[20] For the case of the EU border on

---

[20] | Discussions on the global-local dichotomy echoed Simmel's ambivalent take on the effects of proximity and distance on social relations (Robertson 1994; Massey 2005,2006). Recently, this tension has been widened to discussions on uneven development (Harvey 2005) and "spatial justice" (Soja 2010). Manuell Castell's network-society is not organized around the ordering principle of distance and proximity; instead, one is either in or out of the network. Inside the network, distance approaches zero. According to Castells, black holes stand for radical exclusion (Castells 1996; Schweitzer 2011). Marc Augé argues that under

the Mediterranean Sea, the tension could be measured as noted above by comparing geographic distance to time, money, and resources invested in migration, as well as to the time individuals wait or are detained. Reformulated as tension, Simmel's fourth quality of space, "proximity and distance" is also valuable when investigating border-spatialities.

Fixity

"Fixity" (*Fixierung*) describes the extent to which a particular social content is fixed or localized on a place or a building such as the house or the clubroom. Under this quality of space, Simmel addresses questions of belonging as they relate to physical presence or absence, and he discusses the function of a pivotal point to social relations. With regard to the latter, he writes that "meaning, as the fulcrum (*Drehpunkt*) of sociological relations, is held by a fixed spatiality wherever the encounter or the engagement of otherwise separated elements can only occur in a particular place" (Simmel 1992: 708).[21] By means of the fulcrum, relations that otherwise might have remained invisible appear, at least to the sociologist. These relations serve to support the continuation of social processes. Simmel's elaborations are perfectly compatible with the idea of virtual space, and the meaning of the chat room experience functions as a fulcrum for societal relations which otherwise would not occur or be tangible.

Another interesting example that illustrates the spatial quality of "fixity" is the difference between individual and numeric naming of houses:

The 'being numbered' of urban houses signifies, in a higher sense, the spatial fixation of individuals, as they can be traced with the help of a mechanical method. Obviously, this traceability differs in nature from the designation of particular quarters and streets to certain classes and professions and from the separa-

---

the condition of supermodernity there is merely the near, anything of no concern to the self would occur elsewhere (Augé 2008 [1992]) – a nuance not captured in the German translation "Das Nahe und das Ferne".

21 | "Die Bedeutung als Drehpunkt soziologischer Beziehung kommt der fixierten Örtlichkeit überall da zu, wo die Berührung oder Vereinigung sonst voneinander unabhängiger Elemente nur an einem bestimmten Platze geschehen kann."

tion into Christian, Jewish, and Muslim quarters in oriental towns (Simmel 1992: 712).[22]

Contrasting houses that are numbered as parts of an ordering inventory and houses with names, Simmel works out the advantages and disadvantages of aggregate and individual classifications. Simmel's rather innocent example should not hide the momentousness of the underlying thought: different ordering logics have different implications for sociation.

Movement, Migration

Under the concept of "movement or migration" (*Bewegung, Wanderung*) Simmel analyses the extent to which the structure of a social group is affected when some or all members of a group are migratory. Simmel argues that a sociological assessment which looks at the "effects of migrating" (*Wirkung des Wanderns*) (Simmel 1992: 748) does not have to distinguish between nomadism and migration, for the reason that "the effect on the form of society is typically the same in both cases: oppression or removal of the internal differentiation of the group, a subsequent lack of actual political organization, which, however, is often compatible with despotic leadership" (Simmel 1992: 748f).[23] When describing the advantages and disadvantages in social status of itinerant and sedentary individuals, Simmel writes, "the person who is sedentary in principle can at any time move anywhere, so that he, in addition to his sedentariness, enjoys all advantages of mobility, whereas not all advantages of sedentariness apply to the same extent to the person who is mobile in principle"

---

22 | "Die Nummeriertheit der Stadthäuser bedeutet in einem höheren Sinne überhaupt erst die räumliche Fixierung der Individuen, indem diese nun nach einer mechanischen Methode auffindbar sind. Diese Auffindbarkeit ist ersichtlich ganz andrer Natur, als sie in der mittelalterlichen Designierung besonderer Quartiere und Straßen für bestimmte Stände und Berufe liegt oder in der Trennung von Christen-, Juden- und Mohammedanerquartieren orientalischer Städte."

23 | "Denn jene Wirkung auf die Gesellschaftsform ist typischerweise in beiden Fällen die gleiche: Niederhalten oder Aufhebung der inneren Differenzierung der Gruppe, daher Mangel eigentlicher politischer Organisation, der sich aber oft mit despotischen Einherrschaften durchaus verträgt."

(Simmel 1992: 764).[24] According to Simmel, mobility implies more advantages when combined with a sedentary status. Simmel does not describe migration as a global phenomenon that affects local circumstances; instead he is interested in processes of sociation within the migrating group itself. Moreover, he takes up the relationship between migrants and non-migrants but does not necessarily assume different group affiliations. Note that, concerning membership, the itinerant is not the same thing as the stranger.[25] Itinerant and the sedentary individuals compete for social resources. Subsequently, sociation implies a tension over negotiating membership policies. Reading Simmel, it becomes clear that movement policies and spatial clustering of social groups are interrelated, and this deserves attention.

Fixity and Movement with Regard to Bordering Spaces?

In times of globalization, Markus Schroer argues, asking about space corresponds to asking about one's origin, destination, and level of access in respect to a certain area (Schroer 2006). Similarly, Zygmunt Bauman considers mobility as the key condition of social stratification in a globalizing world. "The dimension along which those 'high up' and 'low down' are plotted in a society of consumers, is their *degree of mobility* – their free-

---

24 | "Es scheint überhaupt, als ob, je näher der Gegenwart, um so günstiger die Position des Seßhaften gegenüber dem auf Bewegung angewiesenen Gegner sei. Und dies ist durch die Erleichterung der Ortsveränderung begreiflich. Denn sie bewirkt, daß auch der prinzipiell Seßhafte dch jederzeit sich überallhin begeben kann, so daß er neben seiner Seßhaftigkeit mehr und mehr noch alle Vorteile der Mobilität genießt, während dem Unsteten, prinzipiell Beweglichen nicht im gleichen Maße die Vorteile der Seßhaftigkeit zugewachsen sind."

25 | In his essay, "The Stranger" (1908), Simmel writes in the section on proximity and distance: "The stranger will thus not be considered here in the usual sense of the term, as the wanderer who comes today and goes tomorrow, but rather as the man who comes today and stays tomorrow – the potential wanderer, so to speak, who, although he has gone no further, has not quite got over the freedom of coming and going. He is fixed within a certain spatial circle – or within a group whose boundaries are analogous to spatial boundaries – but his position within it is fundamentally affected by the fact that he does not belong in it initially [...]" (Simmel 1972).

dom to choose where to be" (Baumann 1998: 86). According to Baumann, the consumer society has created the social figures of tourist and vagabond. Vagabonds are stuck in a place because of their limited possibilities, watching the world go by. Tourists, however, move around the world as they please. In contemporary debates, the term "migrant" is commonly used for those whose mobility is restricted, whereas the term "mobility" is used to describe something possessed by "global elites," who are able to overcome geographic distance quickly and with little disruption of their personal lives. This distinction is clear from the perspective of border management: the "bona fide" passenger is supposed to be helped across the border as seamlessly as possible, but those who are not allowed to cross must be held up. Considering that movement can also be conceptualized as power, as Trutz von Trotha (2006) argues with reference to Albert O. Hirschman, mobility constraints cannot simply be reduced to an issue of resources. Rather they reveal asymmetric power relations, traceable within migration patterns and border control policies. With regard to the EU's external border in the Mediterranean, practices such as interception operations at sea, the detention of migrants and asylum seekers, and the acquisition and storage of individual travel records or personal data in databases[26] result from the tension between fixity and mobility as a quality of bordering spaces. The small boat, with its undocumented (read un-fixed) passengers, has thus not emerged by accident as the preferred means of transport into the EU. It rather indicates a constant maneuvering through fixity and movement.[27]

---

26 | The tensions between visibility and invisibility and between fixity and movement overlap in the example of databases as Leon Hempel (2011) shows in his essay "Das Versprechen der Suchmaschinen. Der europäische Sicherheitsraum als Sichtbarkeitsregime."

27 | In her 2011 monograph, Silja Klepp provides compelling examples of the transit economy based around the small boat. Sicco Rah (2009) explores in detail the different legal arguments relating to the small boats transporting asylum seekers, migrants, and refugees on the high seas and across territorial waters. In his lecture "Where are the missing vehicles?," William Walters describes these small boats as the "anti-ship of state" (Walters 2011).

AMPLIFYING SIMMEL:
SOME GENERAL QUALITIES OF BORDERING SPACES

This essay set up a communication between Simmel's qualities of space and contemporary analysis of migration and border control policies in the Mediterranean. Simmel's qualities of space were examined to asses their potential merit for border studies and for further development when appropriate. The qualities of bordering spaces (*Grenz-Raumqualitäten*), extrapolated from this conceptual experiment, are meant to spur further debate.

Qualities of space, it was found, reflect social interactions and formations as much as they affect them. In the specific case of bordering spaces, their qualities reflect and perpetuate social tensions, differences as well as mechanisms for the regulation of membership, and for the granting and negating of liberties. The qualities of bordering spaces, proposed here as tensions, are based on the premise that demarcation occurs as these tensions are negotiated and resolved.

Discussing Simmel's quality of exclusivity against selected analysis of contemporary EU migration and border control policies indicated two general tensions inherent to bordering spaces. Both an *inside-outside* tension which captures distinction and an *open-closed* tension which addresses selection, revolve around the quality of exclusivity and should be separated when analyzed and deployed as qualities of bordering spaces. Two further tensions, namely those between *visible and invisible* as well as between *natural and cultural* have proven relevant for bordering spaces when examining the decomposability and delimitation of borders. Whereas the latter tension addresses the legitimizing narrative of borders, the first revolves around the scope, range, means of law enforcement on the one hand, and around the practices of border-crossing on the other. Although Simmel's quality of space *proximate-distant*, proved applicable to bordering spaces, this did not work without the reinterpretation of geographic distances to uneven development, a reinterpretation which would require further investigation and critical reflection. Finally, Simmel's qualities fixity as well as movement and migration, could be applied to bordering spaces and taken together as the tension between *fixed and mobile*. This tension allows for capturing policies regarding mobility, data storage, and detention. Table 1 provides an overview of both Simmel's qualities of space and spatial formations and the extrapolated tensions that are characteristic of bordering spaces.

Simmel's five qualities of space (and his examples)	six proposed general tension characteristic of bordering spaces	practices and policies which negotiate the proposed tensions of bordering spaces
exclusivity (territorial nation-state)	inside-outside	othering, exclusion
	open-closed	selection, biopolitics
decomposability and delimitation (Gebietshoheit, Zentralität)	visible-invisible	cat and mouse game, sovereign and deviant
	natural-cultural	routing borders, legitimising them
fixity (club, house, numbering of houses)	fixed-mobile	data storage, politics of identity
movement and migration		politics of mobility
proximity and distance (empty space, the in-between)	proximate-distant	uneven distribution of resources and infrastructure

Table 1: Tensions of bordering spaces as extrapolated from Simmel's qualities of space

Bordering spaces are characterized by the negotiation of these tensions. Demarcation is marked through a decision to inhibit these dichotomies. The proposed six tensions characteristic of bordering spaces should allow for a more methodical approach to those spatial formations which have emerged as the constitutive "architecture" of the EU border control regime in the last 20 years. For the purpose of testing its value, the proposed bordering tensions need to be applied to different empirical sites of European demarcation, such as, for instance, the French waiting zone, the European Surveillance System, the small boat, the court, the detention center, the island of Lampedusa or Lesbos etc. Only then can we decide whether this approach, derived from Simmel, fulfills its promise of conceptual rigor regarding the qualities of bordering spaces or whether it leads to essentially descriptive outputs. Yet, in this first experimental step, Simmel's way of thinking sociology about space has indeed pointed to some possible general qualities of bordering spaces, applicable to many empirical cases of demarcation.

REFERENCES

Agnew, John (1994): "The Territorial Trap: The Geographical Assumptions of International Relations Theory", in: Review of International Political Economy 1 (1), pp. 53-80.

Agnew, John (2007): "No Borders, No Nations: Making Greece in Macedonia", in: Annals of the Association of American Geographers 97 (2), pp. 398-422.

Agnew, John (2008): "Borders on the mind: re-framing border thinking", in: Ethics & Global Politics 1 (4), pp. 175-191.

Agnew, John (2010): "Still Trapped in Territory?", in: Geopolitics 15 (4), pp. 779-784.

Allen, John (2000): "ON GEORG SIMMEL. Proximity, distance and movement", in: Mike Crang/Nigel Thrift (eds.), Thinking space, London: Routledge (Critical geographies 9), pp. 54-70.

Augé, Marc (2008 [1992]): Non-places. An introduction to supermodernity, London/New York: Verso.

Balibar, Etienne (2002a): "World borders, political borders", in: PMLA 117 (1), pp. 71-78.

Balibar, Etienne (2002b): Politics and the other scene, London: Verso.

Balibar, Etienne (2004a): We, the people of Europe? Reflections on transnational citizenship, Princeton: Princeton UP.

Balibar, Etienne (2004b): Europe as borderland: The Alexander von Humboldt Lecture in Human Geography. Lecture given at University of Nijmengen, Netherlands.

Bauman, Zygmunt (1998): Globalization. The human consequences, Cambridge: Polity Press.

Buckel, Sonja (2011): "Das spanische Grenzregime. Outsourcing und Offshoring", in: Kritische Justiz 44 (3), pp. 253-261.

Buckel, Sonja/Wissel, Jens (2010): "State Project Europe: The Transformation of the European Border Regime and the Production of Bare Life", in: International Political Sociology 4 (1), pp. 33-49.

Cantó Milà, Natàlia (2006): "Die Grenze als Relation. Spanische Grenzrealität und europäische Grenzpolitik", in: Monika Eigmüller/Georg Vobruba (eds.), Grenzsoziologie. Die politische Strukturierung des Raumes, Wiesbaden: VS, pp. 185-197.

Castells, Manuel (2000): The rise of the network society, Oxford et al.: Blackwell.

Cuttitta, Paolo (2006): "Points and Lines: A Topography of Borders in the Global Space", in: Ephemera: theory and politics in organizations 6 (1), pp. 27-39 [accessed via: www.ephemeraweb.org/journal/6-1/6-1cuttitta.pdf (30.03.2010)].

Cuttitta, Paolo (2007): "Le monde-frontière. Le contrôle de l'immigration dans l'espace globalize", in: Cultures & Conflicts 68, pp. 61-84 [accessed via: www.cairn.info/load_pdf.php?ID_ARTICLE=CC_068_0061 (28.03.2010)].

Cuttitta, Paolo (2010): "Das europäische Grenzregime: Dynamiken und Wechselwirkungen", in: Sabine Hess/Bernd Kasparek (eds.), Grenzregime. Diskurse, Praktiken, Institutionen in Europa, Berlin: Assoziation A, pp. 23-40.

Durkheim, Émile (1904): "Simmel, Georg, Über räumliche Projectionen sozialer Formen. Review", in: Année sociologique 7, pp. 646-647.

Dijstelbloem, Huub/Meijer, Albert (eds.) (2011): Migration and the new technological borders of Europe, New York: Palgrave Macmillan.

Elden, Stuart (2010): "Thinking Territory Historically", in: Geopolitics 15 (4), pp. 757-761.

Eigmüller, Monika (2006): "Der duale Charakter der Grenze. Bedingungen einer aktuellen Grenztheorie", in: Eigmüller/Vobruba (eds.), Grenzsoziologie, pp. 55-73.

Fall, Juliet J. (2010): "Artificial states? On the enduring geographical myth of natural borders", in: Political Geography 29 (3), pp. 140-147.

Fischer-Lescano, Andreas/ohidipur, Timo (2007): "Europäisches Grenzkontrollregime. Rechtsrahmen der europäischen Grenzschutzagentur FRONTEX", in: Zeitschrift für ausländisches öffentliches Recht und Völkerrecht 67, pp. 1219-1276.

Flusser, Vilém (1991): "Räume", in: Heidemarie Seblatnig (Ed.): außen räume innen räume. Der Wandel des Raumbegriffs im Zeitalter der elektronischen Medien, Wien: Universitätsverlag, pp. 75-83.

Glauser, Andrea (2006): "Pionierarbeit mit paradoxen Folgen? Zur neueren Rezeption der Raumsoziologie von Georg Simmel", in: Zeitschrift für Soziologie 35 (4), pp. 250-268.

Harvey, David (2005): "Space as a key word", in: David Harvey (Ed.): Spaces of neoliberalization. Towards a theory of uneven geographical development. [Eighth] Hettner-lecture [from 28 June to 2 July] 2004. Stuttgart: Steiner, pp. 93-115.

Hempel, Leon (2011): "Das Versprechen der Suchmaschinen. Der europäische Sicherheitsraum als Sichtbarkeitsregime", in: Leon Hempel/ Susanne Krasmann/Ulrich Bröckling (eds.), Sichtbarkeitsregime. Überwachung, Sicherheit und Privatheit im 21. Jahrhundert, Wiesbaden: VS, pp. 124-142.

Kasparek, Bernd (2010): "Laboratorium, Think Tank, Doing Border: Die Europäische Grenzschutzagentur Frontex", in: Hess/Kasparek (eds.), Grenzregime, pp. 111-126.

Karafillidis, Athanasios (2009): "Entkopplung und Kopplung. Wie die Netzwerktheorie zur Bestimmung sozialer Grenzen beitragen kann", in: Roger Häußling (Ed.), Grenzen von Netzwerken, Wiesbaden: VS, pp. 105-131.

Kaufmann, Stefan (2006): "Grenzregimes im Zeitalter globaler Netzwerke", in: Helmuth Berking/Ulrich Beck (eds.), Die Macht des Lokalen in einer Welt ohne Grenzen, Frankfurt a.M.: Campus, pp. 32-65.

Kaufmann, Stefan (2008): "Technik als Politik. Zur Transformation gegenwärtiger Grenzregimes der EU", in: Comparativ. Zeitschrift für Globalgeschichte und vergleichende Gesellschaftsforschung 18 (1), pp. 42-57.

Klepp, Silja (2011): Europa zwischen Grenzkontrolle und Flüchtlingsschutz. Eine Ethnographie der Seegrenze auf dem Mittelmeer, Bielefeld: transcript.

Konau, Elisabeth (1977): Raum und soziales Handeln. Studien zu e. vernachlässigten Dimension soziolog. Theoriebildung, Stuttgart: Enke.

Köster, Werner (2002): Die Rede über den "Raum". Zur semantischen Karriere eines deutschen Konzepts, Heidelberg: Synchron.

Läpple, Dieter (1991): Essay über den Raum. Für ein gesellschaftswissenschaftliches Raumkonzept, in: Hartmut Häußermann et al. (eds.),

Stadt und Raum. Soziologische Analysen, Pfaffenweiler: Centaurus, pp. 157-207.
Löw, Martina (2001): Raumsoziologie, Frankfurt a.M.: Suhrkamp.
Massey, Doreen (2005): For space, Los Angeles: Sage.
Massey, Doreen (2006): "Keine Entlastung für das Lokale", in: Berking/Beck (eds.), Die Macht des Lokalen in einer Welt ohne Grenzen, pp. 25-31.
McConnell, Fiona (2010): "The Fallacy and the Promise of the Territorial Trap: Sovereign Articulations of Geopolitical Anomalies", in: Geopolitics 15 (4), pp. 762-768.
Neal, Andrew W. (2009): "Securitization and Risk at the EU Border: The Origins of FRONTEX", in: JCMS: Journal of Common Market Studies 47 (2), pp. 333-356.
Newman, David (2010): "The lines that continue to separate us", in: Progress in Human Geography 30 (2), pp. 143-161.
Newman, David (2010): "Territory, Compartments and Borders: Avoiding the Trap of the Territorial Trap", in: Geopolitics 15 (4), pp. 773-778.
Nosh, Christopher (2008): "Exterritoriale Lager in Libyen und der Ukraine", in: Bürgerrechte und Polizei/CILIP 89 (1), Berlin, pp. 26-33.
Panagiotidis, Efthimia/Tsianos, Vassilis (2007): "Denaturalizing camps. Überwachen und Entschleunigen in der Schengener Ägais-Zone", in: Transit Migration Forschungsgruppe (Ed.), Turbulente Ränder, Bielefeld: transcript, pp. 57-85.
Pries, Ludger (2008): Die Transnationalisierung der sozialen Welt. Sozialräume jenseits von Nationalgesellschaften, Frankfurt a.M.: Suhrkamp.
Rah, Sicco (2009): Asylsuchende und Migranten auf See. Staatliche Rechte und Pflichten aus völkerrechtlicher Sicht, Berlin: Springer.
Robertson, Roland (1994): "Glocalization: Time-Space and Homogeneity-Heterogeneity", in: Mike Feathersone/Scott Lash/Roland Robertson, Global Modernities, London et.al.: Sage, pp. 25-44.
Rumford, Chris (2011): Cosmopolitan Spaces. Europe, Globalization, Theory, New York/London: Routledge.
Schroer, Markus (2006): Räume, Orte, Grenzen. Auf dem Weg zu einer Soziologie des Raums, Frankfurt a.M.: Suhrkamp.
Schweitzer, Doris (2011): "Grenzziehungen und Raum in Manuel Castells Theorie der Netzwerkgesellschaft, in: Christoph Kleinschmidt/Christine Hewel (eds.), Topographien der Grenze: Verortungen ein-

er kulturellen, politischen und ästhetischen Kategorie, Würzburg: Königshausen & Neumann, pp. 49-62.

Simmel, Georg (1992 [1908]): "Der Raum und die räumliche Ordnung der Gesellschaft", in: Georg Simmel, Soziologie. Untersuchungen über die Formen der Vergesellschaftung, edited by Otthein Rammstedt, Frankfurt a.M.: Suhrkamp, pp. 687- 803.

Simmel, Georg (1909): "Brücke und Tür", in: Der Tag. Moderne illustrierte Zeitung 683, Morgenblatt, 15 September 1909, Berlin, pp. 1-3 [accessed via: http://socio.ch/sim/verschiedenes/1909/bruecke_tuer.htm (15.04.2012)].

Simmel, Georg (1972 [1908]): "The Stranger", in: Georg Simmel/Donald N. Levine, On Individuality and Social Forms. Selected Writings, Chicago: Chicago UP, pp. 184-189.

Soja, Edward W. (2010): Seeking spatial justice, Minneapolis: University of Minnesota Press.

Strassoldo, Raimundo (1992): "Lo spazio della sociologcia di Georg Simmel", in: Annali di Sociologia 8 (II), pp. 319-329.

Trotha, Trutz von (2006): "Von der Ohnmacht der Flucht zur Macht der Kündigung. Flucht als 'bewegtes' Machtverhältnis – Ein theoretischer Essay", in: Katharina Inhetveen/Trutz von Trotha (eds.), Flucht als Politik: Berichte von fünf Kontinenten, Köln: Köppe, pp. 17-38.

Vobruba, Georg (2010): "Die postnationale Grenzkonstellation", in: Zeitschrift für Politik 57 (4), pp. 434-452.

Walters, William (2008): "Bordering the Sea: Shipping Industries and the Policing of Stowaways", in: borderlands ejournal 7 (3), pp. 1-25.

Walters, William (2011): Where are the missing vehicles. Lecture given at the Hanyang University. 2nd Flying University of Transnational Humanities. 25.-29. Juni 2011. Seoul.

Weibel, Peter (1989): "Territorium und Technik", in: Jean Baudrillard (Ed.), Philosophien der neuen Technologie/Ars Electronica 89, Berlin: Merve, pp. 81-111.

Wimmer, Andreas/Glick Schiller, Nina (2002): "Methodological nationalism and beyond. Nation-state building, migration and the social sciences", in: Global Networks 2 (4), pp. 301-334.

Ziemann, Andreas/Simmel, Georg (2000): Die Brücke zur Gesellschaft. Erkenntniskritische und topographische Implikationen der Soziologie Georg Simmels, Konstanz: Universitätsverlag.

European Border Regions as "Laboratories" for Cross-Border Cooperation

Euroregions

Emerging New Forms of Cross-Border Cooperation

Barbara A. Despiney Zochowska

> "When an industry has chosen a locality for itself it is likely to stay there long: so great are the advantages which people following the same skilled trade get from near neighborhood to one another." Alfred Marshall, Principles of Economics, London, Macmillan, 1920.

INTRODUCTION

One motivating factor driving the accession of Central European countries to the EU in 2004 and 2007 was the intention of preventing these countries from becoming economic backwaters in a "multi-speed Europe" (DATAR 1996). In this new context, economic clusters, which are thought to be more readily adaptable to unique or changing circumstances, may prove to be able to foster new and maintain established market actors and jobs in central Europe. Many examples from around the world demonstrate that clusters are more stable than market sectors. Even when sectors are in decline, clusters are at times able to adapt and avoid crisis. Clusters may, then, emerge as even more important for less affluent regions in the future.

In the context of eastward EU expansion, it was necessary to integrate new member countries into the European Spatial Development Perspective (ESDP) with its polycentric model of development. The three objectives of the ESDP are: (1) social and economic cohesion, (2) sustainable development, (3) improved competitiveness of European regions (SDEC

2000). Regional production systems grouped together on the spatial level and integrated company networks at the regional level could become a basis for local hubs of competition. The problem lies in identifying assets held by central Europe for future endogenous development. This contribution concentrates on identifying these assets, looking for the possible emergence of local competitive productive systems in Central European countries. The paper concentrates on instances of positive development in "industrial districts," built around networks of small and medium-sized firms that survived the decline of industrial mass production in the transition countries after 1989.

Before the transition to market economies, communist economic strategy favored a concentration of industry in highly specialized industrial districts with priority given to heavy industry over consumer goods (Despiney-Zochowska 1982; Andreff 1986). After the dissolution of the COMECON in 1989-1990, the globalization of previously protected markets obliged national economic actors to adapt to new competition. The rationalization strategies of multinational firms, which include among other things the international outsourcing of production processes, entails the loss of autonomy of national productive systems and their eventual dissolution (Andreff 1994). However, the contribution of new flexible methods of production to local development and to the dynamics of regional integration is not as negligible as has been suggested (Pellegrin 1999). The traditions and production experience of any given local economy may fit well to global needs, yielding products that are well-accepted in the marketplace or new ideas regarding production that can be used elsewhere, such as in processes of standardization, in the organization of production lines, in the reorganization of work, or through subcontracting. If local knowledge of productive techniques, material usage etc. fails to find a place in the global organization of production, it falls into the realm of folklore (Becattini/Rullani 1995).

To place the recent changes in regional and local economies into global perspective, we must look at multinational firms. They still constitute the main creative economic force (Amin and Robins 1992). Localized productive systems (LPS) should be studied empirically, from a multidisciplinary perspective, with field studies and a qualitative adaptation of statistical measurements. Studies should investigate local players with the goal of anticipating future developments. On the macro-economic front, the problem is to decide whether or not localized productive systems constitute a new form of industrialization in which small and medium-sized companies can flourish. This is the goal of the study discussed below, which considers local characteristics in the context of macro-economic factors tied to the transition in the 1990s.

Theoretical Framework

Today, we can look back on a "geographical turn" in economics that encouraged three areas of research: (1) the spatial agglomeration of economic activity; (2) the dynamics of regional growth convergence; and (3) neo-Marshallian district economics (Martin 2001). This contribution briefly explains the Marshallian district concept and offers some reflection on its relevance for the analysis of regional development in Central Europe, looking specifically at cross-border cooperation.

It its initial conception, the industrial district was presented as a productive complex created by market behavior and the rules of civil society (Azais 1997). The notion of localized productive systems emerged at the same time as the term "flexible production" (Piore/Sabel 1984). Piore and Sabel argue that a new logic of production, "flexible specialization," emerged to challenge mass production after markets for standardized goods became saturated and higher quality and more specialized goods attracted more consumers. This flexibility is based on small-sized production units, on the density of links between them and on the rapid reaction time of companies when faced with new internal and external conditions (Courlet 2000). This flexibility also implies the capacity to adapt to new technologies.

One of many problems linked to the notion of flexibility is that the debate has centered on the organization and spatial dynamics of the economic system in its role as a productive system. If in the world of capitalist production, production is nothing more than a broader means of accumulating capital, then the district phenomenon should be understood from within a broad political economy framework concerned with the nature of development and the ongoing transformation of capitalism. According to the American geographers Scott and Storper, there has been an "evolutionary tendency" towards flexible specialization as a form of industrial organization, but also towards "flexible accumulation," which they see as harkening a new historic social era (Scott/Storper 1989). Flexible specialization and flexible localization find their significance in the broader socio-historic context, they write. The competitive advantage of flexible specialization strategies and networks of small-sized companies is based on very specific historical and social conditions. The advantage depends on irregular and differentiated demand and on low start-up costs (Dunford 1992). Various other factors may encourage a certain degree of regional concentration, such as, for example, certain sectors' dependence on economies of agglomeration and the need for a faster and more flexible adaptation of the productive system in all stages, from conception to final manufacturing. Geographic proximity may help companies meet these challenges. Spatial concentration may also be made more likely by job insecurity in a traditional industrial zone, making it less necessary for companies to search for more flexible, less costly labor abroad (Martinelle/Schoenberger 1992). Flexible specialization also brings about more flexible spatial relationships and competition between regions for industrial development, as the regions themselves face the problematic development of underprivileged regions and the gap between the center and the periphery. The emergence of industrial districts is an answer to this new problem; it is a type of industrialization that is particularly well adapted to the need for flexibility, and it may serve the needs of industrial companies both in emerging countries and in transition countries (Courlet 2000).

Another perspective on these issues is presented by the French regulation school, which argues that the previous paradigm of mass production is not dead yet. Its research program has been informed by contributions from history, sociology, and political science. It focuses on how economic logic, social ties, and political power are combined to resolve conflicts that inevitably arise in socio-economic systems (Boyer/Saillard 1995). One of its founding principles is the hypothesis of the historicity of the development process of capitalist economies. Special attention is paid to the territorial dimension of the regulatory processes (Benko/Lipietz 1992). The economic geography of the era of "post-Fordism" presents the territory as a mosaic (or "leopard skin") of different types of regional economies (Krätke 1997b). This is particularly applicable to the economies of central and eastern Europe. As in the industrial district debate, doubt has arisen in this school, too, about whether it is possible to explain all geographical clusters in terms of any single, universal theory (Martin 2001).

The Marshallian District: A Toolbox

The notion of the localized productive system (LPS) is based on the industrial district model proposed by Alfred Marshall (Marshall 1920). His insistence that the location of companies is important brought the notion of "territory" into the economic discourse (Azais 1997). He was the first to propose a new interpretation of the market, leaving the perfect competition framework in favor of an analysis of companies gathered together in "industrial districts." He described the specific socio-historic trajectories of territories and the territoriality of industrialization. Alfred Marshall's work forms a starting point, or a toolbox, but it needs to be adapted in order to study company behavior, market structures, and industrial performance. The revival of the industrial district concept was initiated by Beccatini in 1979 following the renewal of this type of local system in Italy in the form of a high geographic concentration of small companies active in the same sector.[1] Another typical case is that of Silicon Valley in Santa Clara, California, although growth in this case was linked to the first stages of the life cycle of computers. The Marshallian district of Greater Los Angeles and the flexible industrial systems of Hong Kong are also noteworthy (Scott 1992).

The industrial district is based on the external economies of agglomerations and the economics of urbanization. Those agglomeration economies can be intra-industrial or inter-industrial. Urban economies are external to the firm and to the branch, but they are internal to the urban region.

A Marshallian district designates a collective way of living, thinking, and producing that is characteristic of a given society, space, and milieu. It is a socio-territorial entity characterized by the presence of an active community of people and a population of companies in a given geographical space. In his arguments, Alfred Marshall strongly emphasized the part played by human factors, pointing out "mental and moral" qualities such as integrity, self-confidence, patience temperance, honesty, loyalty, et cetera (Arena 2000). The local productive system creates an "industrial atmosphere," in which an osmosis of know-how is made possible.

---

1 | Early Italian research dates to the 1960s, so a great number of theoretical, historical, and socio-economic studies on this subject have been undertaken there.

Its most noticeable characteristic is its relatively homogeneous system of values and thought, which may be seen as the expression of a certain system of ethics concerning work, activity, family, and reciprocity (Becattini 1992; Becattini et al. 2009). The industrial district is governed by a set of community and religious values or corporatist practices. It has its own specific forms of know-how that are inimitable and deeply anchored in the territory, being the know-how of local artisans. Yet, economically relevant knowledge and customs are not unchangeable. Cultural change due to economic change was postulated by Alfred Marshall more than a century ago. Marshall understood that customs, making up a part of what economists today call "informal rules," are not immutable but "have been imperceptibly growing and dwindling again, to meet the changing exigencies of successive generations" (quoted in Winiecki 1998).

The Emergence of New Forms of Governance and Regulation

It seems that it takes a long time to establish a Marshallian "atmosphere" in central European enterprises (Duche 2001). We may, however, see the rise of a culture of capitalism in central Europe sooner than in other former socialist countries, especially Russia. In central European countries, economic history and the capitalist culture that make up the national heritage have encouraged a new commercial and entrepreneurial spirit, especially in those countries in the German neighborhood. Poland, Hungary, and Slovakia are located between the richest and the poorest countries of Europe and suffer from considerable asymmetries and distortions of regional markets. The emergence of small and medium-sized companies acts as a motor for growth and job creation, whereby their presence is stronger near the German, Czech, and Baltic borders (Despiney/Baczko 2001). Although the majority of small and medium-sized industries and firms were created in the commercial sector, new entrepreneurs are now beginning to redirect capital accumulated there into manufacturing enterprises. This is true especially in the Polish case. During the years of communist rule, Poland had large private agricultural, retail, and private crafts sectors. Furthermore, in the 1980s, the government introduced several pro-market reform measures (economic self-government, relative autonomy for enterprises, and partial price liberalization) as well as a basic law in 1988 that allowed the creation of private commercial firms and remained in force until late 1989. In the 1980s, social approval increased for entrepreneurship and of the role of financial incentives in the regulation of economic behavior – important social preconditions of a private market economy. By the end of 1989, there were approximately 500,000 private enterprises outside agriculture, most of them created in the late 1980s (Surdej 2000). But the emergence of small and medium-sized industries and firms has been particularly visible since the beginning of the transition (Chmiel 1997; Grudzewski/Hejduk 1998; Duchêne/Rusin 2002). Small, private, and locally grown activities are the foundation stones of the Polish economic revival and the motor behind the relatively good performance of the Polish economy. As an outcome of pro-market reform measures of the 1980s, relations between the central state and business enterprises had already begun to be shaped by indirect control mechanisms like market price-setting and the taxation of revenue. Thus, in Poland, the decentralization process did not start with the transition, but some years before (Rogulska 1985; Despiney-Zochowska 1988, 2001).

In Russia, the situation is different. Small companies reappeared after becoming legalized in 1988, but they now play no role in the various plans of economic modernization. In fact, they were never an official priority. In the 1990s, the Russian state preferred to give priority to the resolution of macroeconomic problems. After 2000, it paid attention almost exclusively to heavy industry (Kisline 2009).

New Forms of Governance: Euroregions

The three necessary preconditions of healthy localized productive systems in post-socialist Europe are decentralization, the resolution of disputes over property ownership, and personal mobility. Although the first condition has been touched upon by administrative reforms, the recent admission to the EU seems increasingly vital in order to meet the second and third conditions.

The regions need autonomy and the capability to carry out their own policies, all of which depend on territorial decentralization. In central Europe, state territorial structures are now decentralized. Can decentralized territories help spur an evolution toward improved productive organization (Despiney 2001)? Will the two processes of decentralization and the possible revival of localized production systems reinforce each other, or will they follow separate paths? To answer these questions, we turn in the analysis below to two examples of LPS emergence: one on the Polish-Czech-German border and one on the new eastern border of the EU. With their appearance, we can trace the development of a new system of dialogue between the respective central states, now also members of the EU, and local communities (Courlet 2000).

Legal and tax frameworks, research institutions, and social relationships are areas for innovation and entrepreneurship. The incompleteness of market and institutional reforms in the three countries studied heightened the risk of trans-border economic relationships (Krätke 1997a). However, the greatest barrier to the proliferation of clusters in our studied regions is the lack of a tradition of cooperation among companies, especially among competitors. These businesses avoid sharing information, and they do not communicate about dividing the market by specialization. This is closely related to the infancy of capitalism in this region and the heritage of the communist regime. Businessmen are more focused on competition and rivalry, not on partnership cooperation.[2] Another serious barrier to cluster formation in the Polish regions is the lack of financial resources to establish and support such clusters. Most measures to support local economic initiatives aim to improve local entrepreneurs' access to credit (Lewitas/Gesicka 1994). However, local entrepreneurs are few and the distance between these regions and their country's financial centers discourages those who would like to create a family business. The Polish experience of the 1990s confirms the weak role played by local institutions in the fostering of entrepreneurship.

Although individual entrepreneurs can best move technology, industry, and regions forward, local government policy also plays a role in promoting entrepreneurship and clustering in central and eastern Europe. In fact, localized production systems will only emerge with the active support of regional authorities aiming to develop a network of diffuse industries. This was the case of the former East Germany, where the transition process was not spontaneous and new economic development depended on massive financial transfers from the central state (Samson/Goutin-Bourlat 1995; Nivet 2002).

---

2 | Other studies on localized productive systems in Polish industry confirm the same phenomenon. See Duche (2000).

Local authorities and the legal framework for cross-border cooperation (CBC) along Poland's borders have been particularly important since the 1990s, when former communist countries signed the Convention of Madrid and the European Charter of Territorial Self-Management. This clarified the legal status of foreign activity for local and regional authorities, including those located near the borders, by unambiguously authorizing foreign contacts and establishing EU standards of cooperation. CBC is a specific form of international regional cooperation. Its territorial scope and content are shaped in large part by political factors, but their development is also determined by socio-economic, technological, institutional, and geographic conditions on both sides of the border, as well as by more general factors like European integration. Regional CBC was regarded as a transitional phase for Poland, the Czech Republic, Slovakia, and Hungary. These countries were thought to be on their way to incorporation into the uniform economic system of the Europe Union, a development that would obviate traditional borders. However, previously established CBC will remain an issue, particularly in the form of Euroregions, because political decisions to remove borders do not automatically liquidate longstanding differences in social and economic life (Starzyk 1996).

As of 2012, sixteen Euroregions had been established along Poland's borders[3] (see figure 1). Two of them, the "Neisse" and the "Carpathian" Euroregions, serve as our laboratories of local governance.

---

3 | These are: "Neisse – Nisa – Nysa" (December 1991), "Carpathian" (February 1993), "Spree –Neisse – Bober/Sprewa – Nysa – Bóbr" (September 1993), "Pro Europa Viadrina" (December 1993), "Tatras" (August 1994), "Bug" (September 1995), "Pomerania" (December 1995), "Glacensis" (December 1996), "Neman" (June 1997), "Praděd" (July 1997), "Cieszyn Silesia" (March 1998), "Baltic" (February 1998), "Silesia" (September 1998), "Beskydy Mountains" (February 2000), "Białowieża Forest" (May 2002), "Lyna-Lawa" (March 2003).

Figure 1: Euroregions localized on Polish borders

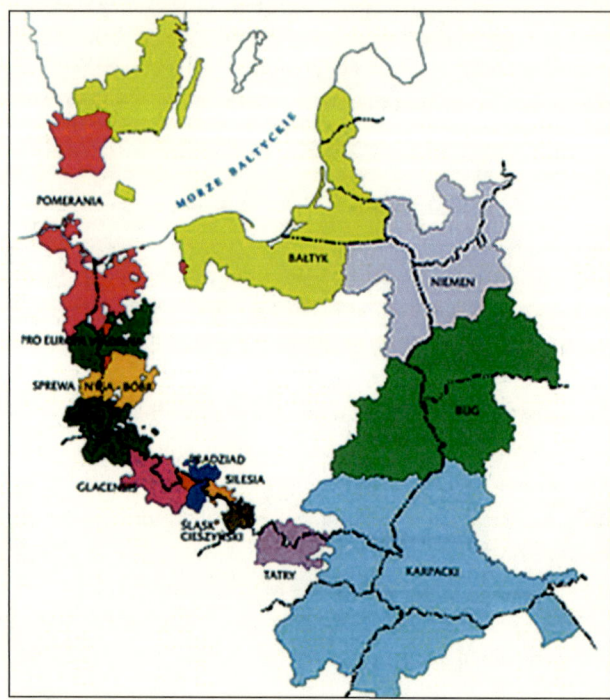

Source: *Euroregiony na granicach Polski 2007, WUS, Wroclaw, 2008.*

For studying our two Euroregions, we employ the GREMI approach pioneered in 1984 by Philippe Aydalot and associated with French economic thought. Within the GREMI approach,[4] post-Fordism is seen to have opened the way to the new "territorial" type of development based on a capacity for innovation better adapted to the task of encouraging local social and industrial networks (Aydalot 1985; Maillat 1988; Perrin 1989). The new spatial dynamics appear to be associated with innovation as expressed by the concept of "milieu innovateur." The local *milieu* or *the local*

---

4 | The GREMI (Groupe de Recherche Européen sur les Milieux Innovateurs – European Research Group on Innovative Areas) has been based at University Paris 1 Pantheon-Sorbonne since 1984 with the support of the Ministry of Urbanization and Housing and *the Caisse de Dépôts et de Consignation*.

environment of the firm may perhaps be considered to be one of the most important sources of innovation on the local level. The approach emphasizes that a region's development does not depend only on its capacity to attract external firms but also on its capacity to promote local initiatives and to activate a territorial dynamic of innovation. GREMI's research methods approach, used throughout its empirical enquiries (GREMI I, II, III, IV and V), is divided into three phases (Ratti/Bramanti/Gordon 1997): (1) elaboration of the objectives and articulation of a common framework for territorial teams; (2) fieldwork; (3) analysis of the results with theoretical synthesis and policy recommendations.

The most recent GREMI phase, the GREMI VI inquiry, is dedicated to a new empirical phenomenon: *milieux* and local production systems operating around natural and cultural resources (Camagni et al. 2004). This approach is used in urban studies, but it could also be useful for studying areas like the Carpathian region, which is rich in natural resources and in cultural heritage (Despiney/Tabaries 2008; Despiney 2011).

CASE STUDY 1: THE NEISSE EUROREGION

In order to study the emergence of local productive systems under the conditions of globalization, we take up the case of the *Neisse* Euro region, situated along the Oder and Neisse rivers on the Polish-German-Czech border. This region is useful for studying both historical continuity and regional dynamics. In our work carried out for DATAR[5] in 1996, the border is, in fact, presented as having a strong growth potential (Samson et al. 1996). This work revealed the emergence of a dynamic peripheral crown in the western and southern part of the country along the German and Czech borders. This growth may be similar to European Alpine growth, based not only on economies of agglomeration but also on industrial and tertiary activities linked to tourism in the Sudety Mountains.

Situated between the *Spree-Neisse-Bober* and the *Glacensis* Euroregions, the *Neisse* Euroregion was created in December 1991 and encompasses six districts of the German federal state of Saxony (Bautzen, Kamenz, Löbau-Zittau, Oberlausitz, Görlitz and Hoyerswerda), 44 communities (*gminas*) of the Lower Silesia Voivodship, four *gminas* of the Lubuskie Voivod-

---

5 | DATAR: French regional planning authority.

ship, and the Czech administrative units of Liberec, Jablonec, Semily, and Ceska Lipa as well as the Sluknov region. Initially a flourishing economic region, the area unites Lower Silesia, Northern Bohemia, and Upper Lusace and includes nearly 725,800 residents in Germany 1.5 million altogether. The *Neisse* Euroregion, one of four created along the Oder-Neisse border, is considered a model for other initiatives of this type. It is sometimes used, for example, for purposes of statistical inference. The Polish part of the Euroregion is part of a data collection project, entitled "PL-14 Euroregions," conducted by the Jelenia Gora Statistics Office.

Regional Trajectory

Territorial dynamics, judged in terms of individual social interactions and institutional ties, can only be observed over the long-term. In the context of our hypothesis concerning the possible revival of LPS in the *Neisse* Euroregion, we find ourselves faced with the heritage of historic and regional continuity (Despiney 1995). Silesia's economic development made it a remarkably advanced region in spite of its feudal structures. Central Europe's integration with the international economic system was achieved mainly through German channels. The economic and cultural links between Saxony, Polish Silesia, and Czech Bohemia are the legacy of the shared history of these neighboring countries. This history was influenced by the longstanding, strong German presence (Jeannin 1991). The textile industry experienced a period of development in the 16th century that was initiated by German merchants. Silesia, Saxony, and Bohemia sold inexpensive wool fabrics until the middle of the 17th century. From the beginning of the 17th century, villages began textile production and by the 18th century entire families were involved in the work of weaving and spinning. The impetus came from urban centers such as Hirschberg (Jelenia Gora), which were unusual because of their wealthy entrepreneurs. The positive effects created by rural industry – job creation, the stimulation of demographic growth, the activation of the domestic food market – were reinforced by the fact that the manufacturing of fabrics took place within a region rich in a variety of industries. Economic development in Silesia made this province remarkably advanced in spite of its feudal social infrastructure (Henderson 1954). These fabric producers even reached international importance, rivaling the French on Spanish and American markets. The structural crisis in the old mining economy that took place in the 16th century encouraged the appearance of dye producers in Silesia, who brought the seeds of the future chemical industry. The existence of advanced industrial settlement here, with a long history of linkages between science and technology, had a huge influence on the economic development of central European countries. At this time, European industrial geography was characterized by the dispersion of its industries, with pockets of industry sunk into the rural landscape (Veltz 1996).

The Socialist Period 1945-1989

Silesia was an industrial district in the Marshallian sense before the second world war. A large proportion of the industrial workforce was employed east of the Oder and Neisse, which, at that time, was part of Germany. This included 43 percent of the hemp industry workforce, 49 percent of the spinning workforce, and 48 percent of the linen industry (Lepesant 1997). Border changes in 1945 and the expulsion of German residents put an end to the homogeneity of the local productive system in Saxony, Lower Silesia, and Bohemia. During the communist period, the Oder-Neisse line was "split" or "cut," as Claude Courlet wrote, cutting also the industrial district's developmental trajectory (Courlet 1988). On both sides of the Oder-Neisse border, the massive population migrations that took place after the Second World War meant that many people had difficulty identifying with these border regions. It was to this area that a number of ethnic German communities from Central Europe were transplanted (Bafoil 1995). Indeed, the surge of refugees from the East and the migrations following the war modified the population structure on both sides of the Oder-Neisse, blocking the growth of a common economic culture and squelching the practice of regional traditions. These German regions were made up of the lands of the former Junkers, expropriated following the agrarian reform of 1945 and joined into large collective holdings (Lacquement 1993). On the Polish side, too, these lands were confiscated and collectivized (Despiney-Zochowska 1995). The workers who came from Polish lands in the East had no industrial tradition and their integration created a number of problems for the authorities throughout the communist period. Between 1945 and 1989, the East German, Polish, and Czechoslovak authorities pursued a common development policy in the border lands only briefly in the 1970s. In industry, few new industries were created, although coal mining increased in both Lusatia in East Germany and in the Turoszow region in Poland. During the Communist period, there was a strong development in the textile industry, but this took place in isolation in each of the three bordering countries (Bafoil 1995). These border regions are fragile in large part due to an all-too similar industrial structure on either side of the Oder-Neisse border. In Germany, the old administrative districts soon disappeared, replaced by smaller ones that could do nothing but implement decisions made at the central level. In Poland, the party leadership under Edward Gierek carried did the opposite in 1975, liquidating the *powiat* – the intermediate administrative level – and introducing 49 Voïvodhips.

Transition and Globalization

The Euroregion is a legacy of the logic of communist economics. In Poland, textiles are among the branches of the Polish economy that suffered most from the shock therapy introduced by Leszek Balcerowicz in 1990 (Lipowski/Despiney 1991). In eastern Germany, the European RETEX program was supposed to bring massive aid to the textile industry beginning in 1994. The restructuring of textiles and clothing was part of a program of the complete overhaul of Saxony's economic structure (ATLAS), but it never sought to rethink the region's industrial identity. The economic development strategy for the Polish border, called "The chain of pearls along the Neisse," was a concerted development policy scheme planned for Upper Lusatia. Yet, the transition process depended on massive financial transfers from the German central state. This example of industrial restructuring is highly instructive. It enabled the regions to preserve their industrial centers as German textile firms subcontracted to improve international competitiveness. German enterprises have adopted a strategy based on outward-processing trade (OPT) with Polish and Czech partners. A star-shaped relationship links firms who work with each other on a paired basis (Courlet/Pecqueur 1991). This type of relationship can often create a form of dependence for small and medium-sized companies. This brings a danger for the local productive system: the increasing dependence of smaller companies as they become transformed into subcontracting entities for larger firms needing technical know-how, cheap labor, and a pre-existing client network. Nonetheless, subcontracting reinforced the competitive nature of the Polish and Czech textile industry, particularly in the clothing sector. Not only did made-to-order contracts help a number a producers exploit their production capacities, but Polish companies also benefited from technology transfers from German companies (DREE 1998). Nevertheless, subcontracting did have some disadvantages. For instance, it further closed German markets for Polish and Czech products. To cope with the competition of central European countries, this sector has been protected by significant trade barriers. Poland, the Czech Republic, and Hungary were the firsts German partners in Central Europe in the field of subcontracting from 1990 to 1995, but since 1996 re-exports produced in the OPT is decreasing. The situation began changing in 1995, when growth in subcontracting fell considerably. In 1997, for the first time since 1993, OPT is being redirected to countries with even lower wages, including Rumania and Ukraine (Boudier-Bensebaa 2002).

Euro Textile Region

To help small and medium-sized enterprises in the three parts of the Euroregion, the "Euro Textile Region" initiative was launched on the Polish-German-Czech border in late 2000. The Euro Textile Region unites textile and apparel manufacturers in the German federal states of Brandenburg and Saxony and in border areas within Poland and the Czech Republic. It is thus larger than the *Neisse* Euroregion and extends across Plauen-Guben in the west and Liberec-Zielona Gora and Wroclaw in the east (Figure 2). The Euro Textile Region includes 1,460 companies with 71,000 employees (448 companies in Saxony, 54 in Brandenburg, 344 in Lower Silesia, 150 in Lubuskie, and 473 in the Czech Republic). Its first common decision was to organize three associations of producers in the textile and clothing industries to counter Asian competition. The region will specialize in intelligent textiles and automobile components. Today, some manufacturers are expanding into markets in the former Soviet Union.

It might be hoped that cross-border cooperation could make economies of scale possible, cutting production costs, and perhaps compensating for the disintegration of eastern markets (Andreff 1994). Indeed, according to Krugman, regional export hubs whose cohesion is based on external Marshallian economies are more likely to form in areas where the economy is well integrated (Krugman 1993). One thing is certain – the joint territorialization of private and public sectors helps encourage institutional cooperation and stabilizes conditions of production, both of which should help companies accumulate know-how in technology. The major accomplishments of the Eurozone were the creation of a common strategy for light industry, common initiatives in making credit more available, and the provision of more accurate market information.

This Euro Textile Region is a regional knowledge cluster rooted in partnerships between universities and business. It shows that local productive systems can also facilitate the kinds of connections between small business and educational institutions that are vital for improving marketing and technology transfer.

Case Study 2: The "Carpathian" Euroregion

Many contemporary authors argue that the emergence of innovative clusters is to be expected primarily in urban economies because clusters depend on diverse, high-quality infrastructure. However, the agricultural zones of the traditionally underdeveloped "eastern belt" of Europe have been the target of public sector economic development efforts motivated by the hope of encouraging such clusters in rural areas. How might the experience of the *Neisse* Euroregion help us understand regional development in the EU periphery? Could growth here follow the European Alpine model and become based not only in economies of agglomeration but also on industrial and tertiary activities linked to tourism in the Carpathian mountains? To answer these questions, we turn now to an observation of the evolution of cross border cooperation in the Carpathian Euroregion (Despiney 2011).

As the second Euroregion established in central Europe, the Carpathian Euroregion is situated on the southeastern part of the new eastern border of the EU (Figure 1). This Euroregion is composed of regions in Poland, Slovakia, Ukraine, Hungary, and Romania. It encompasses nearly 10 million inhabitants. Not all of the countries have common borders, making this region a special case of regional cooperation (Slim 1998). Created in 1993, the Euroregion includes one Polish voïvodship (Lower Carpathians), five Hungarian regions (Borsod-Abaùj-Zemplén, Hajdù-Bihar, Heves, Jasz-Nagykun-Szolnok, Szabolc-Szatmar-Bereg), four Ukrainian regions (Lviv, Uzhorod, Ivano-Frankivsk, Cernevici), two Slovakian regions (Preszow and Koszice), and seven Romanian regions (Bihor, Botosani, Maramures, Suceava, Satu Mare, Zilah, and Harghita). All of them are underdeveloped regions, depressed by transition, dominated by agriculture, with no important urban centers except for a few medium-sized cities that have just started to emerge (Despiney 2012). Considering the rural character of those regions, the experience of agro-food, agro-tourist, and cultural clusters could be applied here. The concept of "local agro-food systems" (Système Agroalimentaire Local – SYAL) focuses attention on the emergence of agro-food development models based on local resources including regional products, knowledge, specialized skills, businesses, and institutions. SYAL stands for the organization of a local development process based on a concentration of agro-food businesses (farms, input suppliers, processing outlets, marketing units, service, catering businesses etc.) in relative proximity, structured around common activities (Despiney/Szymoniuk 2001; Szymoniuk/Walukiewicz 2004; Despiney 2005).

Agro-tourist clusters have common objectives that justify common action such as joint marketing projects, supervision of the quality of services, joint lobbying, and applications for subsidies. Their interests include the design of tourism products with a specifically local character based around folk art, rituals, local cuisine, and cultural and natural monuments. They also include the development of local infrastructure, regional promotion, and the provision of tourist services such as sports equipment rental, camping sites, ski-lifts, bicycle paths, scenic views, pharmacies, post offices, and internet access.

The move to tourism and agriculture-tourism would appear to be a good solution for some eastern European regions. It may be their only chance to prevent further economic deterioration. If this does not happen, the national economy risks a fall in wealth creation particularly at the regional level. This is all the more urgent now that tourism is becoming a more important strategic means of territorial development (Bensahel/Donsimoni 1997). In certain regions, tourism can be seen as a means of financing regional development because of its stimulating effects on the overall economy and its interaction with other sectors, especially agriculture. A vital territorial potential still exists in these regions within the agriculture-tourism combination, shown by the rate of employment in the service sector, especially in tourism (Samson et al. 1996). On the EU's eastern border there are several examples, including the lakes of Mazuria, the forests of Bialowieza and Bieszczady, and the Puszta in Hajdu-Bihar, which are part of UNESCO's World Humanity Heritage. The prospects for establishing the Bilateral Biosphere Reserve of Bialowieza Wilderness are being studied by Polish and Belarus authorities.

In the case of the Carpathian Euroregion, the biodiversity of the Carpathian Mountains is recognized through its inclusion in the UNESCO biodiversity reserves network *Transboundary Biosphere Reserve "East Carpathian"* (UNESCO 2009). More than classic tourism regions, those rural voïvodships are dependent on the agriculture-tourism combination. Agro-tourism has a long tradition in the region, especially in Poland. Colloquially, they were called "vacations under the pear tree." In Poland, as in other Eastern European countries, agro-tourism will continue to grow. There is a trend now for vacationers to turn away from large tourist centers and resorts. Short weekend trips to the country are becoming popular because of the natural, quiet environment and low prices that agro-tourism farms offer. There about 5,000 agro-tourist farms in Poland alone, approximately 2,000 of which are members of the Polish Federation of Agro-Tourism "Hospitable Farms." The federation is made up of local associations that represent cores of agro-tourism clusters. Member farms, although in competition with each other, are willing to cooperate in coordinating forms of specialization, investment, and mutual assistance. The cluster is also connected, informally, with other bodies such as neighboring farms that provide local produce and additional services, museums, the Regional Center for Agricultural Consultancy, and church organizations. The essential feature of agro-tourist farms and associations is their potential for providing income opportunities for rural women of all ages and educational levels. The traditional skills of the region's women, including household management, cooking traditional dishes, handicrafts, and knowledge of folklore, are in demand.

Important is the establishment of clear ownership and local identity. The local agricultural system needs to be closely identified with the locality's geography, history, and knowledge. Of importance, too, are producer-consumer relationships in the process of establishing this identity, notions of quality and safety, links with tourism, and cultural dynamics. In the "Carpathian" Euro region, we can imagine in the near future the emergence of a cultural cluster based on the common historical heritage of all these countries. There are, for example, religious monuments that could be utilized for culture-driven development processes (Despiney 2011). This region has its own specific forms of know-how that are inimitable and deeply anchored in the territory, such as specific artisan know-how in wood working. This cultural heritage could be utilized to develop local tourism and sport activities like bicycle races, marathons etc.

The role of associations is important in the Carpathian Euroregion for promoting the activities around the wooden churches and natural resources belonging to UNESCO World Heritage. One of them, the French association "Bois debut en Pologne" initiated some cultural activities in Poland and the Ukraine. The first successful Polish-Ukrainian initiative was an exhibition at UNESCO's headquarters in Paris in 2008, dedicated to wood churches from both countries. Two of the region's countries prepared the common bid to put some of these structures in UNESCO's World Heritage Program.

The emergence of a cultural cluster could be added to other economic activities important for the emergence of a localized productive system in the Carpathian Euroregion (Garafoli 1996). In fact, new growth in craft industries is taking place in "Aviation Valley" created in 2003 by 18 enterprises and research and development institutions (Despiney 2012). The Aviation Valley Association currently represents 30 companies and institutions, among them Snecma Poland, Goodrich, Pratt & Whitney, and AvioPolska. The two major objectives of the association are organization and development of a low-cost supply chain and creation of favorable conditions for the development of the aerospace industry in the region. This industry started in the 1920s with the construction of the first Polish aircraft company, which was further developed during the communist period for Soviet aviation and is now continuing in the form of a cluster. The Special Economic Zone (SEZ) created in 1995 in the city of Mielec is a partner of "Aviation Valley." This has improved Mielec's ranking among medium-sized cities in terms of investment attractiveness. Together with the city of Puławy, Mielec is performing better than other medium-sized cities in the Lower Carpathians voïvodship. In this region, the connections between trade schools and universities with corporate businesses are weak, causing barriers to the establishment of clusters. In the case of "Aviation Valley," the situation seems better. Six technical universities cooperate with the association. EU support is given to this new economic activity trough INTERREG III C ADEP, a project executed with partners from northern Finland and northwestern Ireland. The goal of the project is to share best practice within the field of industrial cluster development as well as to tighten cooperation between partner regions.

References

Andreff, Wladimir (1994): "From disintegration to new integration in former Soviet Union and Eastern Europe", in: Marie Lavigne (Ed.), Capitalism in the East. A difficult delivery, Paris: Economica, 16- 52.

Andreff, Wladimir (1986): The End of Planned Industrialisation Model: What the lessons for the Third World?, ORSTOM Conference, Paris, 26-27 February .

Arena, Richard (2000): Economic Institutions and Social Organisation in Marshall's Work: An Evolutionary Interpretation, Conference "Organisations and Institutions", Amiens, 25-26 May.

Aydalot, Philipe (1985): Crisis and Space. Paris: Economica.

Azais, Christian (1997): "Dynamiques territoriales, localisation et systèmes productifs locaux: quelques repères théoriques", in: Christian Palloix/Yorgos Rizopoulos (eds.), Firmes et économie industrielle, Paris: l'Harmattan, 75-102.

Bafoil, François (1995): "Between memory and expectations: A sociological approach of Neisse Euroregion", in: Cahiers du ROSES (1), 3- 18.

Becattini, Giacomo (1992): "Marshallien district: A socio-economic notion", In: Georges Benko/Alain Lipietz (eds.), Les régions qui gagnent. Districts et réseaux: les nouveaux paradigmes de la géographie économique, Paris: PUF, 35-55.

Becattini, Giacomo/Rullani, Enzo (1995): Système local et marché global. Le district industriel, in Economie industrielle et économie spatiale, Paris: Economica.

Becattini, Giacomo/Bellandi, Marco/De Propris, Lisa (eds.) (2009): A Handbook of Industrial Districts, London: Edward Elgar.

Boudier-Bensebaa, Fabienne (2002): "The East German transformation: Between shock therapy and handouts", in: RECEO 33 (2), 9-24.

Boyer, Robert/Saillard, Yves (eds.) (1995): Théorie de la regulation.L'état de savoir, Paris: La Découverte.

Camagni, Roberto/Maillat, Denis/Matteaccioli, Andrée (eds.) (2004): Ressources naturelles et culturelles, milieu et développement local, Neuchâtel: IRER-EDES.

Chmiel, Jan (1997): "SMS and regional development", in: Studia i Prace (243).

Courlet, Claude (1988): "The frontier: Cut or seving?", in: Economie et Humanisme (301), 23-54.

Courlet, Claude/Pecqueur, Bernard (1992): "Localized productif systémes in France: a new development model?", in: Benko/Lipietz (eds.), Les régions qui gagnent, 81-102.

Courlet, Claude (2000): Industrial Districts and Localized Productive Systems in France, Paris: DATAR.

Despiney, Barbara (2005): "Building Entrepreneurial Capacity in Post-Communist Poland. A Case Study", in: Human Factors and Ergonomics in Manufacturing 15 (1), pp. 109-126.

Despiney, Barbara (2010): "Les transformations de l'agriculture polonaise face à la réforme de la PAC", in: Cahiers Lillois d'économie et de sociologie, issue "La Pologne dans l'Europe: une intégration achevée?", University of Lille 1, September, pp.133-165.

Despiney, Barbara (2011): "Patrimoine et développement en zone rurale: le cas des Basses Carpates", in : Michel Vernières (Ed.), Patrimoine et Développement. Etudes pluridisciplinaires, Paris: Karthala, pp. 73-91.

Despiney-Zochowska, Barbara A. (1982): Socialist Countries and NIEO. An attitude towards developing countries since 1974, Thesis, University of Paris 1.

Despiney-Zochowska, Barbara A. (1988): "The Reform of the Centre", in: Le Courrier des Pays de l'Est (332), pp. 60-63.

Despiney-Zochowska, Barbara A. (1995): "Rural restructuring in Oder-Neisse region", in: Cahiers du ROSES (1), pp. 29-64.

Despiney-Zochowska, Barbara (2001): "The Marshallian District – An Attempt to interpret Regional Developpment in Poland", in *Regional Transitions: European Regions and Challenges of Developpment, Integration and Enlargement,* Proceedings of Annual Conference of RSA, Gdansk, 15-18 September 2001, Seaford, 88-105.

Despiney-Zochowska, Barbara (2009): "From marshallian district to Local Productive Systems: the Polish case", in: Zofia B. Liberda/Anna Grochowska (eds.), Civilizational Competences and Regional Development in Poland, Warsaw: Warsaw UP, pp. 122-153.

Despiney-Zochowska, Barbara (2012): "Quelle dynamique économique à la frontière de la Pologne et Ukraine occidentale?", in: Tadeusz Poplawski/Alberto Gasparini (eds.), Overcoming Barriers. Challeges of Cross-border Cooperation in East of Europe, ISIG Journal XXI (1), pp. 23-40.

Despiney, Barbara/Baczko, Tadeusz (2001): On first line, Magazyn Finansowy. Special Issue.

Despiney, Barbara/Szymoniuk, Barbara (2002): From State-owned productivist farms to local agri-food systems: The Polish Case, paper presented to International Seminar "Local agri-food systems: products, enterprises and local dynamics", Montpellier, 16-18 October.

Despiney, Barbara/Tabariès, Muriel (2007): "Ressources patrimoniales et nouvelle gouvernance: le rôle des milieux innovateurs", in: L'Agriculture française et polonaise dans l'Europe de 27: expériences partagées et intérêts communs?, Actes du colloque franco-polonais tenu à Paris du 5 au 6 octobre, pp. 186-210.

DREE (Direction des Relations Economiques Extérieures) (1998): The Textile-Clothing sector in Poland, Warsaw: French Ambassy.

Duché, Genèvieve (2000): "Vers la création d'un nouveau mode de production à Lodz (Pologne). Les freins au développement d'un milieu innovateur", in: RERU (1), 111-137.

Duchêne, Gerard/Rusin, Philippe (2002): "Small innovative firms in transition: the Polish case", in: Wladimir Andreff (Ed.), Analyses économiques de la transition post-socialiste, Paris: La Découverte, 87-120.

Duchêne, Gerard/Rusin, Philippe/Turlea, Geomina (2002): "Entrepreneurship and Institutions in Transition", in: Journal for Institutional Innovation, Development and Transition 6, 57-76.

Dunford, Mick (1992): "Trajectoires industrielles et relations sociales dans les régions de la nouvelles croissance économique", in : Benko Geoges/ Lipietz Alain, Eds., Les régions qui gagnent. Districts et réseaux: les nouveaux paradigmes de la géographie économique, Paris : PUF, pp. 227-264.

Grudzewski, Wieslaw M./Hejduk, Irena K. (1998): SMS in Polish market economy, Warsaw: WSHP.

Henderson, William O. (1954): Britain and Industrial Europe 1750-1870. Studies in British Influence on the Industrial Revolution in Western Europe. Liverpool: Liverpool UP.

Jeannin, Pierre (1991): "Dependency and development capacity in Central Europe at the end of 'ancien régime'", in: Cahiers de Varsovie (22), 85-104.

Kisline, Dimitri (2009): "La petite entreprise face au plan de modernisation de l'économie russe: un oubli regrettable", in : D'autres Russies. Altérité, diversité et complexité dans la Russie d'aujourd'hui, La revue russe 33, 105-108.

Krätke, Stefan (1997a): Regional Integration or Fragmentation? The German-Polish Border Region in a New Europe, Regional Studies Association, International Conference, Frankfurt (Oder), 20-23 September.

Krätke, Stefan (1997b): "Une approche régulationiste des etudes régionales", in: Association Recherche et Régulation (Ed.): L'Année de la Régulation. Vol. 1, Paris: Découverte, 263-296.

Krugman, Paul. R. (1979): "Increasing Returns, Monopolistic Competition and International Trade", in Journal of International Economics (9),. 469-479.

Lacquement, Guillaume (1993): "Rural restructuring in new Länder", in: Les Cahiers de l' Obsérvatoire de Berlin (24), 35-49.

Lepesant, Gilles (1997): Development Strategies in cross-border regions of Poland, Germany and Czech Republic, CERAT Report, Grenoble: University of Grenoble.

Lewitas,Andrzej/Gesicka, Grazyna (1994): Lokalne fundusze gwarancyjne, Warsaw: Oficyna Wydawnicza.

Lipowski, Adam/Despiney, Barbara (1990): "Recession and structurals changes in Poland", in: Revue des études slaves (4), pp. 921-938.

Maillat, Denis (1988): "SMS, Innovations and territorial development", in: IRER-Cahier (18), 21-46.

Marshall, Alfred (1919): Industry and Trade, London: Macmillan.

Marshall, Alfred (1920): Principles of Economics, London: Macmillan.

Martin, Ron (1999): The New 'Geographical Turn' in Economics: Some Critical Reflections, in: Cambridge Journal of Economics 23 (1), 65-91.

Martinelli, Flavia/Schoenberger, Erica (1992): "Les oligopoles se portent bien, merci!", in Georges Benko/Alain Lipietz (eds.), Les régions qui gagnent. Districts et réseaux: les nouveaux paradigmes de la géographie économique, Paris: PUF, pp. 163-188.

Michalet, Charles-Albert (1999): Charming nations or how attract FDI, Paris: Economica.

Nivet, Jean-François (2002): "Economic restructuring in the new Länder: Light from the East", in: RECEO 33 (2), pp. 115-136.

Pellegrin, Julie (1999): German Production Networks in Central/Eastern Europe. Between Dependency and Globalisation, WZB discussion paper FS I, 99-304.

Piore, Michael J./Sabel, Charles (1984): Le second industrial Divide: possibilities for prosperity, New York: Basic Books.

Ratti, Remigio/Bramanti, Alberto/Gordon,Richard (eds.) (1997): The Dynamics of Innovative regions. The GREMI Approach, Aldershot: Asghate.

Rogulska, Barbara (1985): "Indirect regulation and new relations Centre-enterprise in Poland", in: Economie et Société, Cahiers de l'ISMEA (41), pp. 2-31.

Samson, Ivan et al. (1996): Poles of growth and decision in the East. 1994-2015. Rapport pour la DATAR, Paris.

Samson, Ivan/Goutin-Bourlat, Elisabeth (1995): Opening, transition and development in Germany. Rapport pour la CGP, Paris.

Scott, Allen J. (1992): "L'économie métropolitaine : organisation industrielle et croissance urbaine", in: Les régions qui gagnent. Districts et réseaux : les nouveaux paradigmes de la géographie économique, Paris: PUF, pp. 103-120.

Scott, Allen J./Storper, Michael (1986): Production, Work, Territory, Boston: Allen & Unvin.

SDEC (Schéma de développement d'espace communautaire) (2000): La Documentation française, Paris.

Slim, Assen (1998): Intégration et disintegration économique régionale: du CAEM vers de nouvelles unions, Thesis, Université Paris 1 (Panthéon-Sorbonne).

Starzyk, Kazimierz (1996): "Cross-Border Co-operation as a Factor of Poland's Integration into the EU", in: Fritz Franzmayer/Christian Wese (eds.), Polen und die Osterweiterung der Europäischen Union, Berlin: Duncker & Humblot, Berlin, pp. 67-92.

Surdej, Aleksander (2001): Small-and Medium-Sized Entreprises Development in Poland after 1990, UNU/WIDER Working Paper, January.

Szymoniuk, Barbara/Walukiewicz Stanislaw (2004): Setting up rural clusters in Poland, contribution to the RSA Annual Conference, Angers, France, 15-16 April.

Veltz, Pierre (1996): Mondialisation, villes et territoires. L'économie d'archipel, Paris: PUF.

Winiecki, Jan (1998): "Formal and Informal Rules in Post-Communist Transition", in: Journal of Public Finance and Public Choice XVI (1), pp. 3-26.

WUS (2001): Euro-regions in the new territorial division of Poland. Wroclaw: WUS editions.

Territorial Cohesion and Border Areas

Roswitha Ruidisch

INTRODUCTION

Border areas are often described as "laboratories" for European cohesion, as places where European policymakers can experiment (KEG 2009: 15; Rippl et al. 2009). Sometimes they are also called *"petites Europes,"* where processes of change common to all of Europe can be seen taking place on a smaller scale (Luschny 2009: 28). Problems of cohesion, too, are more evident on a scale smaller than that of the European Union or nation-states, so border areas and other sub-national levels would seem the appropriate level to direct our observations. Border areas that straddle the old border dividing western and eastern Europe are especially interesting places, for here disparities are stark and easily seen. Differences and disparities offer opportunities for action in politics, economics, culture, environment, and social welfare. Concerning the interests of politics, border areas are crucial test areas for the instruments of European Regional Policy. One of the central aims of Regional Policy is to reduce disparities and contribute to cohesion in the EU. Cohesion, in the understanding of the European Union, focuses mainly on regional development. Given that European Regional Policy received the second largest share of the EU budget between 2007 and 2013, one might expect that EU Regional Policy exerted great deal of influence on cohesion in the European Union.

Cohesion may be interpreted as economic, social, or territorial cohesion. Territorial cohesion is the least well defined of the three. As it is the most recently added goal of Europe's cohesion policy, there is no clear understanding of what territorial cohesion will mean and no common understanding of which policies best promote it and what effects they have.

In this paper I will therefore analyze the concepts of "territorial cohesion" and "territorial capital," and I will show how these apply to border areas using the example of the Czech-German border area.

Territorial Cohesion: Origins and Significance

"Territorial cohesion" is a relatively new term, coined in the context of European Regional Policy. There has been little time for interpreting the new term and its meaning relative to its two component words "territory" and "cohesion." Not surprisingly, the term has been interpreted in many different ways. Below, some of the main interpretations are reviewed.

Origins

The term "territorial cohesion" was used in an official document first in the Amsterdam Treaty 1997. At that time, territorial cohesion was associated with services of general economic interest. Territorial cohesion within this context was supposed to counteract the liberalization of public services and therefore contribute to the maintenance of standards of living and help keep less populous regions competitive (Faludi 2009). The term has been used often in European political debates since the early 2000s. The Second Report on economic and social cohesion in 2001, for example, devoted an entire chapter to territorial cohesion. It included a statement supporting balanced development and described the development problems of specific regions. Border regions and their specific development situation were also mentioned. In 2004, the Third Report on economic and social cohesion noted for the first time that there is no clear definition of "territorial cohesion." Territorial cohesion was torn at that time between the two opposing goals of European Regional Policy, competitiveness and balanced development. The issue of territorial cohesion and how to interpret it as an objective and as a concept had been discussed long before it was anchored in the Treaty of Lisbon (2009) as an objective equal in priority to economic and social cohesion (Article 3 [3], TEU). In 2005, the planners Wil Zonneveld and Bas Waterhout, for example, suggested that territorial cohesion "will feed into existing EU policies by adding a territorial dimension to them, thereby making them more effective and efficient" (Zonneveld/Waterhout 2005: 18). But being nothing more than a "territorial dimension" was for many interested parties not enough. After territorial cohesion was added to the Treaty of Lisbon in 2009, it became a buzzword for politicians and researchers involved in European Regional Policy. During the preparation of the European constitution, territorial cohesion was the subject of intense lobbying (Robert 2007) and it gained supporters with a variety of interests and views (Böhme 2005; Faludi 2006; Finka 2007; Schön 2005).

The controversial discussion about the term covers a wide range of concerns, further contributing to a lack of precision in its definition (Faludi 2005b: 3; David 2007: 10). The explanation of the planner Jacques Roberts for this problem is that "[...] a definition cannot be derived from current or past practice, because territorial cohesion has so far hardly been applied concretely as an operational policy concept" (Robert 2007: 23). Another outcome of the discussion that territorial cohesion has taken on a normative coloring, being associated with ideals like equity (Faludi 2005b: 5; Böhme et al. 2008: 1), solidarity (Böhme et al. 2008: 1-3), social welfare, or harmonious development (Battis/Kersten 2009: 10; CEC 2008). Territorial cohesion also has been linked to questions concerning the quality of the territorial structure within the European Union. Achieving territorial cohesion requires accounting for spatial needs like accessibility, governance, sustainability, balanced development, services of general economic interest, or spatial planning (Böhme et al. 2008:3; David 2007: 5ff.). The planner Philippe Doucet is quite disenchanted with the term "territorial cohesion": "As for those outside this inner circle of specialized planning experts and officials, we can probably assume that they care little about territorial cohesion [...] Territorial cohesion is probably an unimportant esoteric ideal to many ordinary EU citizens" (Doucet 2006: 1475).

The Commission reacted to the critics in 2008 with a Green Paper on territorial cohesion entitled "Turning territorial diversity into strength." This paper launched a public discussion, inviting interested parties to comment on a set of questions in order to arrive at a definition of territorial cohesion. The effort produced no clear definition, but three narratives associated with "territorial cohesion" dominated this and other discussions: balanced development, competitiveness, and sustainability.

Narratives of Territorial Cohesion

Territorial cohesion has various meanings. However, the basic idea of territorial cohesion is very similar to the basic principles of regional policy:

balance, stability, competition, and sustainability. As territorial cohesion is an aim of the European Regional Policy, it is heading in a similar direction: "[T]he concept of territorial cohesion builds bridges between economic effectiveness, social cohesion and ecological balance" (CEC 2008). Below, the aspects of *balanced development, competitiveness,* and *sustainability* are analyzed with respect to their meaning for territorial cohesion.

Territorial Cohesion and the Aim of Balanced Development

Regional differences in living standards increased with every enlargement of the European Union. Therefore, one of the main aims of European Regional Policy is to balance regional disparities. Balanced development is measured in per capita GDP. Another central goal is that citizens and economic stakeholders have equal access to "services of general economic interest" (GD Regionalpolitik 2004: 3), regardless of where they live. The planner Kai Böhme and others state this goal more precisely: "A vital precondition for balanced development is access to a minimum standard of infrastructures and services" (Böhme 2008: 3). The challenge of territorial cohesion is to improve the development of disadvantaged regions, to promote an effective use of the instruments of regional policy, and to enhance territorial capital. All this is intended to contribute to a balanced development and regional cohesion.

Territorial Cohesion and the Aim of Competitiveness and Growth

Since the adoption of the Lisbon Strategy in 2000, EU Regional Policy has focused strongly on competitiveness and growth. Competitiveness as an aspect of territorial cohesion is relatively new. For years, the focus was rather on equity: "the Community shall aim at reducing disparities between the levels of development of the various regions and the backwardness of the least-favored regions [...]" (Article 130a, TEU). Today the most competitive area of the European Union is the "Pentagon" area framed by the cities of London, Paris, Milan, Munich and Hamburg. Although this core area has different potentials for future development, the challenge for territorial cohesion is to increase the global competitiveness of Europe as a whole as well as the competitiveness of individual regions outside the Pentagon (Faludi 2006: 43). In order to generate competitive advantages, the territorial capital of all areas should be used. Therefore the ball is in the court of the regions themselves: the focus is on regions and their unique, endogenous territorial capital. This contrasts with earlier assumptions in regional policy, whereby cities were seen as the only motors of the economy and of regional development.

Territorial Cohesion and Sustainability

In response to the strongly business-oriented Lisbon Strategy, the Gothenburg Strategy followed in 2001. This strategy is dedicated to sustainable development and takes the European environmental discourse into account. If the idea of sustainable development is transferred to territorial cohesion, it is then often linked to spatial planning. Some authors, like the planner Carl-Heinz David (David 2007: 12), even ascribe to territorial cohesion the role of a new European Spatial Development Policy. Sustainable territorial cohesion promotes the protection of nature and cultural heritage as well as polycentricity. The protection of ecologically sensitive areas in densely populated Europe is thought to be necessary because these areas are often threatened by urban development. To reduce urban sprawl and to enhance sustainable economic development, polycentric spatial structures are thought essential by planners (Battis/Kersten 2009: 11). The task of territorial cohesion is, in this sense, to create good development opportunities for urban areas, small and medium-sized cities, and rural areas. It should contribute to balanced, sustainable development (Faludi 2005a: 107). Polycentric spatial structures are supported by appropriate infrastructure (David 2007: 11) and make use of the territorial capital of the regions.

As the analysis of the different interpretations of territorial cohesion shows, there is a wide range of contents but a clear definition is missing.

The related problem is easy to grasp: as there is no clear target, it is not possible to put target-oriented measures, and it is also impossible to accurately evaluate the measures taken and to improve them. There is a curtain drawn over this problem as the European Union creates its own criteria for evaluation and thus purports itself sovereignty over the interpretation of success and failure of its policy for themselves. Good examples for this procedure are the 'Reports of Economic and Social Cohesion' which have been published since 1996.

Every interpretation of territorial cohesion described above stresses the link of territorial capital to successful regional development. But what is territorial capital and how can it be exploited?

The Cement of Territorial Cohesion: Territorial Capital

The term "territorial capital" was introduced in conjunction with the term "territorial cohesion." Very roughly, territorial capital comprises the assets and limits of a territory. As Europe's territories have very different characters, territorial capital also is associated with "European territorial diversity" (Böhme et al. 2008: 1). This kind of diversity is an important asset, which policy makers wish to transform into strength. This was one of the main points of the Green Paper on Territorial Cohesion in 2008: "Increasingly, competitiveness and prosperity depend on the capacity of the people and businesses located there to make the best use of all territorial assets" (CEC 2008).

What is Territorial Capital?

Territorial capital is the territorial potential of an area: "Each area has a specific capital – its 'territorial capital' – that is distinct from that of other areas[...]" (OECD 2001: 15). Therefore territorial fragilities are not seen as potentials at first sight. In a more economic sense, territorial capital might also be described as its "comparative advantage" (Böhme et al. 2008: 3), as territorial capital can make investments in one region more effective than in other regions. Territorial capital is thus the basis for endogenous growth in cities and regions. Economic growth is generated from an area's potential, and a region's welfare depends crucially on its ability to make use of its unique regional development potentials. The distinct set of territorial potentials that contribute to territorial capital can be factors such as natural and cultural values. Other factors are an area's ability to integrate and connect to other areas (David 2007: 10), which implies accessibility and infrastructure. The Organisation for Economic Co-operation and Development has divided these factors into numerous types, all of which are referred to as territorial capital:

> These factors may include the area's geographical location, size, factor of production endowment, climate, traditions, natural resources, quality of life or the agglomeration economies provided by its cities, but may also include its business incubators and industrial districts or other business networks that reduce transaction costs. Other factors may be "untraded interdependencies" such as understandings, customs and informal rules that enable economic actors to work

together under conditions of uncertainty, or the solidarity, mutual assistance and co-opting of ideas that often develop in clusters of small and medium-sized enterprises working in the same sector (social capital). Lastly, according to Marshall, there is an intangible factor, "something in the air", called the "environment" and which is the outcome of a combination of institutions, rules, practices, producers, researchers and policy-makers, that make a certain creativity and innovation possible (OECD 2001: 15).

Territorial capital is useless without people and businesses that use it locally. It is they who have the best knowledge of their territories, and they who best know how to make the most of its inherent features (Böhme et al. 2008: 2; CEC 2008). In order to get local and regional actors involved, a new approach called "stakeholder policy" has been introduced (David 2007: 8). This approach is, in fact, necessary because the European Union has no legal competence for European Regional Policy and therefore no competence to promote territorial cohesion. The EU gives financial incentives to addressees with the intention of persuading them to voluntarily implement EU territorial cohesion policies.

Measures for Actualizing Territorial Capital

Territorial cohesion lays the groundwork for the political regulation of space. Policy interventions to support regional development do so by "respecting its fragilities" and using its "unrecognized or underexploited potentials" (Böhme et al. 2008: 2). Because European territories possess a great variety of territorial capital, one-size-fits-all development strategies will unlikely achieve territorial cohesion. In order to make the most of their inherent potential, tailor-made measures are necessary.

Political documents of the EU, like the Green Paper on Territorial Cohesion, discuss measures thought to contribute to territorial cohesion such as cooperation, governance, and networks. These measures are supposed to activate territorial capital, but in order to make the most of territorial capital, transportation infrastructure that improves access is crucial (Commission of the European Communities 2008). Better infrastructure reduces travel costs and guarantees access to markets for consumers, workers, and businesses. Therefore, infrastructure development is more popular than ever. As a one-size-fits-all instrument, it seems to fit the goal of territorial cohesion, too. But this idea is not new. Studies (see for example Biehl 1986) have shown that infrastructure is crucial for the development of regional potentials such as labor. Employment does correlate with better infrastructure, hence Biehl argues that regions cannot achieve their highest potential without infrastructure. Unemployed capital could therefore become employed by the "catalyst power" of infrastructure (Kaufmann 1983: 420). The planner Andreas Faludi (2006: 42) also illustrates in the 1999 document, European Spatial Development Perspective (ESDP), that infrastructure was a decisive instrument of "spatial cohesion." Recent studies show that infrastructure can promote the development of regional potential, but not automatically (Schaffer/Siegele 2008: 130). The European Union thus declared that "a good transport system in itself is not sufficient to ensure regional development. The effect of investment in transport [...] infrastructure on economic performance also depends on the region's capacity to use it efficiently [...]." (Europäische Kommission 2010: 55). So what is "the region's capacity," then? The economist Roberto Camagni (2006: 62) argues for "new models of territorial governance" that integrate various levels of territorial management and control. Territorial governance should involve the public as much as possible in decisions regarding territorial changes. Local bodies and municipal authorities are therefore important institutions because they are in direct contact with the inhabitants of a territory and their needs. The most important element, often neglected, is individual citizen participation (Camagni 2006: 63). The inhabitants of a territory, not infrastructure, represent the region's true potential because only they can actualize territorial capital. This way of thinking goes beyond classic, distributive Regional Policy.

What has also becomes evident is the advent of a set of measures like new infrastructure within classic, distributive Regional Policy. The new aspect that is added to conventional strategies is the goal of increasing competitiveness, endogenous development, sustainability, and good governance (Faludi 2006: 43). These ambitious aims in the context of territorial cohesion are useless without taking people into consideration. Areas that are affected by transport infrastructures need local players who make use of both transport infrastructure and territorial capital. As infrastructure connections between eastern and western Europe were cut after the Second World War, border areas had only nationally oriented infrastructure for decades. The European integration process has resulted in a rebuilding of cross-border infrastructure connections, making border areas interesting laboratories for territorial cohesion.

Border Areas as Laboratories for Territorial Cohesion

European integration and the establishment of the Single European Market have made national borders more permeable. The functions and development perspectives of national border areas have changed as a consequence, as they are no longer at the edges of their respective nation-states. National state borders were constructed as an instrument of political power, and as the borders vanish, old strengths of the border areas become fragile and new potentials emerge. Border areas between western and eastern Europe are particularly interesting to study because very different levels of wealth meet in a relatively small neighborhood. The instruments of European Regional Policy intended to overcome regional disparities are especially challenged in this "laboratory". Territorial cohesion is under scrutiny especially in the border areas where western and eastern Europe were once divided. The most commonly used instruments in border areas to promote cohesion include the development and expansion of transport infrastructure and business investment subsidies.

The Czech-German Border Area as a Policy Laboratory

The border between Saxony and Bavaria in Germany and Bohemia is one of the oldest in Europe. For decades, people living on both sides of this border used German as their common language. Settlements and infrastructure on both sides of the border were connected. Until 1918, Bohemia was part of the Austrian monarchy and the area was inhabited by persons of many different nationalities. Certain parts of the Czech border area, where many German settlers lived, were known as "Sudetenland." The Second World War changed the situation in this border area completely. At the end of the war, the German speaking population had to leave Sudetenland and the iron curtain was lowered. This process cut the roots of people and settlements in the border area, and road and railway connections were severed. Whereas the Czech border area of the former Sudetenland was substantially disrupted, there were few changes of population and settlement structures in the Saxonian and the Bavarian border areas. The iron curtain was a strong political dividing line between eastern and western Europe, a circumstance that meant that these border areas took different paths of development over the decades. After the fall of the iron curtain, the territorial diversity of the

Czech-German border areas became visible. This diversity can be regarded as a challenge or as an opportunity (Ahner/Fuechtner 2010: 543).

The iron curtain cut infrastructure connections in the Czech-German border area, including the former transportation links between Nuremberg and Prague. There were motorways from Nuremberg to other points in Germany and from Prague to other points in the Czech Republic, but no connector between the countries. Given the EU's interest in cohesion, Eurocorridors become an important instrument linking big cities in eastern and western Europe. Corridors are bundles of railway lines, motorways, and other kinds of infrastructure. Eurocorridor IV connects Nuremberg and Prague and includes the motorway A6 in Germany and D5 in the Czech Republic. The gap in this motorway between Amberg (Germany) and Plzeň (Czech Republic) was closed in 2008, which improved the accessibility of the German-Czech border area significantly.

The Economy as a Subject of Investigation

The main recipients of regional policy measures are private companies. They initiate investments and create jobs in the region and thus have a decisive influence on regional development. They operate under various conditions. They are supported by Regional Policy measures, but they also face the challenges of the global economy. Companies are embedded in the region and its local socio-institutional structures. The specific forms of territorial capital such as labor, infrastructure, resources, and other factors are used by companies to increase their competitiveness (Bathelt/Glückler 2002: 162). In addition, companies benefit from local relationships, conventions, norms, routines, attitudes, and objectives of regional actors (Storper 1997).

Many entrepreneurs have taken advantage of the particular situation of the German-Czech border area. The economy of the region of Plzeň is dominated by the largest manufacturer in the Czech Republic, Škoda Plzeň. At the end of 1989, more than 33,000 workers were employed there (Toušek 2005: 71). Restructuring and privatization led to thousands of job losses. After 1989, the Plzeň region became attractive for foreign investors due to its location and its labor force. The majority of FDI went into electronics. Panasonic, for example, began the production of televisions, and Alcoa began producing electrical wiring for the car industry. The situation in the German border region Upper Palatinate was slightly different. During the Cold War, Upper Palatinate was a marginal location in Germany. Companies investing there received financial subsidies (*Zonenrandförderung*). The region was known as "the poor house of Bavaria," as the economy was dominated by agriculture and glass and porcelain manufacturing. Although the region suffered from structural changes in the 1980s and 1990s, some family businesses prospered. Quite a few of them have become hidden champions and some of them are world market leaders today. The study, "Zukunft Deutschland 2020" now calls Upper Palatinate a "high-flyer region" (Invest in Bavaria 2008).

Not the region or the border area is the addressee of infrastructure investments, but companies. Thus, it is vital to know who these companies are. Different branches draw on different territorial resources. Today, we have little knowledge about the structure of economic sectors in the German-Czech border area. To generate an overview of the companies located along the new motorway A6-D5, I have mapped the industrial areas at a distance of up to 20 kilometers from the exits. The area I investigated lies between Amberg and Plzeň, the two cities that frame the Czech-German border. I have divided this stretch into six sectors. In the far west is the "Region Amberg-Sulzbach," which is close to the city of Amberg. The "Region Naabtal' is characterized by the intersection of the motorways A6 and A93. Next to it is the "Region Grenzland," adjacent to "Region Böhmerwald" across the border in the Czech Republic. This area belonged to the "Sudetenland" areas mentioned above. During the Cold War, it was mainly occupied by Russian military. The "Region Stribro" is dominated by the city of Stribro, and the "Region Plzeň" is the area next to the city of Plzeň. Roughly speaking, there is a great difference in the age of companies in both countries. In Bavaria, family businesses have been in the region for years. Some of them have expanded their production locations and built new sites close to the new motorway. There has been nearly no FDI. In the Plzeň region there exist many new companies that came from outside the region. Most of them have settled in locations close to the new motorway and were financed by foreign capital.

Apart from Region Stribro, all sectors are dominated by logistics (yellow). The second biggest branch apart from Region Böhmerwald is the metal processing industry (light blue). Region Böhmerwalds' second biggest branch is plastics processing (dark green), which is also dominant in the neighboring German sector Region Naabtal. Even more companies in Region Naabtal belong to the glass processing industry (grey).

Industrial Structure in the Czech-German Border Area

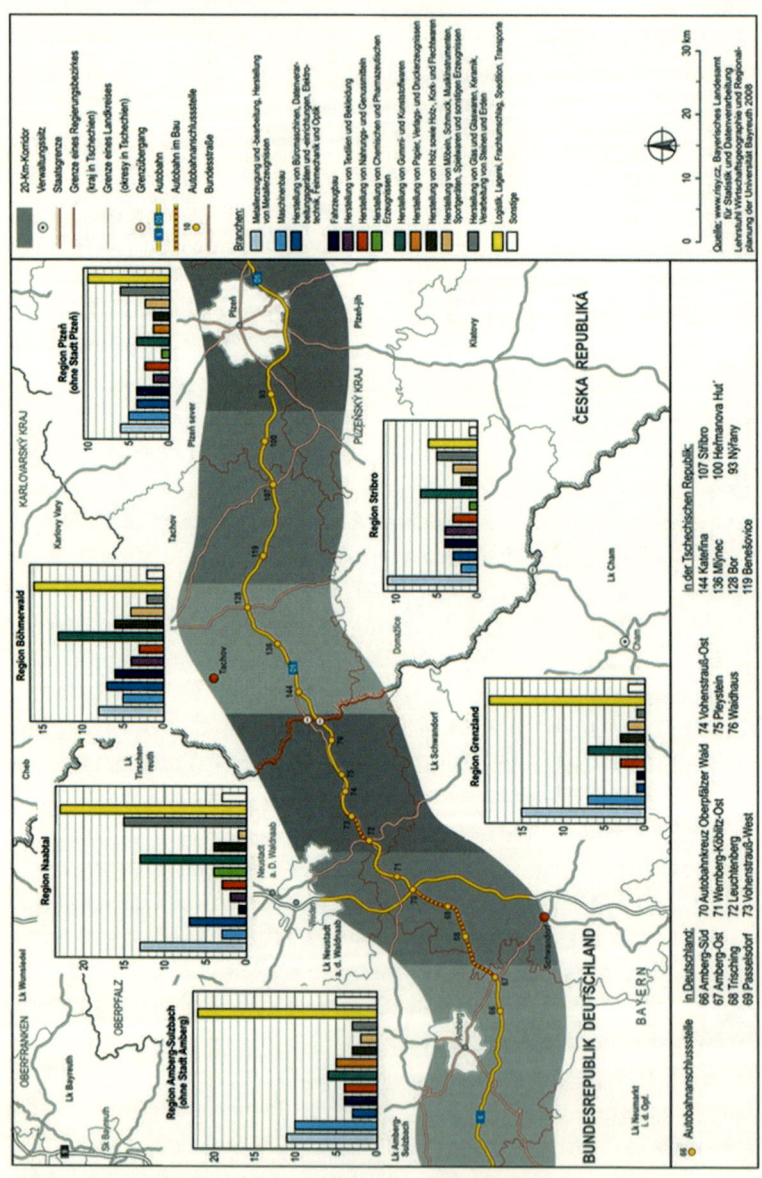

Source: Mapping by Roswitha Ruidisch, 2008-2010

In sum, it is interesting that all regions are dominated by more or less the same economic sectors. One reason for this phenomenon is cross-border investment by a few German, family-owned businesses. In the plastics processing industry the companies Gerresheimer or Inotech for example have their headquarters in Germany's Upper Palatinate but have built production sites just across the border in the Plzen region. They use the territorial potential of easy access to use resources, especially low-wage labor. Logistics is a relatively new branch on both sides of the border. Logistics companies also use the locational advantages of easy access to bigger cities like Nuremberg or Prague.

Conclusion

As stated at the beginning of the article, border areas are quite often described as "laboratories" of European cohesion. But "the region" or the "border area" is not the addressee of European Regional Politics and their infrastructure investments. Therefore, discussions among EU actors regarding "regions" or "areas" are misleading. As the addressees are companies interested in making profit from resources associated with territory, the discussion about territorial cohesion must take them into account. Companies are very much interested in profiting from infrastructure investments, but they are not necessarily interested in territorial cohesion. Yet, the success of subsidies depends on how they are used by companies. Whether transport infrastructure helps to overcome regional disparities in border areas is questionable. Transport infrastructure is used differently by different companies. Companies choose the location of investment for various reasons, motivated in the end by the goal of profit. Regional disparities may therefore be useful for companies, for example in holding down wages. Territorial cohesion as such is a construction of EU politicians. Therefore the term has been used by different lobbyists to follow a range of interests. Planners want territorial cohesion to signify support for their interest in European spatial planning. Economists want territorial cohesion to signify support for competitiveness. Private firms want territorial cohesion measures to subsidize their production processes.

References

Ahner, Dirk/Fuechtner, Natascha-Miriam (2010): "Territoriale Kohäsion: EU-Politik im Dienste regionaler Potenziale", in: Informationen zur Raumentwicklung (8), pp. 543-552.

Bathelt, Harald/Glückler, Johannes (2002): Wirtschaftsgeographie. Ökonomische Beziehungen in räumlicher Perspektive. Stuttgart: Eugen Ulmer.

Battis, Ulrich/Kersten, Jens (2009): "Europäische Raumentwicklung", in: Europarecht 44 (1), pp. 3-23.

Biehl, Dieter (Ed.) (1986): The Contribution of Infrastructure to Regional Development. Final report. European Communities. Luxembourg: Office for Official Publications of the European Communities.

Böhme, Kai/Eser, Thiemo/Gaskell, Frank/Gustedt, Evelyn (2008): The Territorial Cohesion Principles. Position paper to the EU Green Paper on Territorial Cohesion. Hannover Akademie für Raumforschung und Landesplanung (www.spatialforesight.eu/tl_files/files/editors/dokumente/ARL-Position-Territorial_Cohesion.pdf).

BMVBS (Bundesministerium für Verkehr, Bau und Stadtentwicklung) (Ed.) (2006): Territoriale Ausgangslage und Perspektiven der Europäischen Union. Stärkung der territorialen Kohäsion in Europa unter Berücksichtigung der Lissabon- und Göteborg-Strategien. Ein Hintergrunddokument für die Territoriale Agenda der Europäischen Union. (www.bmvbs.de/cae/servlet/contentblob/29702/publicationFile/2621/territoriale-ausgangslage-und-perspektiven-der-europaeischen-union.pdf).

Camagni, Roberto (2006): "The rationale for territorial cohesion: issues and possible policy strategies", in: Luisa Pedrazzini (Ed.): The process of territorial cohesion in Europe. Milano: Francoangeli, pp. 53-67.

CEC (Commission of the European Communities) (2008): Green Paper on Territorial Cohesion. Turning territorial diversity into strength. Brussels (SEC(2008) 2550) (http://eur-lex.europa.eu/LexUriServ/LexUriServ.do?uri=COM:2008:0616:FIN:EN:PDF)

David, Carl-Heinz (2007): "Status and Perspectives of Territorial Cohesion with Respect to European Spatial Development Policy (ESDP) – Normative and Governance Aspects", in: Dietmar Scholich (Ed.), Territorial cohesion. Berlin: Springer, pp. 5-22.

Doucet, Philippe (2006): "Territorial Cohesion of Tomorrow: A Path to Cooperation or Competition? European Briefing, in: European Planning Studies 14 (10), pp. 1473-1485.

Europäische Kommission (2010): In Europas Zukunft investieren. Fünfter Bericht über den wirtschaftlichen, sozialen und territorialen Zusammenhalt. Amt für Veröffentlichungen der Europäischen Union. Luxemburg. (http://ec.europa.eu/regional_policy/sources/docoffic/official/reports/cohesion5/pdf/5cr_de.pdf).

Faludi, Andreas (2005a): "Polycentric territorial cohesion policy", in: Town Planning Review 76 (1), pp. 107-118.

Faludi, Andreas (2005b): "Territorial cohesion: An unidentified political objective", in: Town Planning Review 76 (1), pp. 1-13.

Faludi, Andreas (2006): "The uncertain future of EU territorial cohesion policy", in: Luisa Pedrazzini (Ed.), The process of territorial cohesion in Europe. Milano: Francoangeli, pp. 41-52.

Finka, Maroš (2007): "Territorial Cohesion – Between Expectations, Disparities and Contradictions", in: Scholich (Ed.), Territorial cohesion, pp. 23-39.

GD (Generaldirektion) Regionalpolitik (2004): Territorialer Zusammenhalt. Zwischenbericht. Vorläufige Ergebnisse der Studien von ESPON und EU-Kommission. Amt für amtliche Veröffentlichungen der Europäischen Gemeinschaften. Luxemburg (http://ec.europa.eu/regional_policy/sources/docoffic/official/reports/coheter/coheter_de.pdf)

Invest in Bavaria (2008): Current 'Zukunft Deutschland 2020' Study rates Upper Palatinate as one of the top locations in Germany (www.invest-in-bavaria.de/cn/news/pressemitteilungen/archive-cn/details-cn/archive/2008/august/list/current-zukunft-deutschland-2020-study-rates-upper-palatinate-as-one-of-the-top-locations-in-g/)

Kaufmann, Lothar (1983): "Verkehrspolitik und regionale Entwicklungsmöglichkeiten", in: Internationales Verkehrswesen (6), pp. 419-423.

KEG (Kommission der Europäischen Gemeinschaften) (2009): Bericht der Kommission an das Europäische Parlament und den Rat. Sechster Zwischenbericht über den wirtschaftlichen und sozialen Zusammenhalt. Brüssel (KOM (2009) 295). (http://ec.europa.eu/regional_policy/sources/docoffic/official/reports/interim6/com_2009_295_de.pdf)

Löw, Martina/Steets, Silke/Stoetzer, Sergej (2008): Einführung in die Stadt- und Raumsoziologie. 2. aktualisierte Auflage. Opladen/Farmington Hills: Barbara Budrich.

Mayring, Philipp (2002): Einführung in die qualitative Sozialforschung. Eine Anleitung zu qualitativem Denken. 5. Auflage. Weinheim, Basel: Beltz.

Meidl, Christian N. (2009): Wissenschaftstheorie für SozialforscherInnen. Wien/Köln/Weimar: Böhlau.

OECD (Organisation for Economic Co-operation and Development) (2001): OECD Territorial Outlook, 2001 Edition. Paris: OECD.

Rippl, Susanne/Petrat, Anke/Kindervater, Angela/Boeneke, Klaus (2009): "Zur Bedeutung 'transnationalen Sozialkapitals': Sind Grenzgebiete Laboratorien sozialer Integration in Europa", in: Berliner Journal für Soziologie 19, pp. 79-103.

Robert, Jacques (2007): "The Origins of Territorial Cohesion and the Vagaries of Its Trajectory", in: Andreas Faludi (Ed.): Territorial Cohesion and the European Model of Society. Cambridge, Mass.: Lincoln Institute of Land Policy, pp. 23-35.

Schaffer, Axel/Siegele, Jochen (2008): "Regionale Potentiale – Bedeutung und Nutzung von Potentialfaktoren in den NUTS 3 Regionen Deutschlands und Österreichs", in: Jahrbuch für Regionalwissenschaft 28, pp. 109-132.

Storper, Michael (1997): The regional world. Territorial development in a global economy. New York: Guilford Press.

Toušek, Václav (2005): Czech Republic. Portraits of regions. Praha: Ministry for Regional Development of the Czech Republic.

Waterhout, Bas (2007): "Territorial Cohesion: The Underlying Discourses", in: Faludi (Ed.): Territorial Cohesion, pp. 37-59.

Zonneveld, Wil/Waterhout, Bas (2005): "Visions on territorial cohesion", in: Town Planning Review 76 (1), pp. 15-27.

Identities and Stereotypes in European Border Regions

Identities and Stereotypes in Cross-Border Regions

Antje Schönwald

INTRODUCTION

Identities are socially constructed and dynamic. Some see in this a potential problem, leading in some cases to problems of individual orientation or even to identity crises. This contribution is an examination of identity in what is called the "Greater Region," a large cross-border region that encompasses Saarland, Lorraine, Rhineland-Palatinate, the Grand Duchy of Luxembourg, and both the French-speaking and German-Speaking communities of Wallonia in Belgium. New, multidimensional forms of identity have emerged in this region.

The meaning and relevance of space is changing. Not only territory but also economics, culture, and politics determine space (Krämer/König 2002: 280). Geographic distances can be crossed faster than ever, and personal mobility has increased. Nation states especially seem to be losing more and more functions, and their power of establishing identity is diminishing. In their place, regions are advancing to become "a projection surface of fundamental identity claims"[1] (Buß 2002: 12). Borders, too, are changing in meaning as their barrier function becomes less important. Europe presents itself increasingly as an entity without internal borders, but individual regions, as well as nations, keep their unique characteristics and distinctiveness. Recent research recognizes a connection between globalization and localization much in keeping with Robertson's glocalization thesis: that local and global processes are reciprocally dependent and influential (cf. Robertson 1995, 1998). Thus, a new perspective of the

---

[1] | All quotations translated by the author.

local is possible as global consciousness reinvents the local (Ahrens 2001: 137).

In spite of the fact that identities are constructed, they are able to "have suddenly obvious effects as social facts" (Reese-Schäfer 1999: 7). Because the social world "is made up of actions in concrete interaction situations" (Werlen 1992: 11f.), an influence of identities on action can be assumed. Another impact on action exists through stereotypes, as identities are always influenced by extraneous ascriptions and outward self-presentation. Stereotypes are thus part of every identity and it is necessary to analyze both phenomena simultaneously. Due to increasing tendencies towards individualization and the possibility of self-determination in almost all areas of life, identities are characterized by a continuous dynamic. This "pluralization of possibilities of identity constructions" (Reckinger/Wille 2010: 15) leads to a recurring challenge and checking of existing identities. In the context of the opening of identities and acceptance of plural identities, critics perceive a potential loss of identity due to a lack of orientation. As the nation-state loses its centrality for orienting individual identities, the significance of other territorial units for this function is perceptible. Europe, for example, presents itself as a "Europe of the regions." This reflects the intention of promoting a third level of identity, in addition to the nation and Europe, in bottom-up Europeanization. The nomination of Luxemburg and the Greater Region as European Capital of Culture 2007 can be described as such an attempt.

The example of the "Greater Region", analyzed below, shows that such spaces offer new possibilities for the emergence of new forms of multidimensional identity. It harbors also threats to identity and stereotypes.

In October 1998, the "Charter of Cultural Cooperation in the Region Saar-Lor-Lux-Trier/Westpfalz" was signed. Its declared primary goal was formulated as follows: "As Europe grows together, the partners strive to raise awareness of cultural unity among the population, which is to be deepened by arrangements in the field of the common cultural and historical heritage that create identity" (Charter of Cultural Cooperation in the Region Saar-Lor-Lux-Trier/Westpfalz, 1998). More than ten years later, the question now presents itself of whether any such awareness of common cultural heritage has arisen. If so, what factors have been influential in creating identity and how does any Greater Region identity or identities effect social action, if at all? The study below is based mostly on qualitative interviews with Greater Region stakeholders from various sectors (education, economy, culture, politics, work, and environment), conducted in 2009 and 2010.[2]

The analysis begins with a brief description of the Greater Region, after which the formation and influence of social categories and stereotypes are outlined. Subsequently, the components that contribute to identity and the effects of identifying with the Greater Region are discussed. The article ends with a typology of Greater Region identities.

THE CROSS-BORDER AREA "GREATER REGION"

The Greater Region, as defined today, extends over an area of 65,401 square kilometers and has more than eleven million inhabitants. It is Europe's largest cross-border region. In everyday use, the term "Saar-Lor-Lux" is more frequent than "Greater Region." It owes its prominence to its long tradition, being first used in 1969. At that time, the executive of the Saar-Bergwerke introduced the term for the region to emphasize the importance of the cooperation of the three regions Saarland, Lorraine, and Luxembourg in the coal and steel industry (Glöckner 2001). Later, the Greater Region expanded, and its name changed frequently to reflect these territorial modifications. The Saar-Lor-Lux region thus became Saar-Lor-Lux-Trier/Westpfalz and then Saar-Lor-Lux-Rheinland-Pfalz-Wallonie or "Greater Region."

CATEGORIZATION AS A BASIS FOR STEREOTYPING AND AS PART OF THE CONCEPT OF THE SELF

Social identity theory (SIT) in social-psychology, developed by Tajfel, applies to inter-group processes and conflicts. Its main focus lies on the individual's behavior in groups (cf. Zick 2002). An individual's social identity is based on group membership. Before the formation of groups, categori-

---

2 | The research was developed within the MORO-project "Überregionale Partnerschaften in grenzüberschreitenden Verflechtungsräumen" (Super-Regional Partnerships in Cross-Border Regions) of the Federal Institute for Research on Building, Urban Affairs and Spatial Development and the Saarland Ministry of the Environment.

zations are made that allow individuals to define themselves in relation to social context (Hastedt 1998: 6). They serve as orientation systems (Tajfel 1982: 103). The categories become part of the self-concept (Turner 1982: 16). Due to the division of the social environment into categories and groups (ingroup and outgroups), whenever social identity overrides the salience of personal identity individuals often act not as individuals but as group members. Acting as group members, individuals tend to perceive groups as homogenous, overlooking internal differentiation to focus on differences between groups. This categorizing impact of perception is interesting because the "way we perceive others will influence indirectly how we act towards them" (Turner 1982: 29). Thus, social categorization supports stereotypes and affects our behavior towards stereotyped persons. Tajfel's experiments demonstrated that a trivial categorization into two groups "can suffice to initiate discriminatory behavior towards an outgroup" (Petersen/Blank 2008: 203).

There are four categorization bases of vital importance among stakeholders: political borders and nationality, language boundaries, geographical distance to the national border, and legal competencies. These categorization bases, as shown by interviews, often cause an interviewee to perceive another person "in the light of his belonging to a social category" (Mielke 1999: 5). Evaluating a person based on a categorization is called stereotyping (cf. Mielke 1999: 5). Perception is not passive, it is a matter of "information research" rather than "information processing" (Briesen 1994: 41).

Serving as an example for a stereotype that developed from several categorization bases, the stereotype of the different working methods of Germans and French may be mentioned. According to this stereotype, the work styles of Germans (some interviewees expand this to include "German speaking") and French (or 'French speaking') vary in terms of organization and effectiveness. The German work style is seen, depending on one's point of view, as either over-organized and thus inflexible or as well organized and thus efficient. French and French-speaking persons by analogy are perceived as less organized and less efficient or less fixed and more flexible. This is a good example of how inner-group heterogeneity is ignored and how groups and their individual members become subject to categorical ascription.

STEREOTYPES AND THEIR IMPACT ON CROSS-BORDER COOPERATION

Originating in typography, the term "stereotype" is composed of "the two Greek words *stereos* (fixed, hard, firm) and *typos* (concept, fixed form, characteristic imprint)" (Petersen/Six 2008: 21). Stereotypes are opinions and probability judgments (Ganter 1997: 6). They can be positive or negative (cf. Hahn/Hahn 2002: 20), correct or incorrect (Filipp and Mayer 2005: 26). They tap into "socially shared structures of knowledge" (Klauer 2008: 23) and can be dangerous, particularly because they are used to justify behavior towards members of other groups (Tajfel 1982: 44).

Stereotypes are characterized by durability. If a stereotype is attributed to a category, in most cases it won't change even when the stereotype contradicts reality. Before a stereotype is called into question, individuals are more likely to cancel out their intellectual knowledge "on an emotional basis" (Hahn/Hahn 2002: 27).

Interviews with stakeholders in the Greater Region verified that stereotypes can have both positive and negative consequences for cross-border cooperation. As an option for individual orientation, stereotypes have a mainly positive function: "The essential cognitive function of stereotyping is thus to systematize and simplify information from the social environment in order to make sense of a world that would otherwise be too complex and chaotic for effective action" (Tajfel 1981: 148). Stereotypes facilitate dealing with a culture that has been foreign. In the best case, this stimulates interest in learning more about the unknown group and to question the stereotype. One interviewee, Ms. "O.L.," experienced the lack of stereotypes as obstructive for cross-border identity construction because stereotypes are needed to create an image of other people. She prefers having an image, even if it's probably a false one.

Apart from the positive functions of orientation, stereotypes have two other possible positive functions: positive discrimination and the stabilization of social identity. Luxembourg provides an example of positive discrimination: "Luxembourgers" are often attributed with above-average openness. The interviewee Mrs. R.I., for example, was of the opinion that they have "always" had a Greater regional identity. Positive discrimination exists when groups are attributed with positive characteristics or are more readily trusted: "discrimination is when a person treats another person due to his group membership better or worse than a member of another group" (Förster 2007: 33).

Even when preferences have positive effects, they must still be considered an "inadmissible generalization" because the positively stereotyped person is thereby "confronted with excessive peer pressure and his individuality and singularity is denied" (Filipp/Mayer 2005: 30). Stereotyping comparison groups can strengthen one's own social identity if the ingroup is judged to be better than the outgroup (Roth 2005; Tajfel 1981, 1982). Stereotyping an outgroup can serve as a defensive mechanism if a negative stereotype about one's own ingroup is threatening: "stigmatized groups turn the negative attributions into positive qualities" (Keupp et al. 1999: 180). The reciprocal stereotyping of German and French work styles demonstrates this. Indeed, stereotypes often arise from reactions to attributions from outside. The dependence between auto-stereotypes and hetero-stereotypes is evident in this example. "Almost every time, when using a negative hetero-stereotype, the positive auto-stereotype is in mind at the same time" (Hahn/Hahn 2002: 31).

The interviews revealed three negative effects of stereotypes: justification of the status quo; social discrimination and avoidance; and the perception of threat or the weakening of social identity. Justification of the status quo is present in the stereotyping of regions situated at the geographical edges of the Greater Region. Some interviewees are convinced that the inhabitants in those areas are less interested in cooperation and do not identify with the Greater Region. Obviously, the category "inhabitant at the edge" is itself a stereotype. That stereotypes can lead to social discrimination is also obvious in the Greater Region: the idea of the "Greater Region with two speeds" was a common theme. Mummendey and Wenzel see in this a common form of social discrimination: when two categories exist as subcategories of the same overarching category, whereby one is portrayed as the better prototype of the superior category, necessarily deprecating the other (Waldzus/Wenzel 2008).

Luxembourg's special position in the Greater Region can lead to the perception of threat or a weakening of social identity. Luxembourg is the strongest economic region in the Greater Region. It also has the greatest number of in-coming commuters. It is the only nation-state completely contained within the Greater Region and thus has greater legal competencies than the other subregions. This is not regarded positively by all stakeholders. Mrs. H.S., for example, feels that Luxembourg exploits the surrounding areas because it benefits from commuters with skills but does not honor social obligations to the outlying areas such as contributing to the maintenance of education systems. The positive stereotype of Luxembourg as "Greater Region's stimulation" may be evaluated negatively when other subregions feel their social identities threatened.

Identity-Creating Factors

Different factors create identity: territory, language, symbols, history, contact, functional relations, mutual interest, and education. The manifestation of each in the Greater Region is discussed below.

Starting with territory, recent approaches in the sociology of space proceed from the assumption that "social and historically relevant space is the result of human actions and perceptions" (Mein 2008: 33). Nonetheless, space remains important because of relationships to a specific geographic location, especially in the postmodern era when, as Giddens argues, people desire to re-embed themselves in reaction to the dislocation and detachment caused by globalization (Kühne 2006: 112ff.). Although the enormous size of the Greater Region is criticized by many stakeholders, few demand a rearrangement. The stakeholders are conscious of the malleability of frontiers and of their arbitrariness, yet, they accept the demarcation as it stands. The fact that all regions are located at a national border is seen as common ground by stakeholders.

That language plays an important role in creating identity was emphasized repeatedly by interviewees. One stakeholder saw in the bilingualism of colleagues a point of shared identity. Additionally, language is described as something that enables contact and provides material for conversations, for example about the same television programs. And language itself is described as an important cultural force, whereby language boundaries are considered to be cultural boundaries. High linguistic competence is said to express openness and interest, a language boundary on the other hand can serve as means of exclusion.

Symbols, both spatial symbols and space-related symbols, are important. Furthermore, the name "Greater Region" itself has a symbolic character. The name Greater Region is well known to all stakeholders and is also used as a term for the cooperation area. But most criticize its arbitrariness, its lack of significance, its ambiguity, and, finally, its interchangeability, especially for persons outside the Greater Region. The term plays no role in creating identity. Natural geographic symbols, for example the Moselle or the Eifel, are better for establishing connections. Borders are of special importance for spatial symbolism. The opening of borders is a symbol of putting away a warlike past. The border area symbolizes values like peace and liberty and thereby an openness between cultures. Spatial symbols offer the possibility of establishing categories that are less exclusive than categories based on linguistic area, nation, or subregion. So far, there exist few space-related symbols in the Greater Region.

Memories evoked by symbols are much more important than their actual meanings. Many cross-border areas emphasize the historical commonalities of the several subregions. In general, a common history is thought to create common identity. "Memory, on the individual level, has the function of attributing consistency and meaning to [...] existence. One's own past, thereby, always serves the validation of the present" (Flender 1994: 109). Some argue that a common history should legitimate political goals or serve generally to demarcate spaces in the Greater Region, although others argue that there "can be no question of a historically grown Greater Region or a 'natural' growing together of the population in the Greater Region" (Pauly 2009: 29). Few interviewees expressed belief in a common historical legacy within the Greater Region. The border's delineation is widely held to be arbitrary. The commonality of being located on a national border seems to be more important than any historical commonality. Thus, for creating a common identity, common history is not useful, although some do mention it. Nonetheless, it does have meaning as a connecting factor for some common projects. The goal of breaking with the warlike past and preserving peace is more important than historical unity for current identity constructions.

Both personal contact across borders and informational exchange can arouse interest and reduce fears. If contact is lacking, interest is more likely to be lacking as well. The mainly positive attitude of the interviewees towards the Greater Region is probably attributable to a previous job-related interaction with the Greater Region. There is a positive correlation between information and interest. Pierre Bourdieu calls attention to persons in relations of propinquity: "They meet more often, they get into contact, sometimes in conflict, but this is also a kind of relationship [...]. Knowing each other personally becomes easier the closer you are, physically" (Bourdieu 2005: 36). But in Bourdieu's opinion, it is also quite clear that propinquity does not suffice to promote exchange. For contact, social space is at least as important as physical space.

Functional relations in common institutions play an important role in creating identity. Functional interdependence promotes consciousness of the meaning of the Greater Region in everyday life. Yet, stakeholders noted that border commuters, who are affected most by functional interdependency, do not necessarily identify more closely with the Greater Region. Local public transport, which is insufficiently developed, is considered to be a barrier for creating a regional identity.

Many interviewees were of the opinion that shared identity can be increased by an awareness of common goals and of the mutual profit that cooperation can bring. Lack of motivation and lack of interest in cross-border questions or in language acquisition is often considered to be the result of a lack of awareness of these advantages. Cross-border cooperation is not only a matter of philanthropy with the goal of "building of areas of solidarity," it is also a "material, lucrative goal" (Gaunard 1999: 119).

Finally, lack of knowledge of other educational systems has negative effects on intercultural communication. Learning about and understanding other educational systems increases sympathy, tolerance, and cooperation even if differences persist. In the Greater Region, there are at present several cross-border schools including the Schengen-Lyzeum in Perl or the Deutsch-Französisches Gymnasium in Saarbrücken. Furthermore, young people have the possibility to attend cross-border programs of study at the University of the Greater Region.

TYPOLOGY AND CONCLUSION

Multidimensional subidentities or patchwork-identities are gaining in importance. This postmodern trend is recognizable in the Greater Region. National identities are still clearly fundamental for most ingroup and outgroup categorizations, but different identities can be activated and are relevant to action in several contexts. A Greater Regional identity, if it emerges, is going to be composed of many patchwork identities. This would possibly reduce group conflicts if "either-or" identities become weaker and if "as well as" identities become more predominant (cf. Beck 2004). There are rudiments of a regional awareness or a regional identity in stakeholders' minds. Which identity is activated at any particular time depends on the group with which individuals identify themselves at the moment. The "Greater Region" category is rarely salient; other categories such as language or nationality are more fundamental.

The Greater Region's stakeholders can have multidimensional identities. It might seem like a patchwork-like coexistence at first glance, but it is in fact a patchwork-like cooperation because, even when there is no hybridization of identities, mutual interaction takes place. The borders within the Greater Region have a constitutive effect for Greater Regional identities. Diversity is considered to be characteristic of the region, and heterogeneity is expressly desired. So borders continue to be important to identity, but they become more permeable. As described in postmodern thought, residents think of themselves as belonging to several groups, and these groups are not always mutually exclusive. Clear delineations are hardly possible today. The Greater Region shows that delineation does not require exclusion. Borders continue to be important, especially symbolically, but a there is no demand for clear contrast.

The study suggests a typology of identities, all of which can exist in combination with the others. The first type, *Territorial Greater Region identity*, is very similar to national identity. This identity form has yet to arise, and it can be assumed that it never will due to the diversity of national and Greater Regional or cross-border identities. Cross-border identities are not comparable to national identities. There are intended to be non-exclusive. Greater Regional identities cannot be described with national terminology, thus, nation-like symbols and identities do not and will not exist. "But Europe is still considered national as an 'uncompleted nation,' an 'uncompleted federal state,' and it is treated as if it must be both – nation and state. Not least, it is this inability to comprehend and understand this historically innovative reality of Europeanization that causes the European malaise. And this is an essential reason why EU-institutions, which should help people, are considered unreal and even threatening to the population" (Beck 2005: 7). Beck's idea is transferable to the Greater Region. It is impossible, either from the inside or the outside, to sense the Greater Regional reality.

One can talk of *advantage-identity* in the Greater Region because the promise of advantage through cooperation motivates many stakeholders to contribute to the success of the Greater Region. Some justify their group membership in terms of the advantage it brings. The form of advantage need not be clearly defined.

The type *sub-identity of European identity* is characterized by the idea that the Greater Region is a model for Europe. It lacks a unique value and serves only as a model. This type is very similar to *value-identity* because general European values are very important for both. It seems to be obvious that the progress of cross-border identities requires strong European identities.

For *cross-border identity*, borders themselves play an important role. Experiences of borders in everyday life, together with the advantages and disadvantages associated with them in the past and present, create a feeling of togetherness.

Cultural identity with cultural commonalities, focused on feelings of togetherness, is as common as *value-identity*, which is characterized by common general values like peace, tolerance, or liberty. Cultural-identity and value-identity are often closely tied to language and are thus not completely inclusive.

The two final types, *transnational identity* and *cosmopolitan identity* require closer examination because they have a special meaning in cross-border regions.

Transnationalism is characterized by long-term, pluri-local, structured relations across national borders (Pries 2008). The importance of national identities is maintained. According to Ludger Pries, a transnational social world is a world characterized by cross-border phenomena that are everywhere identical (Pries 2008). Transnationalism may be more pronounced in cross-border regions than in the midlands. Many interviewees mentioned personal transnational networks in addition to professional linkages. The continuing significance of space and the nation-states stands, according to Pries, in no contradiction to transnationalization.

Cosmopolitanization "is a non-linear, dialectical process, where the universal and the contextual, the homogeneous and the heterogeneous, the global and the local aren't cultural dualisms, but connected, interacting principles" (Beck 2004: 113). Contrary to nation states, where the foreign is delimited, "the cosmopolitan era is based on a *dialogue-based imagination of the internalized others*" (Beck 2004: 122). Rudimentary indications of the idea of the equality of all and of interdependence was observable in the content of the interviews, although differences were not abolished. The stakeholders feel enriched by "others." Ingroups and outgroups influence each other and appreciate this mutual influence. In spite of this, there is no unification and no desire for standardized culture. Outgroups have a constitutive effect on ingroup identity. In the case of the Greater Region, this means that every subregion continues to be a unique area for culture and identity, but each is influenced by the other, even as subregional and national identities continue to be important. The influence of subregions will not be liquidated in a unified identity. Rather, neighboring subregions will become integrated into subregional identities as the significance of relations to the "other" is recognized.

Identities in the Greater Regional community are far from an ideal cosmopolitanism where "the acknowledgement of otherness becomes a maxim of thought, common life, and action [and where] differences aren't considered hierarchical nor are they liquidated, but they are accepted and considered positive" (Beck 2006). But even if stakeholders emphasize the positive features of diversity and do not seek to abolish them, a hierarchical order can be noticed. The best illustration of this might be the commonly used phrase of the "Greater Region of two speeds." Even if social cosmopolitanism does not exist in its pure form yet, the interviews leave the impression that cross-border regions may be taking on a pioneering role. "Unity in diversity" is the one idea that enjoys the greatest consensus among the stakeholders. This is no completely hybridized society but a society that allows differences without ordering them hierarchically and that enables sub-identities (national, local, cultural etc.) to continue to exist.

The interviews show that postmodern concepts of identity need not lead to rootlessness and instability. All respondents give the impression that a patchwork of plural identities is possible. Their social identities are strong enough to allow other sub-identities in addition to the "classic" identities. But it should be remembered that the interviewees are not representative of the Greater Region's general population. The postmodern patchwork-identity, which recognizes the search for identity as a creative process of self-organization, where the self "is to be recreated continuously in a process of self-reflection and self-stylization" (Eickelpasch/Rademacher 2010: 22), does not affect everyone equally. Individuals need "sufficient material security, relationship skills, communication skills, negotiation skills, and creative structural competence" (Eickelpasch/Rademacher 2010: 29) to take advantage of a flexible identity. Social, economic, and cultural capital (Bourdieu 1987) is, in certain ways, a prerequisite for the formation of Greater Regional identities. The identity-types demonstrated here are more permeable than, for example, national identities, but resource inequality limits many individuals' access to these new identities.

References

Ahrens, Daniela (2001): Grenzen der Enträumlichung. Opladen: Leske+Budrich.
Beck, Ulrich (2004): Der kosmopolitische Blick oder: Krieg ist Frieden. Frankfurt a.M.: Suhrkamp.
Beck, Ulrich (2005): "Das kosmopolitische Empire", in: Internationale Politik (IP), July, pp. 6-12.
Beck, Ulrich (2006): "Wer die nationale Karte zieht verliert", Interview with Goethe Institute (www.goethe.de/ges/eur/eid/de1767656; visited 17/03/2010).
Bourdieu, Pierre (1987): Die feinen Unterschiede. Kritik der gesellschaftlichen Urteilskraft, Frankfurt a.M.: Suhrkamp.
Bourdieu, Pierre (2005): Die verborgenen Mechanismen der Macht. Schriften zu Politik und Kultur 1, edited by Margareta Steinrücke, Hamburg: VSA.
Briesen, Detlef (1994): "Historische Ausprägung und historischer Wandel von regionaler Identität in ausgewählten Montanregionen", in: Detlef Briesen/Rüdiger Gans/Armin Flender (eds.), Regionalbewußtsein in Montanregionen im 19. und 20. Jahrhundert. Saarland – Siegerland – Ruhrgebiet, Bochum: Brockmeyer, pp. 7-47.
Buß, Eugen (2002): Regionale Identitätsbildung, Münster: LIT.
Charter of Cultural Cooperation in the Region Saar-Lor-Lux-Trier/Westpfalz (1998).
Eickelpasch, Rolf/Rademacher, Claudia (2010): Identität. Bielefeld: transcript.
Filipp, Sigrun-Heide/Mayer, Anne-Kathrin (2005): "Zur Bedeutung von Altersstereotypen", in: Aus Politik und Zeitgeschichte (49-50), pp. 25-31.
Flender, Armin (1994): "Vom Saargebiet zum Saarland: Zum Gebrauch kollektiver Erinnerungen in einer Grenzregion nach dem Ersten Weltkrieg", in: Briesen/Gans/Flender, Regionalbewußtsein in Montanregionen, pp. 107-143.
Förster, Jens (2007): Kleine Einführung in das Schubladendenken, München: DVA.
Ganter, Stephan (1997): Stereotype und Vorurteile: Konzeptualisierung, Operationalisierung und Messung, Mannheim: MZES.

Gaunard, Marie-France (1999): "Transformation of border regions in France through the creation of Euro-Regions. Analysis of the multiculturalism in this European integration process", in: M. Koter/K. Heffner (eds.), Multicultural regions and cities, Lódź: University of Lódź, pp. 117-124.

Glöckner, Christian (2001): "Die Großregion – Bilanz der bisherigen Zusammenarbeit und Potentiale ihrer Entwicklung", in: Jo Leinen (Ed.), Saar-Lor-Lux. Eine Euro-Region mit Zukunft? St. Ingbert, pp. 83-88

Hahn, Hans Henning/Hahn, Eva (2002): "Nationale Stereotypen. Plädoyer für eine historische Stereotypenforschung", in: Hans Henning Hahn (Ed.), Stereotyp, Identität und Geschichte. Die Funktion von Stereotypen in gesellschaftlichen Diskursen, Frankfurt a.M.: Peter Lang, pp. 17-56.

Hastedt, Claudia (1998): Selbstkomplexität, Individualität und soziale Kategorisierung, Münster: Waxmann.

Keupp, Heiner et al. (1999): Identitätskonstruktionen. Das Patchwork der Identitäten in der Spätmoderne, Reinbek: Rowohlt.

Krämer, Raimund/König, Frank (2002): "Vernetzung europäisierter Regionen: Zwischen Regionalisierung und Europäisierung", in: Thomas Conzelmann/Michèle Knodt (eds.), Regionales Europa – Europäisierte Regionen, Frankfurt a.M.: Campus, pp. 279-296.

Kühne, Olaf (2006): Landschaft in der Postmoderne, Wiesbaden: VS.

Lesse, Urs/Richter, Emanuel (2005): "Einleitung", in: Almut Kriele/Urs Lesse/Emanuel Richter (eds.), Politisches Handeln in transnationalen Räumen. Zusammenarbeit in europäischen Grenzregionen, Baden-Baden: Nomos, pp. 7-12.

Machunsky, Maya (2008): "Substereotypisierung", in: Lars-Eric Petersen/Bernd Six (eds.), Stereotype, Vorurteile und soziale Diskriminierung, Weinheim, Basel: Beltz, pp. 45-52.

Mein, Georg (2008): "Heterotopien und andere Gegenorte. Raumtheoretische Konzeptionen von Regionalität und Globalität und ihre politischen Implikationen", in: Wilhelm Amann/Georg Mein/Rolf Parr (eds.), Periphere Zentren oder zentrale Peripherien? Heidelberg: Synchron, pp. 31-45.

Mielke, Rosemarie (1999): "Soziale Kategorisierung und Vorurteil", in: H. Mummendey (Ed.), Bielefelder Arbeiten zur Sozialpsychologie. Nr. 192, Universität Bielefeld.

Petersen, Lars-Eric/Blank, Hartmut (2008): "Das Paradigma der minimalen Gruppen", in: Petersen/Six (eds.), Stereotype, pp. 200-213.

Petersen, Lars-Eric/Six, Bernd (eds.) (2008): Stereotype, Vorurteile und soziale Diskriminierung, Weinheim, Basel: Beltz.

Pries, Ludger. (2008): Die Transnationalisierung der sozialen Welt. Frankfurt a.M.: Suhrkamp.

Reckinger, Rachel/Wille, Christian (2010): "Identitätskonstruktionen erforschen", in: IPSE (Ed.), Doing Identity in Luxemburg. Subjektive Aneignungen – Institutionelle Zuschreibungen – sozio-kulturelle Milieus, Bielefeld: transcript, pp.11-36.

Reese-Schäfer, Walter (1999): "Einleitung: Identität und Interesse", in: Walter Reese-Schäfer (Ed.), Identität und Interesse. Der Diskurs der Identitätsforschung, Opladen: Leske+Budrich, pp. 7-43.

Robertson, Roland (1995): "Glocalization: Time-Space and Homogeneity-Heterogeneity", in: Mike Featherstone/Scott Lash/Roland Robertson (eds.), Global modernities, London et al.: Sage, pp. 25-44.

Robertson, Roland (1998): "Glokalisierung: Homogenität und Heterogenität in Raum und Zeit", in: Ulrich Beck (Ed.), Perspektiven der Weltgesellschaft, Frankfurt a.M.: Suhrkamp, pp. 192-220.

Roth, Marita (2005): Stereotype in gesprochener Sprache. Tübingen; Staufenburg.

Tajfel, Henri (1981): "Social Stereotypes and Social Groups", in: J. Turner/H. Giles (eds.), Intergroup Behaviour, Oxford: Blackwell, pp. 144-167.

Tajfel, Henri (1982): Gruppenkonflikt und Vorurteil. Entstehung und Funktion sozialer Stereotype, Bern et al.: Huber.

Turner, John (1982): "Towards a cognitive redefinition of the social group", in: Henri Tajfel (Ed.), Social identity and intergroup relations, Cambridge: Cambridge UP, pp. 15-40.

Waldzus, Sven/Wenzel, Michae (2008): "Das Modell der Eigengruppenprojektion", in: Petersen/Six (eds.), Stereotype, pp. 240-248.

Werlen, Benno (1992): "Regionale oder kulturelle Identität?", in: Berichte zur deutschen Landeskunde, Band 66, Heft 1, pp. 9-32.

Zick, Andreas: (2002): "Die Konflikttheorie der Theorie sozialer Identitäten", in: Thorsten Bonacker (Ed.), Sozialwissenschaftliche Konflikttheorien, Opladen: Leske+Budrich, pp. 409-426.

Between Borders
France, Germany, and Poland in the Debate on Demarcation and Frontier Crossing in the Context of the Schengen Agreement

Angela Siebold

INTRODUCTION

The events of 1989 changed Europe. Protests and regime changes in Central and Eastern Europe, including the fall of the Berlin wall and the resulting end of the cold war, marked the beginning of a process that brought a fundamental reconfiguration of European social, political, economic, and cultural spaces. During this process, the nations of Europe negotiated new national and European identities within the broader culture of a newly unified Europe that was itself undergoing major revision.

The transitions in Central and Eastern Europe, including the former East Germany, were particularly intense. The simultaneous transitions of both political and economic systems meant that virtually every aspect of everyday life was changed for most individuals. One might argue that these institutional changes were the *short-term* result of the political transformation of 1989. Historical research, however, highlights that while the transformation may have come to a head in 1989, it was the result of convergence of a variety of long-term factors that were not restricted geographically to the countries directly participating in the social upheavals of 1989. Bearing in mind the experience and viewpoints of eastern *and* western Europe, we can analyze the meaning of the 1989 transformation in a broader context, taking into account not only institutional transitions but also the transition of patterns and structures of cultural communication and of mentalities.

These include changes that have yet to reach completion and forms of continuity that still persist today. This contribution elaborates the argument that such forms of long-term continuity lasting well after the transformative year of 1989 can best be explained from historical perspective.

Useful for discussing the meaning of the 1989 transformation in historical context is one debate that is highly symbolic for the present construction of Europe: the laws regulating cross-border movement within the context of the Schengen Agreement. This debate allows us to discuss the many forms of collective identity in Europe and to talk about what a national "boundary means to people, or, more precisely, about the meanings they give to it." (Cohen 1985: 12) Reports on the implementation of the Schengen Agreement in 1995 and its eastward expansion in 2007 appearing in the French, Polish, and German print media are analyzed below using articles from six major daily newspapers.[1]

WESTERN PLANS FOR A BORDERLESS EUROPE AND THE FALL OF THE "IRON CURTAIN"

After a long period of rigid boundaries in Cold War Europe, two processes fueled a heated debate about borders and demarcations beginning in the 1980s: the implementation of the Schengen Agreement in the context of European integration and the political and economic transformations of Central and Eastern Europe. The Schengen Agreement had its origins in Helmut Kohl and François Mitterrand's decision in 1984 to create a border-free zone in what would become the Schengen area. One year later, the Schengen Agreement was signed by the governments of France, West Germany, Belgium, Luxembourg, and the Netherlands. It was considered to be the next logical step toward a single European market. The agreement's implementation procedure took ten years, much longer than planned, and finally came into effect in early 1995. By 1997 the additional signatories of Spain, Portugal, Italy, and Austria were also on board. The Schengen area currently encompasses 26 countries.

---

1 | The newspapers are: *Le Monde* (LM) and *Le Figaro* (LF), the *Süddeutsche Zeitung* (SZ) and the *Frankfurter Allgemeine Zeitung* (FAZ), *Gazeta Wyborcza* (GW) and *Rzeczpospolita* (RZ). All cited passages have been translated by the author.

The fall of the "Iron Curtain" fundamentally changed the preconditions upon which the elimination of border controls in Western Europe was founded. Within a very short time span, Europe's eastern border was no longer clearly defined, leading both to hopes for a unified "Europe without borders" and to concerns about future migration patterns and lowered security. German unification had opened up the eminent possibility that a future Europe would comprise both western and eastern European space. Karl Schlögel referred to the year 1989 as a spatial revolution ("Raumrevolution") (Schlögel 2006: 25).

This notable historic constellation raises the question of what happened when the long-term plans regarding the implementation of a "borderless" (Western) Europe within a single European market and a political union coincided with the unexpected fall of the "Iron Curtain." What happened when the transformation processes of Central and Eastern Europe became relevant for Western European integration, which had until then not considered the issue of eastward expansion?

DEBATES ON THE SCHENGEN AGREEMENT IN 1995

The "Agreement between the Governments of the States of the Benelux Economic Union, the Federal Republic of Germany and the French Republic on the Gradual Abolition of Checks at their Common Borders" was signed in 1985. It formulated the plan to establish an unrestricted travel zone in the member states of the European Community. The Agreement was meant to send a signal for the then static process of European Integration. Its economic crisis, then often referred to as "Eurosclerosis," was supposed to be broken with the implementation of the Single European Act in 1986. In 1990, the member states added the "Convention Implementing the Schengen Agreement." In the process leading up to this convention, the new challenges presented by the fall of the Berlin wall had already become apparent. In December 1989, the government of the Federal Republic of Germany delayed signing the treaty, wishing to see a resolution of the question of whether East Germany would automatically become part of the Schengen area after the German reunification.[2]

---

2 | Cf. "Kabinett verschiebt Entscheidung über Schengen", FAZ 15.12.1989: 1.

Abolishing Internal Border Controls

On March 26th, 1995, the Schengen Agreement officially came into force. In France, the plan to abolish border controls attracted much harsher criticism than in Germany. Facing the upcoming presidential elections, many French politicians publicly opposed the opening of the borders or argued for delays.[3] Their opposition coincided with a general concern regarding further immigration to France across the common borders of the Schengen area. The government was afraid of losing sovereignty and control. Opponents were criticized, however, on the grounds that by not entering the Schengen Agreement, France would risk losing influence over European politics.[4]

While newspapers in Poland and Germany had already heralded the opening of common borders (Stabenow 1995: 1; Pomianowski 1995a), French newspapers referred to the date as the beginning of a progressive implementation of the Schengen Agreement in a "probationary phase."[5] As a reaction to bomb attacks in Paris in 1995, among other factors, the French government waited another year to open its borders entirely to the members of the Schengen Treaty (Prantl 1995a: 4).

New "countervailing measures" were also part of the European discourse, especially in German newspapers. Articles focused on conflicts over the right of national police officers to cross borders in "hot pursuit" of crime suspects (Münster 1995: 8). A possible increase in drug trafficking from the Netherlands was also a matter of debate especially in France.[6]

Constructing a Common External Border

Member states were concerned about the new common external borders of the Schengen area. France in particular considered the borders in the Mediterranean regions of Spain, Portugal, Italy, and Greece to be a

---

3 | E.g. Philippe de Villiers ("A l'extrême droite et à l'extrême gauche, les limites du consensus", LM 22.03.1995); Jacques Chirac ("Chirac et les accords de Schengen", LF 07.04.1995: 7); Jean-Marie le Pen ("Le Pen: 'Contrat pour la France'", LF 05.04.1995: 7).
4 | Cf. "Rückzug von Europa?", FAZ 01.7.1995: 2.
5 | "Schengen, une convention en marche", LF 24.03.1995: 10; Bresson (1995).
6 | Cf. "Coke en stock aux Pays-Bas", LF 05.05.1995: 12-C.

long-term security threat for Schengen-area citizens.[7] For many French and German politicians such as Jacques Chirac or Manfred Kanther, the main common goal was to prevent "illegal immigrants" from entering the Schengen area.[8]

Most concerns regarding irregular immigration and increasing crime rates focused on security along the eastern border of united Germany. Erich Inciyan, in *Le Monde*, referred to this as the "most sensitive external border of this new Schengen area" (Inciyan 1995) because it represented the new common border to Eastern Europe. "Sleep well, brave Europeans! German policemen will watch over your security at the borders," wrote Philippe Bernard (1995) in *Le Monde*.

The Schengen Agreement was often criticized on the grounds that the new European situation differed radically from the conditions under which the Agreement had been signed in 1985.

The Schengen Agreement, initiated in 1985 when the Iron Curtain demarcated the eastern border of Europe, was implemented in the completely different context of heavy migratory pressure from Bulgaria, Romania, Russia, and Turkey (ibid.).

The German newspaper *Frankfurter Allgemeine Zeitung* commented on this French concern: "Some people still dream of the old definite boundaries, at least in the east" (Wenz 1995: 8). Although German newspapers generally emphasized high standards of security at the eastern border of Germany (ibid.), the *Frankfurter Allgemeine Zeitung expected "between 5 and 15 million immigrants," especially from Eastern Europe (Zimmermann 1995: 13)*. For the *Süddeutsche Zeitung*, these fears contributed to delays in the implementation of the Schengen Agreement.

The fact that it took almost ten years to forge the first model of a core Europe is not only attributable to normal European infighting but also to the fall of the Berlin wall, which stoked fears of millions of westward-moving immigrants moving out of

---

7 | E.g. "Les exclus de la libre circulation", LM 25.03.1995; "Espace Schengen: l'auberge espagnole", LF 03.05.1995: 16-D; "Espace Schengen: le trou noir albanais", LF 27.04.1995: 12.

8 | Cf. "Justizministerin verspricht verständlichere Gesetze", SZ 30.03.1995: 2; "Chirac: Abkommen eventuell neu aushandeln", SZ 07.04.1995: 7.

a shaken-up Eastern Europe. These fears remain, most especially in Germany, and have resulted in a lack of confidence in "Schengen" (Münster 1995: 8).

According to the *Frankfurter Allgemeine Zeitung*, the need for a stricter surveillance of the German-Polish border resulted from the collapse of the Warsaw Pact and from subsequent changes in Central and Eastern Europe. It would have been necessary to tighten border controls for Germany's Eastern neighbors with or without Schengen, but now that the German-Polish border was the common external border of the Schengen area, stricter controls were even more important (Bannas 1995a: 2).

In its attempt to explain fears concerning the controls at the German-Polish border, the *Frankfurter Allgemeine Zeitung* emphasized that "the poor and the rich part of Europe" meet at this border (Bannas 1995b: 3). The equating of the former "Iron Curtain" with a "prosperity border" was also apparent in French newspapers:

Until 1989, this border was of interest to no one. It only served to separate two socialist states. Today, its rough terrain is a convenient door for our poor cousins from Eastern Europe who are drawn to the West and its plenty (Bernard 1995).

Polish newspapers discussed the new border situation in terms of border traffic issues and delays at border crossing points (Pomianowski 1995a; Alterman et al. 1995: 2). In view of the general significance of the Schengen Agreement, the *Rzeczpospolita* explained that Central and Eastern European states were being kept outside the common space that "was reserved for the members of the European Union."[9] The newspaper also argued that the fear of chaotic situations at border crossing points was accompanied by "xenophobia and negative stereotypes" regarding the citizens of the neighboring states (Pomianowski 1995b). Indeed, Polish citizens no longer needed a visa to enter the Schengen area as a tourist, but some Poles still complained about having to wait in the line of "non-EU citizens" while crossing the German-Polish border (Lentowicz/Sadowska 1995). The *Rzeczpospolita* quoted Poles who felt "discriminated against because they were treated as potential thieves" (Pomianowski 1995a.) or who "first had to prove they were not criminals" (ibid.).

---

9 | "Schengen zamknięte dla Polski", RZ 29.04.1995.

French and German newspapers reported on the Polish reaction to new restrictions at the German-Polish border similarly. "Poland offended"[10] was the headline of an article in *Le Monde*, and the *Frankfurter Allgemeine Zeitung* associated the Polish situation with the time before 1989 with a headline "Grumbling Behind the Curtain" (Rüb 1995: 6). According to these two newspapers, Poles felt like they were being treated as "second-class citizens"[11] because, as non-EU citizens, they had to pass the border in waiting lines separate from those for Schengen citizens, possibly being subject to stricter controls. The *Frankfurter Allgemeine Zeitung* argued that the Poles felt "humiliated because when entering Germany in Görlitz, Poles are not treated like Germans or French but like Russians" (Bannas 1995b: 3). The *Süddeutsche Zeitung* quoted Janusz Tycner, a journalist of the Polish newspaper *Prawo i Życie*: "For Germany," he complained, "the Poles are much like Turks. The Germans treat the French much more respectfully" (Heims/Flottau 1995: 3).

The Symbolic Value of the Schengen Agreement: A Story of Failure?

In an interview with the German radio station *Deutschlandfunk* in 1995, Manfred Kanther, then Minister of the Interior, pointed out the official position of the German government: "The Schengen Agreement was 'an agreement on freedom of movement within Western Europe and an agreement on external security."[12] Print media reports about the abolition of passport controls at the Western European borders in 1995 were ambivalent. On the one hand, German newspapers in particular expressed hope that the Schengen Agreement would serve as a model for the future of a unified Europe (Stabenow 1995:1). The opening of the internal borders was a "notable achievement" (Münster 1995: 8.) for the European integration process.[13] On the other hand, newspapers criticized the removal of border controls for several reasons. First, in the eyes of German and French journalists, it had taken too long to open the borders. *Le Monde* called this process "ten years of hesitancy" (Bresson 1995). The delay of the

10 | "La Pologne s'offusque", LF 27.03.1995: 2.
11 | "La Pologne s'offusque" 1995: 2; Rüb (1995: 6).
12 | "Schengen startet ohne Chaos", SZ 27.03.1995: 6.
13 | See also: "L'espace Schengen a des ratés", LF 27.03.1995: 2.

agreement's implementation symbolized the inability or the unwillingness of national governments to advance the goal of European unification:

> This could have been an historical moment, but all efforts are being made to ensure that it does not become one. There will be no ribbon-cutting. The preoccupation with security and the mistrust of national authorities have run the dynamics into the ground and have spoiled the festivities (ibid.).

Heribert Prantl, writing for the *Süddeutsche Zeitung*, even called the Schengen Agreement a "lie": "No European promise has been broken more often than the promise of a borderless Europe" (Prantl 1995b: 4). He supported his case by stressing that this "borderless Europe" only existed for some European citizens and therefore had created "a first-class and a second-class Europe" (ibid.). He was not referring to Central and Eastern Europe but rather to those EU member countries who were not part of the Schengen Agreement. Furthermore, he criticized stricter controls at the external borders as the construction of a "Fortress Europe." Meanwhile, internal border controls still existed in the form of "mobile controls" (ibid.). Prantl stated that the Schengen Agreement exposed the undemocratic nature of decision-making in the European Union. Moreover, the *Schengen Information System* was criticized for collecting the personal data of EU citizens and distributing this data among several countries. In an article in *Le Monde*, Philippe Bernard pointed out that the promise of free movement inside the Schengen area had a negative "corollary: closed external borders and tighter immigration controls." In addition, Schengen had served as a "justification" for a more restrictive policy towards foreigners and asylum seekers (Bernard 1995).

Le Monde commented on the border opening as follows: "The moment has been historical but it reminds us of historical events that frighten us."[14] Adopting a Central and Eastern European perspective, German newspapers wondered whether Schengen's eastern border had created "new division of Europe" (Rüb 1995: 6).

---

14 | "La peur de Schengen", LM 28.03.1995.

1989 All Over Again? The Abolition of the Eastern Border Controls in 2007

As we have seen, prejudices as well as worries about immigration and rising insecurity – especially with regard to the Eastern borders – found expression in the print media during the implementation of the Schengen Agreement in Western Europe in 1995. In 2007, when Poland and other Central and Eastern European countries joined the Schengen area, similar patterns of argumentation regarding the security of the Eastern European border were apparent.[15] From the longer-term perspective of today, we see that Western stereotypes and the idea of a divided Europe still persist. At the same time, the discourse is Poland reflected its dilemma of maintaining its orientation to the West and the European Union while simultaneously maintaining a relationship with its eastern neighbors.

The Symbolic Value of the Schengen Enlargement 2007

In 1995, the Schengen Agreement was signed by Secretaries of State in the little town of Schengen in Luxembourg (Ruber 2007:2), but on December 21st, 2007, high level European politicians gathered to hail the opening of the Eastern borders. The Polish and the Czech Prime Ministers, Donald Tusk and Mirek Topolanek, the President of the Council of the European Union, José Sócrates, as well as the German Chancellor Angela Merkel and her Minister of the Interior, Wolfgang Schäuble, commemorated the date at the border crossing point between the German Zittau and the Polish Porajów.[16] At the Austrian-Slovakian, the German-Czech, the Polish-Czech and the Polish-Lithuanian borders, barriers were symbolically removed or even sawn through.[17] José Manuel Barroso, President of the European Commission, referred to the expansion of the Schengen area as "the highlight of a process that had started with the fall of the Berlin

---

15 | "Wie einst im November '89", SZ 21.12.2007: 6.
16 | "Europa, einig Schengenland", FAZ 22.12.2007: 2.
17 | "Tag der Symbole", SZ Bayern 21.12.2007: 33; "Europa, einig Schengenland", FAZ:.2; Więcko.2007.

wall" (Ruber 2007: 2) "Today is a truly historic moment,"[18] declared Angela Merkel on December 21st, and Donald Tusk associated this date with a "triumph of freedom, which is a fundamental European value" (Kokot/ Harłukowicz 2007). "For us, it is the return to Europe," explained the Polish Minister of the Interior, Grzegorz Schetyna.[19] "Today, the boundaries have disappeared. Poland has become a free country again" (Celińska 2007). For Władysław Bartoszewski, the implementation of the Schengen Agreement was also "the natural outcome of the policy pursued by Poland since 1994 to join the Union" (Chauffour 2007: 10).

The print media also commemorated the 2007 events. On December 21st, the *Süddeutsche Zeitung* proclaimed that the "last remains of the Iron Curtain" had vanished.[20] The entry of Central and Eastern European states into the EU was considered highly symbolic of an enhancement of the core values of freedom and equality in unified Europe.[21] Finally, Polish citizens were given the same freedom of movement granted to East German citizens in 1990 (Veser 2007: 12). Indeed, western states were told to be pleased at the sight of their cheering neighbors (Bacia 2007: 1), who "had been deprived for decades."[22] Western Europeans, it was said, would always remember the importance of open borders for those whose characters "were shaped by the oppressive thought of potentially being locked behind the 'Iron Curtain' forever" (Bacia 2007:1).

The New Internal Border Between Germany and Poland

German and French newspapers foresaw problems arising from the new freedom of movement. The *Frankfurter Allgemeine Zeitung* declared, for example, that the accession of Central and Eastern European countries to the Schengen Agreement was an "historical event" (ibid.), but that "in the old member states, joy is limited."[23] The new Schengen members had

---

[18] | REGIERUNGonline: "Freie Fahrt durch 24 Länder", URL: www.bundesregierung.de/nn_914476/Content/DE/Archiv16/Artikel/2007/12/2007-12-21-schengenerweiterung.html, 26.07.2011.
[19] | "Offene Schlagbäume", SZ 20.12.2007: 5.
[20] | "Freie Fahrt für Europa", SZ 22.12.2007: 5.
[21] | E.g.: "Le défi de Schengen", LM 21.12.2007; Chauffour (2007: 10).
[22] | "Un espace unique pour 400 millions d'Européens", LM 21.12.2007.
[23] | "Seid umschlungen, Millionen!", FAZ 20.12.2007: 1.

benefited from a "leap of faith," and further controls were necessary (Bacia 2007: 1). *Le Figaro* expected "the accession of Poland to accelerate Western migration," including potentially illegal immigration (Thedrel 2007).

According to Wolfgang Schäuble, new mobile border controls at Germany's eastern border were more "intelligent" than old border controls.[24] From now on, life for criminals would become more difficult, "because they do not know where the police are."[25] Nonetheless, fears of increasing criminality – often illustrated by the stereotype of the Eastern European car thief[26] – were expressed in demands to slow down implementation of full freedom of movement across the Eastern borders so as to create time to "install a few additional alarm systems," as Joachim Herrmann, the Bavarian Minister of the Interior, suggested.[27]

The old image of the "prosperity border" experienced a revival at this time, too, with a new focus on Poland's eastern neighbors (Ruber 2007:2). Inside the Schengen area, as *Le Figaro* noted, it was expected that salary differentials would cause increased migration flows from east to west (Thedrel 2007) A well-known result was the decision to delay freedom of movement for Central and Eastern European workers in France until 2008 and in Germany until May 2011.

Polish newspapers were sensitive to German concerns. They claimed that most Germans feared things would "get dangerous because the Poles will come and steal" (Kokot/Harłukowicz 2007). The Polish press also raised its own concerns about the border opening. While it was described as "an epochal event" (Magierowski.2007: A-002), the *Rzeczpospolita* asked whether Poland would experience a loss of national identity or sovereignty (Ibid.; Brill 2007:3). Drug trafficking from the Netherlands to Poland also appeared on the list of possible future problems.[28]

---

24 | "Wie einst im November '89" SZ 2007: 6.
25 | "Europa, einig Schengenland" SZ 2007: 2.
26 | Cf. Burger (2007: 3); "Seid umschlungen, Millionen!" FAZ 2007.
27 | "Tag der Symbole" SZ Bayern 2007: 33.
28 | "Zniknęły granice, pozostał przemyt", GW 23.12.2007.

A Borderless Europe or a New "Iron Curtain"?
The External Border of the Enlarged Schengen Area

In 2007, as a consequence of the enlarged Schengen area, Poland took over responsibility for controls along a large portion of the new external border. In order to support Poland in this task, a high-tech infrastructure funded by the EU and Germany was established. While the *Süddeutsche Zeitung* headlined "Thousands Celebrate the End of the German External Border,"[29] Grzegorz Schetyna warned the EU of isolating itself from its Eastern neighbors. The new external border should be tight, "but it must not become a new Iron Curtain."[30] In 2009, an article in the *Gazeta Wyborcza* also predicted Schengen would become "for Poland's Eastern neighbors a symbol of the EU's growing isolation from the post-Soviet countries." (Wojciechowski 2009) In fact, Poland had waited until the last possible moment in 2003 to tighten visa restrictions for Ukrainians entering Polish territory. In 2007, the *Gazeta Wyborcza* regarded these stringent conditions as "Schengen's drawback (Wojciechowski 2007). The newspaper demanded that the Polish government stand up for visa-free travel for Poland's eastern neighbors (ibid.).

On the other hand, Poles considered the Schengen Agreement an important step toward full membership in the European Union. It also strengthened the Polish state, in particular with regard to "illegal immigration."[31] This argument raises the question of whether Polish concerns about increased "illegal immigration" had been adopted from discussions in Western Europe. Although Poland is currently attracting more and more migration flows, the number of foreign nationals living in Poland is still extremely low and is estimated to range between 0.1 and 1.9 percent of the population.

Simultaneously, German newspapers transferred worries about "illegal immigration" from the old to the new external border. In Germany, the main political parties as well as the *German Police Trade Union* stressed that gangs of human traffickers in the Ukraine and Belarus posed a threat

---

29 | "Wie einst im November '89" SZ 2007: 6.
30 | "Offene Schlagbäume" SZ 2007: 5; this Polish fear of a "new Iron Curtain" was also discussed in the French and German media: Veser (2007:12); Chauffour (2007: 10); Thedrel (2007).
31 | "Biernacki: wejście do Schengen zwiększa bezpieczeństwo naszego kraju", RZ online, 21.12.2007.

to Europe.[32] *Le Figaro* also announced in December 2007: "Our borders are open for 75 million Eastern Europeans."[33] The "pressure of migration," especially in Southern and Eastern Europe, would not decline (Fauvet-Mycia 2007). Ikka Leitinen, Head of the Warsaw-based EU agency *Frontex*, added to these concerns by stating that in the future more immigrants would be able to enter the European Union secretly from the east.[34]

However, in the opinion of Christine Fauvet-Mycia (*Le Figaro*), the Schengen Agreement is best seen as a concept, drawn up before the fall of the "Iron Curtain," that has managed to survive over the years (Fauvet-Mycia 2007). This is "a great challenge" for unified Europe (Kovacs 2007). Frédéric Fritscher made a plea in *Le Figaro* not to be afraid of a new "massive wave of 'Polish Plumbers'" or of "illegal immigrants" (Fritscher 2007: 14). He explained the importance of the new "borderless Europe" as follows: "Schengen, in this sense, is a first step proving that we are able to live in this freedom, an unexpected gift of the fall 1989" (ibid.).

Conclusion

The historical break of 1989/90 contributed decisively to a change in the meaning of the Schengen process. Starting in 1985 as a technocratic process mainly ignored by the public, it kicked off a passionate discussion about identity, belonging, differentiation, and security.

With regard to concerns about border crossing, French and German newspapers were influenced by general fears of increased migration to the European Union. The French discussion was more intense in 1995, when France had to open its own borders, than in 2007, when border controls in Eastern Europe were abolished. Polish newspapers focused on the perception that Poland had finally achieved equal rights within Europe in 2007. The border opening illustrated the highly symbolic value of borders in Poland. At the same time, however, worries about a loss of national sovereignty, recently achieved, appeared in Polish debates. With reference to the new external borders of 2007, newspapers made use of the image of a "new Iron Curtain." By citing fears of a divided Europe, the

---

32 | "Offene Schlagbäume" SZ 2007: 5.
33 | "Nos frontières s'ouvrent à 75 millions d'Européens de l'Est", LF 20.12.2007.
34 | "Offene Schlagbäume" SZ 2007: 5.

reports revealed that the problem of geographic borders in a unified Europe had reanimated old thought patterns. In this context, negative stereotypes were again exposed and seem to have only slightly changed during the past twenty years. When the German-Polish border opened in 2007, Wolfgang Schäuble noted that the concerns of an increasing crime rate in Western Europe were "fully understandable," but that these concerns had "also existed when the border controls between Germany and France were abolished."[35] As we have seen, these fears of 1995 had also been focused on Europe's eastern borders and those who live behind them.

REFERENCES

Alterman, Małgorzata/Bielecka, Beata/Kęsicka, Katarzyna (1995): "Przejścia z granicami", in: GW 18./19.03.
Bacia, Horst (2007): "Vertrauensvorschuss", in: FAZ 21.12.
Bannas; Günter (1995a): "Außengrenzen werden zu Binnengrenzen, Grenzhäuschen werden abgerissen", in: FAZ 25.03.
Bannas, Günter, (1995b): "An der deutsch-polnischen Grenze treffen sich der arme und der reiche Teil Europas", in: FAZ 17.08.
Bernard, Philippe (1995): "Les contrôles sont renforcés aux frontières de l'espace Schengen", in: LM 28.03.
Bresson, Henri de (1995): "Les contrôles aux frontières disparaissent dans l'espace Schengen", in: LM 25.03.
Brill, Klaus (2007): "Der Segen der Säge", in: SZ 22.12.
Burger, Reiner (2007): "Die Autodiebe auf der Wiese", in: FAZ 21.12.
Celińska, Kalina (2007): "Dzięki Schengen jeszcze bardziej jesteśmy w UE", in: GW 23.12.
Chauffour, Célia (2007): "L'entrée dans l'espace Schengen, aboutissement du parcours européen de la Pologne", in: LM 20.12.
Cohen, Anthony P. (1985): The Symbolic Construction of Community, London: Routledge.
Fauvet-Mycia, Christine (2007): "Un espace Schengen à 400 millions de citoyens", in: LF 20.12.
Fritscher, Frédéric (2007): "L'Élargissement de l'espace Schengen et l'Europe des libertés", in: LF 24.12.

---

35 | "Europa, einig Schengenland" FAZ 2007: 2.

Heims, Hans-Jörg/Flottau, Heiko (1995): "Grenze der Empfindlichkeiten", in: SZ 30.06.

Inciyan, Eric (1995): "Les euroflics, sentinelles inquiètes de la forteresse Schengen", in:LM 30.03.

Kokot, Michał/Harłukowicz, Jacek (2007): "Czesi się cieszą, Niemcy się boją", in: GW 22.12.

Kovacs, Stéphane (2007): "L'Europe central entre dans l'espace Schengen", in: LF 20.12.

Lentowicz, Zbigniew/Sadowska, Jolanta (1995): "Uni tuż za mostem", in: RZ 28.03.

Magierowski. Marek (2007): "Schengen, czyli odrobina radosnego patosu", in: RZ 21.12.

Münster, Winfried (1995): "Frankreich darf im Schwarzwald Verbrecher jagen", in: SZ 25.03.

Pomianowski, Wojciech (1995a): "Siódemka na szlabanem", in: RZ 27.03.

Pomianowski, Wojciech (1995b): "Konsekwencje układu Schengen", in: RZ 13.03.

Prantl, Heribert (1995a): "Nachruf auf den Schengener Vertrag", in: SZ 08.09.

Prantl, Heribert (1995b): "Kein Tag für Feuerwerk und Böllerschüsse", in SZ 25.03.

Rüb, Matthias (1995): "Grummeln hinter dem Vorhang", in: FAZ 29.03.

Ruber, Jeanne (2007): "Kleine Schritte Richtung Zukunft", in SZ Bayern 21.12.

Schlögel, Karl (2006): Im Raume lesen wir die Zeit. Über Zivilisationsgeschichte und Geopolitik, Frankfurt a.M.: Fischer

Stabenow, Michael (1995): "Am Sonntag fallen die Grenzkontrollen zwischen sieben europäischen Ländern", in: FAZ 25.03.

Thedrel, Arielle (2007): "L'adhésion de la Pologne va accélérer la migration de populations vers l'Ouest", in: LF 20.21.

Veser, Reinhard (2007): "Neue Freiheit, neue Grenzen", in: FAZ 23.12.

Wenz, Dieter (1995): "Fähnchen und offene Flanken", in: FAZ 08.08.

Więcko, Wojciech (2007): "Podwójne świętowanie w Ogrodnikach", in: GW 21.12.

Wojciechowski, Marcin (2007): "Ciemna strona Schengen", in: GW 23.12.

Wojciechowski, Marcin (2009): "Schengen: New Iron Curtain Rising", in: GW 11.05.

Zimmermann, Klaus F. (1995): "Ansturm auf die Festung Europa", in: FAZ 17.06.

Cultural Distinction and the Example of the "Third East German Generation"

Jaqueline Flack

> "Central Europe is hardly a geographical notion... The ways of feeling and thinking of inhabitants must thus suffice for drawing mental lines which seem to be more durable than the borders of the states" (Czesław Miłosz, 1986)

When in 1989 the Berlin Wall collapsed, both East and West Germans experienced an existential shock as those walls, which once seemed so permanent, very suddenly became permeable and changeable. Today, despite the fact that all Germans experienced this change together, Germany is still divided. The division has outlived the wall.

The biographies and daily lives of West Germans did not change much after 1989, but East Germans saw the coordinates of their lives change dramatically as they faced the new challenge of crossing the invisible border that remained. We know today that this border was more durable than the political border that once separated the two Germanys. From the moment the Berlin Wall fell, East Germans were enveloped by a new and different social, economic, and cultural system to which they had to adapt. However, neither East nor West Germans realized then just how durable, subtle, and deep the differences between the two societies had become during the years of separation.

East-west differences in cultural, social and communication practices, values, and norms quickly became a standard subject for German magazines, newspapers, and research grant proposals. They have been widely analyzed in the last twenty years by many researchers from different fields as well as by writers, journalists, and politicians. Despite the fact that the unification process has become one of the most studied phenomena in German history, it still makes sense to inquire into its continuing progress, even over twenty years later, because the transformation has affected each generation differently and this influence sometimes becomes clear only decades later.

THE "THIRD EAST GERMAN GENERATION"

In the course of the last few months, a new voice has strengthened in the din of public discourse: the voice of the "Third East German Generation", a group that includes Germans born between 1975 and 1985 in the GDR[1]. These individuals experienced the impact of the fall of the Berlin Wall during childhood or adolescence. We do not need much knowledge in developmental psychology to understand how deep the social and psychological impact of this historic moment must have been on individuals at such an important period in personal development. The questions they pose for themselves about this impact and the answers they provide are important, and they differ from the questions and answers of their parents and grandparents.

We are all familiar with the social and economic particulars of this change, but we know very little about the individual circumstances and experiences of this important generation.

---

1 | The term "Third East German Generation" is inspired by the concept of "third-generation migrant," which is used in the migration literature in discussions of how the grandchildren of immigrants live between two different cultures. The term is used metaphorically to liken the shared experiences of the last generation of adult East Germans to the experiences of third-generation immigrants. Hence it is set in quotation marks. The sociological research on East Germany uses different terms to describe the same group, such as the "Fourth Generation" or the "Unadvised Generation," while the journalist Jana Simon talks in an essay about the "Generation Zero" (Lindner 2003; Simon 1998). According to the Mannheimian generation concept, which defines a generation as the result of shared historical events by individuals of a similar age who develop a collective and distinctive consciousness, the effect of the fall of the Berlin Wall in 1989 and the sweeping social changes that ensued on East German adolescents demarcates the main generation-building event defining the "Third East German Generation."

What did it mean to grow up in social and economic instability and uncertainty, with family members who lost their jobs, and with parents and teachers who themselves were disoriented in the new social and economic system, often unable to give advice about important school and career choices? Who explained the world to this generation after the established social knowledge of the older generation appeared to have been made obsolete?

Further, what lasting influence did these experiences have? In what manner did their experiences shape the way they see the world and act in it today?

The members of the "Third East German Generation" ask themselves these questions and some have publicly articulated their specific experiences. This contribution analyzes the experiences of this generation as discussed in two sets of interviews published in Der Spiegel (Hollersen/Gutsch 2009; Kastner 2011). In these interviews, ten East Germans discussed their individual experiences in East Germany during the social transformation process and its impact on their present lives. These texts of the East German transformation experience are analyzed as border-crossing experiences, focusing on their relevance to the lives of members of the "Third Generation" today. I will therefore characterize these East Germans' specific transformation experience since 1989 as a border experience.

Important to the analysis is the concept of cultural distinction, defined as cultural practices that *draw a cultural borderline*. This act is realized either consciously or unconsciously by a person or group who makes a distinction between other persons or other groups. Acting distinctively characterizes an important aspect of constructing personal and cultural identity.

The question of "who we are" is also the question of what makes us distinctive from others. We can find out the answer to this question by experiencing actual or constructed differences in how people act and think in other cultures or societies. The construction of a post-unification eastern German identity began with the confrontation with the "different other," in this case defined by the norms, roles, values, and social practices of West German society. Although Germans from the east and from the west are both "German" and share a common ongoing history that has lasted much longer than the forty years of post-war national separation, many observers underestimated the intensity of the differences forged in those forty years. Expectations and reality differed greatly.

As a result of the confrontation with the "other Germany" after 1989, western Germans began to construct an image of *the* eastern German that reproduced many of the already existing prejudices about the citizens of the German Democratic Republic (GDR). These images were projected through the media and became very dominant in the public discourse (cf. Ahbe et al. 2009; Pates/Schochow 2013).

Of course, eastern Germans constructed an image of western German at the same time, and these were often based on prejudices too. Easterners' image of westerners, however, was not reinforced through the mass media as were western German perceptions of eastern Germans. The media construction of eastern Germans began soon after the Wall fell and anchored itself securely in the public discourse on both sides of the old border. In contrast, eastern German perceptions of westerners circulated for the most part only in the east. Although the self-perception of eastern and western Germans was for both mostly positive, westerners' perceptions of easterners in the media tended to be negative and undifferentiated.

Many more eastern Germans migrated to the west than vice-versa, so easterners' opinions about "the other Germany" were often based on personal experience and was thus subject to modification and differentiation. Eastern German migrants in western Germany were confronted with negative public ascriptions on a daily basis, but many fewer westerners were affected similarly. Accordingly, those born in the east have been forced to reflect and cope with what were mostly negative stereotypes and, as a result, many more easterners have undergone a process of personal redefinition within the context of negative perceptions.

One gets the sense from the interviews below that young eastern Germans have acquired a self-confidence not very widespread among their elders. Public forms of reflection on the questions of "who we are" and "where we come from" represent an expression of this new self-confidence and indicate a desire among young eastern Germans to understand and reflect upon their origins.

As mentioned, the western German media not only influenced the self-perception of eastern Germans after unification but also the way that eastern German identity is constructed by others. For outsiders, eastern German identity is often reduced to the product of socialization during the GDR period, while the experiences of unification and transformation after 1989 are largely ignored.

With regard to the formation of a specific eastern German identity, however, the transformation years are just as important as life before

1989. The interviewee C., for example – an eastern German woman born in 1983, explains the meaning of this period as follows:

I have only recently come to realize just how big an influence the transformation period after 1989 had on me – as suddenly all the adults around me, including parents and teachers, had to reorient themselves (Kastner 2011).

M., born in 1979, discusses the difficulties then faced by the adults who were close to him, as parents and teachers tried to adapt to new and different social structures and had to reorient themselves entirely. He describes his first impressions after the reunification as a culture shock:

The west was not totally new for me, in East Berlin we had bananas and could watch West German TV. After the collapse of the government, West German products were suddenly everywhere on the shelves and that was the first culture shock [...]. The second culture shock was seeing homeless people and junkies. I have no idea what they did with them in East Germany, but you never saw anything like that (ibid.).

The essential point here is that he was experiencing culture shock *without having moved* from where he grew up. Culture shock is generally described in ethnology as a typical reaction of individuals to a foreign culture or a different country. For most East Germans, however, the defining experience after 1989 took place at *home*, where ordinary things like groceries or the educational system changed "overnight." M. also describes how social instability and insecurity in East German society increased tremendously. Before 1989, homelessness and drug abuse had been virtually unknown.

Radical social, cultural, and economic change as well as the awareness of opportunities for a new beginning are characteristic experiences of the "Third Generation" during the transformation process. "Anxiety about the future," "uncertainty," and "disorientation" are commonly mentioned as negative aspects of the transformation process. Yet some individuals claim to have been "crisis-proofed," "liberated," or left "without fear of their own future" and have assumed personal responsibility for their own lives. A., born in 1978, expresses herself as follows:

We survived a complete transformation. At that time, our parents did not know what to expect or how the new system works. So you learn that it is possible to adapt to new circumstances (Hollersen/Gutsch 2009: 66).

D., born in 1973, noted:

For me it was a feeling of great liberation..., that in the future, everything will depend on me and on what I can do, not on the system (ibid.).

Confronted with mainly negative public images constructed by the media, eastern Germans started to reflect upon and criticize them. Young people today still struggle with unsophisticated generalizations and stereotypes. D. summarizes these stereotypes: "Easterners of all ages are on the dole, complain, are not willing to work, vote for the *The Left* party, and are atheists..." (ibid.: 67). A. and D. express themselves similarly:

A : "They always say that easterners complain too much and too loudly. But I have seen the same thing with West Germans who have rigid, pre-formed expectations about their own future, and when these are not fulfilled, they get scared" (ibid.: 66).

D : "It happens constantly to me. Nine times out of ten, people assume I am a westerner. They just can't fathom how the young attorney in front of them could possibly come from the east" (ibid.: 69).

S., born in 1982, remarks that the public often associates East Germany with "Nazis" (Cf. Kastner 2011). In contrast to ascriptions made by the media, interviewees formed a self-image distinct from the public image of eastern Germans in their personal processes of contemplating the existence of a specific East German identity. In this context, D. emphasizes the importance of integrating East German history into the whole of German history instead of erasing it:

"During all the media coverage of the 60th anniversary of the founding of the Federal Republic of Germany, what I noticed and what makes me so angry is that they always only report the history of the Federal Republic: the end of the war, the economic recovery, the new *Ostpolitik*, the 1968 generation, the R.A.F. The GDR is covered only in passing with the construction and fall of the Wall. What happened in this country during all those years is not covered. The GDR is treated as a foreign country.... You'll never get a westerner to think of GDR history as a part of his own history. But they expect us easterners to adapt the history of the Federal Republic before 1989 as our own" (Hollersen/Gutsch 2009: 69).

East German history is seen as an essential part of eastern German identity. To have grown up in the GDR, having experienced the fall of the Berlin Wall as well as the impact of the transformation process – all of these aspects are understood as essential to the development of what they call *Ostprägung* or *Ostidentität* (eastern coloration or eastern identity). Those experiences shape a feeling of being different from western Germans of the same age, as reflected in the following exchanges between D. (1973) and C. (1978):

Der Spiegel: "How long do you think your eastern coloration will last?"

D.: "It will always be there. I was 16 when the Wall fell, that was my youth" (ibid. 66).

Der Spiegel: "Do those younger than you have this eastern identity, too? That feeling of being different from westerners in the same age group?"

C.: "Theirs is a diffuse eastern identity, a kind of distinction... It will continue to be passed along for a long time..." (ibid.:67).

Even if the eastern Germans who were interviewed were not able to describe what *Ostidentität* exactly means, they feel it still exists:

Der Spiegel: "Sometimes it is argued that there are no differences any longer among eastern and western Germans in our generation."

C.: "That argument is made all the time. You start a conversation with someone your age from the west and everybody starts out saying, 'there are no differences anymore.' But in the course of the conversation the consensus grows between east and west that these actually do still exist" (ibid.: 68).

Members of the "Third East German Generation" claim now to have found their own voice, now articulating their own experiences instead of allowing themselves to be characterized and stereotyped by others. In the rise of Angela Merkel, an eastern German, to the position of Federal Chancellor, D. once saw a potential end to prejudice against eastern Germans:

"When Merkel was elected I thought that the east-west discussion would be over after one legislative period. Now that an eastern German is Federal Chancellor, then every westerner [should] know that eastern Germans can do every other damn job in Germany." But D. noted that this hope remained unfulfilled due to the fact that Angela Merkel is "completely unrecognizable as an East German." At the same time, he argues: "If Angela Merkel takes a long time to formulate a clear opinion, some call that typical of eastern Germans. They say she learned that in the GDR. It makes me want to scream" (ibid.: 69).

Cultural Distinctions

Individuals of the "Third East German Generation" have begun to discover a self-confidence about their East German origins. Being East German and having "this different, exciting past" (ibid.: 67). C. describes as "trendy" (ibid.). When the younger generation wears T-shirts with the logo of East Berlin, it can be considered an act of expressing East German distinctiveness.

At the same time, East German identity is described as a "diffuse" (ibid.) feeling, objectified, for example, through an emotional affinity to other eastern Germans.

C.: "My university was in Baden Württemberg. The strange thing was that easterners hung out together there. Now a lot of alumni are moving to Berlin, but both westerners and easterners keep to themselves" (ibid.: 68).

Der Spiegel: "How did you recognize each other?" (ibid.).

C.: "It may be that I felt more protected among my own crowd, so to speak. Or that I simply thought I can trust them more. I have the feeling that you can talk about weaknesses and difficulties more openly among easterners" (ibid.).

A.: "I also have the feeling that easterners are more direct and open" (ibid.).

Based on his work as a clinical psychologist, Hans-Joachim Maaz confirms this impression: "West Germans keep up appearances even when a crisis has erupted on the inside. Eastern Germans are more typically ready to talk about anxiety or insecurities. This creates a warmer interpersonal connection" (Maaz 2009).

D. objects to this generalization based on his experience of having close western German friends, who are "just as authentic and open and… willing to admit that they have weaknesses" (Hollersen/Gutsch 2009: 68).

The construction of an eastern German identity was described above mainly as a *reaction* to ascriptions made by others, especially by the mass media. Below, the focus switches to the distinctive socio-cultural practices of eastern Germans.

The wish to keep souvenirs of the GDR, to sing old songs, and to tell family stories appear to be important social practices used by individuals of the "Third Generation" to deal with their own history. These activities indicate a wish to understand and conserve their own cultural and historical roots, despite the fact that these activities are sometimes perceived as ambivalent or shameful:

C.: "On my 25th birthday somebody took up a guitar and we started singing old songs. That was pretty borderline, and the westerners were thinking 'we've never seen that before.' It was 'interesting' for them" (ibid.: 67).

When C. uses the term "borderline" to evaluate the described situation, he instinctively realizes what is going on with regard to culture at that moment. While eastern Germans are drawing a cultural borderline by singing "old songs," thereby excluding those who do not know them, western Germans see the border as something unfamiliar. In addition, the term "borderline" in the original German also carries an undertone of ethical critique of the distinction thus drawn.

K., born in 1975, mentions another way of preserving personal memories: taking pictures of specific East German subjects such as old shop signs or collecting old GDR product packages. This practice she describes as an act of *Ostalgie*, a neologism that combines the German words for "nostalgia" and "east": "I've preserved a bit of *Ostalgie* in me. I take photos of old shop signs from GDR times in eastern German cities and I collect old GDR product packages: gelatin, pudding, soap" (Kastner 2011).

An example of how identity is narratively constructed can be seen in the experience of having to tell the "Wall story" over and over again, which is described as being typical for young East Germans. It demonstrates how the narrative construction of an East German identity by themselves and others takes place. C. states that there is a "need for those stories as well as for young people telling them" (Hollersen/Gutsch 2009: 67).

D. and A. similarly explain: "We constantly have to retell the Wall story. Where were you?"

All: (laughing) "Yes! Where were you!" (ibid.).

A.: "I spent some time in England and sometimes I had to tell the Wall story to the same person three times in the same week. Oh please, tell me again. I was shown all around: an East German! They kept offering me food, I guess because they thought I grew up hungry" (ibid.).

The importance of the act of story-telling for cultural self-placement, especially for young eastern Germans, becomes clear in the following quotation from C., born in 1983:

"I don't have any personal memories. I never even went to the Pioneers [a party youth organization]. I was in kindergarten when Germany unified. I can tell a couple of stories, but they are the stories of my parents or my big brother. I only remember the three-cornered bags that milk used to come in" (Kastner 2011).

Hence, *telling* and *being told* these stories by family members became an important cultural practice that allowed eastern Germans to pass down specific eastern German experiences to the younger generation. Furthermore, these stories help to reproduce East German socio-cultural specifics. Above all, comprehending these social practices helps us to understand why very young people still consider themselves to be "eastern German" even without having experienced the GDR.

D.: "Some young people who never experienced the GDR use that country or the east as a basis for their identity" (Hollersen/Gutsch 2009: 67).

A.: "When I am in Thuringia [a new federal state], the kids down there don't say "I'm a Thuringian." They say: I'm an easterner. There's this feeling that we are something special" (ibid.).

In addition, these individuals emphasize the fact that the period *after* the fall of the Berlin Wall, the process of social transformation, is just as important for the development of an eastern German identity – especially to the younger generation – as having experienced the GDR first hand. In contrast, C., born in 1983, tells that she feels "much more European than German or even eastern German" (Kastner 2011). Furthermore, she emphasizes her distinctive interest in traveling and considers herself cosmopolitan and open-minded. She notes that until graduating from high school she lived in a small suburban village. She then moved to the nearby city to study social work, "but not necessarily in order to stay in the east; it was simply the most convenient place" (ibid.). After that, she went to South Africa for six months and then moved to a large city in western Germany. She says that she travels a lot and does not feel that the world ends at the eastern German or European borders (Cf. ibid.).

Despite the collective experiences they described, the interviewees have different concepts of life and personal values as well. Reflecting on what they consider to be the "right way" to provide for themselves in the future, D. and C. remark:

D.: "I have some stocks."

C.: "Investments don't interest me, and I don't want to own real estate" (Hollersen/Gutsch 2009: 66).

As we can see, members of the "Third East German Generation" describe distinctive identity-establishing cultural practices, but they are not all alike. They reflect also on observed transformations and differences in the mentality of young East Germans born after 1989.

C.: "It will interesting to see how the next generation turns out, those who were one or two during unification... there were many young eastern Germans... They talked about how their résumés define their lives... I had the impression that they've completely internalized the mechanisms that are necessary for success."

A.: "I notice that too... The haste and ambition they have to improve their résumés. Everything has to fit just right" (ibid.: 66).

However, in drawing comparisons to young west Germans, the interviewees explain these changes as a product of financial insecurity.

C.: "People in the west at my age or even younger have a different level of security. They get money, even the 32-year-olds, even if they don't finish college right away, sometimes quite a lot of money. In the east, you know that you have to do everything on your own. There's no safety net" (ibid.: 67).

Conclusion

Eastern German identity has been discussed as a product of a reaction against negative ascription and socio-cultural practices. The construction of an eastern German identity, I suggest, should be seen as a complex interaction between both. The ascriptions made by the media are an externally drawn distinction. And although many heterogeneous practices among individual easterners and westerners can be observed, many social practices are unique to young easterners and these create a line of cultural distinction from the inside. Both mechanisms are a substantial part of the construction and reproduction of an eastern German identity.

References

Ahbe, Thomas/Gries, Rainer/Schmale, Wolfgang (Eds.) (2009): Die Ostdeutschen in den Medien. Das Bild von den Anderen nach 1990, Leipzig: Leipziger Universitätsverlag.
Geißler, Ralf/Machowecz, Martin (2011): "Wir suchten Sicherheit, nicht Abenteuer", in: Die Zeit, 29.12. [www.zeit.de/2012/01/index].
Hollersen, Wiebke/Gutsch, Jochen-Martin (2009): "Wir werden nie etwas erben", in: Spiegel Special 1/2009.
Kastner, Daniel (2011): Ostdeutsch geboren. Damals, als der Westen kam, Spiegel Online 08.07.2011.
Lindner, Bernd (2003): "Die Generation der Unberatenen. Zum Profil der letzten DDR-Jugendgenerationen", in: Berliner Debatte Initial 14 (2), pp. 28-34.
Maaz, Hans-Joachim (2009): 20 Jahre Mauerfall: Viele Ostdeutsche sind nicht geheilt, Spiegel Online 14.08.2009.
Mannheim, Karl (1928): "Das Problem der Generationen", in:. Kölner Vierteljahreshefte für Soziologie 7 (2), pp. 157-185, 7 (3), pp. 309-330.
Miłosz, Czesław (1986): "Central European Attitudes", in: Cross Currents 5, pp. 101-108.
Pates, Rebecca/Schochow, Maximilian (Eds.) (2013): Der "Ossi". Mikropolitische Studien über einen symbolischen Ausländer, Wiesbaden: VS.
Simon, Jana (1998): "Die Generation Null". in: Tagesspiegel, 22.10.

Views on the History of Polish-German Border Regions

Anthropology of Borders and Frontiers
The Case of the Polish-German Borderland (1945-1980)

Agata Ładykowska and Paweł Ładykowski

INTRODUCTION

In this paper we illustrate social processes, practices, and views that historically preceded the most recent formation of Polish-German borderland. With the enlargement of the European Union, scholarly attention has turned to new configurations of political community and economic cooperation at and across its borders. The claim has been made that there is an increasing need to reconceptualize the meanings and functions of state and national borders and frontiers (e.g. Wilson/Donnan 2005). However, in so doing, we believe that an exploration of the history of those regions that experience political reconfigurations is essential as well, as it helps clarify the ambiguous relationship between the concepts of "frontiers" and "borders" as analytical categories. At the end of World War II, the new international arrangement meant that the former East Prussian regions of Silesia, Lubuskie, Pomerania, Warmia and Masuria were subsumed under the Polish state. This entailed the forced expulsion of the large populations of Germans living in those areas. The territory became inhabited by Polish settlers arriving in waves that included mainly those who had been living in the so-called eastern borderland of the Second Republic of Poland, which was lost by Poland as a result of the Yalta agreement. In this paper, we demonstrate how the politically demarcated borderline, which formally separated Poland and the German Democratic Republic after 1945 quite sharply, was in fact relatively porous. It was gradually appropriated by incoming inhabitants from the eastern border region, who, under special state regulations that changed over time, worked out the conditions and, indeed, even the area of their settlement, and thus negotiated the border "from below." We provide the account of how those Poles who were forced westward experienced their migration and later narrated those experiences, and how the emigration experience shaped emigrants' perception of geography as expressed in their attitudes about their new places of residence. Also, we demonstrate how in the three periods between the end of World War II and 1947, the 1960s, and between the 1st of January, 1972 and the 20th of October, 1980 the borderline was in fact permeable and created a situation conducive to intercultural contact beyond state control .

THE CURRENT SETTING:
THE POLISH-GERMAN BORDERLAND NEAR SZCZECIN

In what follows, this contribution inquires into the history of a new "borderland" that emerged near Szczecin. This area that is not an historical "border region."[1] After Poland joined the EU in 2004, and especially after Poland's ratification of the Schengen Treaty in December 2007, there has been greater economic, social, and cultural interaction involving movements of goods and jobs and permanent cross-border resettlement. The opening of the German labor market for Poles in April, 2011 and the depressed condition of the real estate market on the German side of the border have created new incentives for Polish settlement in Germany, and, consequently, for the ethnic recomposition of the borderland region. In particular, three east German border counties – Uecker-Randow[2], Ostvorpommern, and Uckermark – have become an attractive destination for

---

1 | This section is based on Pawel Ładykowski's project. The fieldwork was conducted jointly by Paweł Ładykowski (Polish Academy of Science), and Łukasz Kaczmarek (Department of Ethnology and Cultural Anthropology at the University of Szczecin) within the project entitled "The Resurgence of the German-Polish Borderland," launched in 2008. Some of the conclusions included here are also described in Ładykowski (2011).

2 | Recently, in September 2011, due to administrative reforms, the county was merged into the Vorpommern-Greifswald district and ceased to exist as an independent administrative unit.

Poles looking for new housing.³ This mobility has been accompanied by the emergence of a trans-border market characterized by the principles of border economies: for unemployed Germans, it has become less complicated and demanding to search for legal jobs in Poland in construction, services, local branches of EU institutions. And for the better-off in Germany, Poland offers specialized services at a relatively low price, e.g. private medical care (in vitro fertilization, dental surgery etc.). Imbalances in price and perceived quality have stimulated economic and cultural exchange and new developments on the real estate market, in education, in medical care, in services, and in many other areas.⁴

Since 2004 at least, the act of crossing the Polish-German border has been increasingly perceived as a "private" matter, not very different from crossing an internal administrative border (Wedel 2009). Although the

---

3 | In the year 2003, 2,140 Poles were legally registered residents of the federal state (*Bundesland*) of Mecklenburg-Vorpommern. By 2007, there number had grown to 3,637 and to 4,500 in 2011 (Segeš Frelak and Kriszan 2012: 38). The Uecker-Randow district has the highest population of Poles, with 1,258 registered Polish citizens in 2010 (ibid.). In 2009, 83 % of the migrant Polish population lived in the two towns of this district, namely Löknitz and Penkun. In Löknitz 10 % of the population (242 persons in 2008) is of Polish origin (Barthel 2010). The trend these numbers show is significant when seen against the backdrop of population decline in eastern Germany. For example, the district of Uecker-Randow had 96,043 inhabitants in 1990; 85,086 in 2000, 77,152 in 2005, and 72,137 in 2010 (Statistisches Amt Mecklenburg-Vorpommern, 2010; Segeš Frelak/Kriszan 2012: 37). In 2009, Poles formed 12-17 percent of the local population in the settlements of Grambow, Ramin, and Nadrensee. The latter statistical data were accessed in 2009 from the website of the district authorities, www.lkuer.de, before the district was merged into the Vorpommern-Greifswald district. The site is currently unavailable. Interestingly, the website of the Uckermark district (www.uckermark.de) lacks current statistical data that feature the inhabitants nationality, which might be interpreted as an expression of the new policy adopted in response to NPD activity in the region (personal communication with one of the commune's officers).

4 | This fact has attracted the attention of the regional authorities and led them to develop high levels of cross-border cooperation. For instance, there are considerable attempts to establish political institutions of supra-local importance, such as the Polnisch-Deutsche Gesellschaft "Pomeraniak e. V.".

border is still visible in political space, it is gradually losing relevance for everyday life.[5] The greater Szczecin area has a strong potential to become a fixed transnational space where political, cultural and social identities not only coexist but also fuse. With these facts in mind, in this contribution we inquire into the cultural mechanisms driving the development of a borderland. In so doing, we explore the historical particularities of the Polish-German border region after its creation in 1945.

The following section summarizes the social-cultural anthropology discussion on borders and frontiers as background knowledge for approaching narratives and practices of social, political, economic, and cultural interaction.

Anthropology of Borders and Frontiers

The anthropology of borders typically entails the study of the cultural, territorial, and social dimensions of those borders. Boundaries are symbols through which localities, states, and nations define themselves: they delineate at once territorial limits and socio-cultural spaces (Berdahl 1999: 3). As borderlines that simultaneously separate and join different entities, borders are ambivalent, as discussed in the classic works by Arnold van Gennep (1909), Victor Turner (1967; 1969), or Mary Douglas (1966). By the same token, borderlands as the spaces-in-between characterized by a cultural overlap are liminal spaces. They are simultaneously dangerous sites and sites of creative cultural production open to cultural play and experimentation as well as domination and control (Donnan 2001: 1290).

The relevant research on borders in anthropological literature concentrates on two complementary trends and see borders both as social and symbolic and as territorial and political. The first trend in anthropological theory owes much to Frederik Barth (1992 [1969]), who draws attention to social boundaries between ethnic groups. He points out that cultural differences persist despite inter-ethnic contact and that social relations are organized and maintained across such boundaries. The symbolic construction of community and cultural boundaries is stressed in works of

---

5 | The border is obviously marked by the linguistic barrier, but these too are tending to fade as free language courses are offered. Moreover, courses in the respective neighbor's language are part of school curricula in both Germany and Poland.

Anthony Cohen (1985; 1986). In his view, boundaries are symbolic entities constructed by people in their interactions with others, from whom they wish symbolically to distinguish themselves. By marking out one's social identity, boundaries symbolically demarcate one's sense of similarity and difference.

The second line of inquiry presents borders as territorial and political entities and implies a fruitful conceptual link between borders, state, and society. State borders mark the limits of sovereignty and of state control over citizens and subjects. Anthropological border studies were pioneered at the University of Manchester in the 1960s. The "school" that emerged in Manchester produced several works dealing with borders, each influenced by Max Gluckman who was Departmental Chair at that time (Donnan 2001: 1291). However, they did not take up the issue of national state borders, and the value of localized studies for understanding how cultural landscapes are superimposed across social and political divides was not recognized until 1974, when *The Hidden Frontier: Ecology and Ethnicity in an Alpine Valley* by John W. Cole and Eric R. Wolf appeared. This became the cornerstone work for subsequent anthropological research on national and international borders. Cole and Wolf found it interesting that in South Tyrol, the cultural frontier continued to manifest itself as important in everyday life long after the politically defined state borders had shifted. In this focus, they shared Barth's view of social boundaries. The major contribution of this study, however, was in demonstrating the usefulness of including both local and supra-local influences in research on this process. The work has informed many subsequent border studies in the way it focused on how social relations, defined in part by the state, transcend the territorial limits of the state and transform the structure of the state at home and its relations with its neighbors (Donnan 2001: 1292).

A more recent approach to national borders focuses on the states of the European Union and asks question of how culture inhibits and enhances cross-border cooperation in the context of various state and supranational initiatives undertaken in order to transform the economic, political, and social structures of people's everyday lives (for an overview see Wilson and Donnan 2005). Such an approach is best suited for the study of state-society relations. Instead of being fixed and static, state-society relations are currently seen as dynamic, processual, and permeable (Hann/Dunn 1996). What happens along the border can support or undermine national government policies, and borders are good locations for studying the features of state-society relations in general (Wilson/Donnan 2005). The enlargement of the European Union is bringing about fundamental changes in the nature of European states and of their relationships with each other. These recent changes call for field studies of the current borders and borderlands designed so as to contribute to the advancement of anthropological theory.

The changes discussed above are very relevant to our present case. However, we argue that focusing only on current developments would block the opportunity to place the emerging Polish-German borderland within a broader historical perspective that would enable us to better grasp cultural patterns and meanings that are framing current events. The social effects of the recent dismantling of the border regime separating Poland and Germany must be seen in relation to the effects of the border's construction: forced expulsions of previous German inhabitants of the lands merged into Poland resulting in incoming waves of Polish settlers who inhabited an area emptied of people. In our further analysis, we employ the theoretical distinction between the notions of a "border" and "frontier." In order to make this distinction visible both on the theoretical and ethnographic level, it is important to situate the concepts within the frame of existing anthropological analysis.

For example, social anthropologist Michał Buchowski reflects (in Polish) on the meanings of terms employed in English such as:

[...] *limit, border, boundary, frontier.* Typically *boundary* should be a line, while the *border* [is] the zone around this line [...]. We may further distinguish between a border line, a border, and a borderland. The first category, *border line* (*linia graniczna)*, would be the equivalent of [...] *boundary,* and as such would be a line designated in space that is in fact invisible but is made tangible by natural signs and symbols that give it a political significance. The notion of *border* (*granica*) would indicate the zone around the boundary. It spreads over the area in which the presence of a demarcation line has a direct impact on daily economic, social, and cultural relations of the residents living in the border areas. *Borderland* (*pogranicze*) would mean an area that is wider than border area, and would include the long-term phenomena characteristic for such zones, as for instance bilingualism, intermingling, or interpenetration of cultures (in this case understood as ethnic or national cultures), or assimilation of customs (Buchowski 2004: 9).

Indeed, there is a variety of typologies of what we call frontiers and borders.[6] These chiefly articulate a relationship between state and local community. For example, Anthony Giddens (1987: 49) distinguishes between "frontiers" and "borders" borrowing from political geography, where the term "frontier" "means either a specific type of division between two or more states, or a division between settled and uninhabited areas of a single state." "Frontier" in his analysis refers to an area on the peripheral regions of a state in which the political authority of the centre is diffuse or thinly spread. Frontiers exist where a state is expanding outwards into territory previously either having no inhabitants or populated by tribal communities. Also, frontiers describe areas within one state inhabited sparsely, for example due to "the general inhospitality of the terrain" (Ibid: 50)). A "border," on the other hand, would be a known and geographically drawn line separating and joining two or more states. Borders are clearly delineated limits of a state's sovereignty, although their nature can be fluid as they are located on the edges of the modern state, often the sea (cf. Roszko 2011). Borders, in contrast to frontiers, make the presence of the state clearly manifest through military posts, border guards, and customs checkpoints.

The distinction articulated above by Giddens has not always been obvious. For example, Wendl and Rösler (1999: 3) provide insights into the genesis of these concepts by tracing etymologies of the notions of "border" and "frontier":

Both terms "frontier" and "border" are respectively of Latin and Frankish ancestry and convey a different range of implicit meanings. Both found their way into English through Middle French, and both are finally rooted in the perceptual experiences of the human body [...]. The frontier (Latin *frons* or forehead) is always "in front of" the subject. It denotes a flat, horizontal view from an absolute, anthropocentric body-based standpoint [...]. The border, on the other hand, derives from the Frankish "bord," literally the two wooden sides of a ship, or the fringes of textiles (German "borte, French "bordure"). It denotes a bird's-eye view, with the observer not bodily involved, but rather looking down at the outline of objects on the ground. In today's English, to some extent, both terms are used interchange-

---

6 | For a detailed overview see Wendl and Rösler 1999; for the classical study of frontier society see Frederick Jackson Turner (1994 [1893]), and for a comparative frontier history see Lamar and Thompson (1981).

ably [...]. It seems however, that the notion of "frontiers" is more elaborated, popularly as well as scientifically, in the American than in the British imagination. The reason for this [...] comes from the American expansionist experience of moving west. While in British English the term "frontier" also refers to remote backwoods regions [...] that differ significantly from areas of metropolitan refinement, it is used in American-English speech and thought without these negative attributions. Here, it rather has come to mean pioneerism, dynamism and advancement.

This semantic shift appears for the first time in the classical study of frontier society by Frederick Jackson Turner (1994 [1893]). The image used in his study was that of an anonymous force that swept like a slow tidal wave from east to west across North America, bringing with it smaller waves. First pioneers then settler communities (cf. Wendl/Rösler 1999: 3-4). In African historiography, "frontier" came to be used for description of European penetration into southern Africa. A refined definition of Thompson and Lamar (1981:7, quoted in Wendl/Rösler 1999: 4-5), states that a "frontier" is a "zone of interpenetration between two previously distinct societies," and this is the way it has been used often in the description of hybrid cultures in postcolonial studies.[7]

In our analysis, we wish to explore the problematic representation of space embodied in the Turnerian image of the moving frontier and in the Giddensian sense of a remote, uninhabited peripherality into which a state is expanding. The new territories joined to Poland were emptied of people but not of buildings, factories and infrastructure. This made the new links forged between place and identity especially problematic (cf. Gupta/Ferguson 1992). The new settlers slowly appropriated the new territories: the advancing frontier was reterritorializing the emptied land. In the next sections we demonstrate the impact this had on their percep-

---

7 | This reductionist view of "frontiers" as "colonial intrusions" was challenged and further differentiated by Igor Kopytoff (1987). His cyclical model encompasses "external" frontiers that arise when metropolitan cultures expand and extend political hegemony (like colonial tidal waves), and "internal" frontiers found in the less populated fringes between two or more organized societies, where intruding settlers create new societies on their own; smaller groups split-off from their cities move into the interstitial zones where they continue to intermingle with other similar groups in an institutional vacuum until they grow to form a new city. This process may continue in a number of cycles (Wendl/Rösler 1999: 5).

tion of the new space and on the social process of constructing it as "their place." Also, we investigate the modalities of cultural interpenetration over time of the two previously expulsed communities that inhabited the lands divided by the border.

AFTER THE WAR: MOVING INTO THE "WILD WEST"

The Potsdam Conference of 1945 gave the Polish state control of Silesia, Lubusie, Pomerania, Warmia, and Masuria. The meridional line of two rivers, Lusatian Neisse and the Oder defined the new western Polish borderline. The decision to shift the Polish-German border decided the fate of millions of Poles and Germans who were forced to resettle from the east to the west. The territories previously inhabited by over 8 million Germans became inhabited by 4 million Poles (Eberhardt 2010).[8] Most Polish emi-

---

[8] | The drama of forced expulsions is a sensitive issue in Polish-German relationships: there is an enormous literature tackling the topic from the perspective of political history. We do not wish to engage in this discussion. Our aim is to highlight the scale of relocations and the problem that a region that was built for about 8 million people was emptied and inhabited by a new population of approximately half that size. According to the census carried out in 1939, the territories that later became part of Poland under the Potsdam agreements had been inhabited by 8,885,400 German citizens at that time (Eberhardt 2010:127). This number gives a sense of how densely this region was inhabited under normal conditions. Clearly, the number of people living in these areas was constantly changing during the final months of the war. Some approximations go as high as 12,339,400 Germans living in 1944 (Nitschke 2000: 232-233, quoted in Eberhardt 2010: 128). All these numbers should be treated with caution (they use different criteria to determine ethnicity, for example), however, they are indicative of the scale of relocations. Estimates of the number of Germans who left forcibly or willingly from 1944 to 1950 varies between between 8 and 11 million ((Eberhardt 2010: 187, 191), as noted in the Polish and the German sources respectively. In the three year period between 1945 and 1948, a total exchange of population occurred in the lands adjoined to Poland (Ibid.: 209). Cautious estimates are that in 1945-47 about 4 million people settled and started a new life (Ibid.: 208). The waves of newcomers in 1948-9 were significantly smaller, and from 1950 onward the process of stabilization started. The census carried out in 1950 confirmed that the lands

grants were from the so-called eastern borderland of the Second Republic (*kresy wschodnie*). Those Germans living to the east of the newly demarcated border were similarly forced to move west. The newly acquired territories in the west, the Polish "Western Lands" (*Ziemie Zachodnie*), were called in Polish propaganda the "Recovered Territories" (*Ziemie Odzyskane*), which alluded to the historical presence of the first Polish state in the reign of the Piast dynasty in the 10th century. This rhetorical formula was meant to legitimize both the presence of the Polish state in formerly German territories after the war and the forced resettlements.

Constant migration, a lack of permanence, the lack of stable state control or provision of basic services, a widespread sense of insecurity experienced by newcomers – including the uncertainty about the eventuality of another global conflict – all this contributed to the settlers' permanent sense of temporariness (cf. Polski 2005: 20). Their migrating was a process requiring many years and became such a special feature of their lifestyle that it strongly determined their perception of space, i.e. their attitude toward their new place of residence. Polish immigrants' diaries and official archival government documentation of the period clearly show that the Western Territories were perceived as a dangerous area, subjected to colonization by people uncertain of their future. They considered their new residences in the former German villages, towns, and cities only as the one stop on an endless journey. Often, the situation forced them to share a house or an apartment with Germans who had not yet managed to repatriate to Germany.[9] All these experiences during the first several years

---

discussed were populated by 5.6 million people or about 3 million fewer than in 1939 (Ibid.: 213). The number rose to 7.8 million in 1960 and to 10 million in 2010 (ibid.). These figures, of course, include those born after the 1950s.

9 | Regarding the situation in 1945, the Report on the Western Lands from 15.05. to 15.06.1945 (the AAN, the Government Delegate to the RP, 202/III/36, k. 151-210, Part E – k. 205-210) stated that in the belt between the West and the Silesia voivodeship the population consisted of 30 % Poles and 70 % Germans, in the belt from the Baltic to the Poznań voivodeship the population consisted of 20 % of Poles and 80 % Germans and in the Silesian belt the population consisted of 15 % Poles and 85 % Germans. In various cities on the basis of rough data : in Szczecin 40,000 Germans and 1,500 Poles; in Gorzów (Landsberg) 20,000 Germans and 3,000 Poles; in Skwierzyn (Schwerin) 2,000 Germans and 1,500 Poles; in Legnica, 10,000 Germans and 2,000 Poles; in Wrocław 25,000 Germans and 1,800

after the war strongly influenced the attitudes of newly settled residents. A temporary state was the ordinary state of life, and this left a strong imprint on the Polish settlers and the first generations born in the lands adjoined to Poland.

This constant movement was accompanied by the lack of clear idea of the exact location of the border delineating the new acquisitions. This was well captured by two journalists from Cracow, Maciej Malicki and Tadeusz Żychiewicz, who went on a tour of the Western Lands in 1957. It resulted in three articles written in a form of a diary published by the newspaper *Tygodnik Powszechny*. Malicki and Żychiewicz's (1957) described their disorientation regarding the area they were required to portray, the Western Territories. Asked to write material from the "Zgorzelec – Szczecin line" that would provide an account on the situation "as close to the border as possible" they wrote:

Our assumption is that we need a material from the "Zgorzelec – Szczecin line, as near the border as possible," but the assumption is also that this area will provide us with conclusions that can be generalized to the whole Western Territories. Therefore, we cannot travel [from Cracow] to Zgorzelec with our eyes closed. From the west it is clear, the state border demarcates the boundary. But from the east? For instance, today no one would think of classifying Gliwice, Bytom, or Zabrze as part of the Western Lands. Similarly, for an average Pole, Wrocław and Szczecin represent some kind of special enclave, of "equal importance and rank" to the other voivodeship cities. However Opole, Jelenia Góra, Koszalin are [...] somewhat different. There is one idea of the Western Lands adjacent to our former Polish border and another idea among those situated by the Oder River (ibid.).

Since it was not clear for the Cracovian intellectuals where the Western Territories begin, it would not have been clear for the average Polish citizen either. This certain lack of familiarity with the new territorial acquisitions and toponymy in the social imagination, observed twelve years after the war, went on to last for decades. The process of gradual integration of all the lands into a coherent body became part of the experience of several generations of settlers. The Western Lands area was perceived as quite different than the rest of the Polish state. The recollections of the settlers

---

Poles; in Świebodzin 2,000 Germans and 800 Poles; in Gryfino 1,500 Germans and 400 Poles; in Zagórze 1,800 Germans and 600 Poles (Pietrowicz 2005: 125).

contain accounts of a shocking confrontation with completely different aesthetics, the cities' skylines, the churches, completely different infrastructure, as well as a different principle of administrative jurisdiction. The newcomers noted the ubiquitous ex-German factories and ex-German cemeteries, contributing to the overwhelming feeling of "not being at home" (see e.g. Polski 2005: 21).

The inhabitants of the Western Territories were in constant motion as millions of people continuously sought for new places to settle. A sense of uprootedness and a devastation of the goods entrusted to these individuals were the consequence; many made a living by "looting." Polish administrators could not fully control these phenomena, and in popular diction the term "Regained Land" quickly gave way to "The Wild West." This expression denoted both individual freedom and impunity to law as experienced there. Sparsely populated territories in the west suffered from demographic collapse, which in turn prevented the normal inclusion in the economic system of the country unifying after the turmoil of war. The proverbial "wild(er)ness" reflected the nature of the new relationship between identity and place, as well as the emotions evoked among people migrating there. "The Wild West" was a place where "civilization," understood as government and the rule of law, was established only against the resistance of the inhabitants. The main factors that hindered the establishment of an orderly government in the area directly after 1945 were constant population movement, which involved also movement first to the Western Territories and then to central Poland; "looting" (*szaber*); the large numbers of Germans still residing in the area; and the way the new Polish-German border was drawn, which later would have significant repercussions.

The Oder and Neisse Border Line in 1945-1949: A Matter of Negotiation

The radically different expectations of each nation made the process of forming a new Polish-German border difficult and caused many misunderstandings. While the German side still hoped that the unfavourable loss of the lands East of the Oder River and Lusatian Neisse would be reversed (Kochanowski 2008: 31f.), the Poles demanded that the line be moved even farther to the West (Ibid.: 35), arguing that not only Szczecin but also the island of Rügen are necessary for national defence purposes (Ibid.: 34). Even after the Potsdam conference ended, the Polish Foreign Ministry tried to negotiate a new demarcation of the border line so that the Szczecin Lagoon as a whole would came into Polish possession, demanding that the whole of the Oder River "must be in the hands of one state, Poland, with all three delta beds" (Ibid.: 36). Poland also endeavoured to articulate its expectations to global public opinion in the directives received by Polish delegation at the mid-November 1946 session of the UN in New York; Poland argued that "[n]ot leaving the Oder River in one hand [...] will spark constant disputes and border conflicts in Europe" (Ibid.: 38). It was contended that an effective military defence of the Oder–Neisse line could be only provided by the expansion of Polish territory beyond the area of Świnoujscie, Szczecin, Frankfurt, Görlitz, and Gubin. Poland argued that such an attempt would contribute to the re-unification of the divided cities, this time within the Republic of Poland. Pragmatic and economic arguments were presented: industry and the most important components of urban infrastructure remained on the German side under the Potsdam agreement, which should be rectified (Ibid.: 38f.). The Polish political goal of uniting both sides of the Oder remained a sensitive issue in relations with the USSR and East Germany long thereafter.

However, despite Polish demands, the border was finally set at the Lusatian Neisse and Oder.[10] Ironically, despite the fact that the border was set on waterways and thus sharply divided the two nations, it became – contrary to the probable intentions of its creators – a space of German-Polish relations. Polish concerns that the suburbs of cities remaining in Poland on the east bank of the Oder and Lusatian Neisse (like Guben, Frankfurt, Görlitz) would be cut off from necessary infrastructure – proved to be warranted. These less urbanized and poorer eastern parts of Polish cities almost lost their practical viability almost altogether. To remedy this problem, people began spontaneously establishing relationships with residents on the other side of the river. The interest turned out to be mutual, as part of the urban infrastructure essential for city functions on the German side was in fact located in Poland.

---

10 | Excluding the area of Szczecin, Szczecin Lagoon, and the Western outskirts of Świnoujscie on the Usedom island.

The atmosphere of suspense and uncertainty accompanied the people on both sides of the border river.[11] Despite devastation, unemployment, housing shortages, and a terrible supply situation, a significant proportion of expatriated persons wished to remain as close as possible to the new border, believing – as reported in February 1946 from Guben – that "one fine day they will cross the Neisse again" (Ibid.: 31). By the end of 1947, however, German expatriates had gradually begun to lose hope for return. In Guben, in January 1948, rumours spread that the Poles would take over the railway station; this caused many German families to leave the border region (Ibid.: 34).

Overcrowding and unemployment on the German side of the river was as permanent as underpopulation and chronic lack of manpower on the Polish side.[12] Running the industries located on the eastern side of the Oder required qualified and skilled workers able to competently manage and operate the infrastructure. Power plants, sewage treatment plants, drinking water supply pumps, and other equipment similarly required the skills of specialists. These were possessed only among the German

---

11 | The expatriates were considered a serious problem for the Soviet Occupation Zone (SBZ) and later the German Democratic Republic. In the years 1949-1950 in the SBZ/GDR area there were about 4.5 million expellees while in the much larger Western Germany there were just under 8 million. The concept of "expellees" also implied that these people were had been wronged and might hope to return to their homes. Thus, in official diction, expellees were deliberately renamed the "displaced" and later also "new citizens" (*Neubürger*), to shatter any hope for a return to the former eastern territories of Germany. This, however, did not resolve the problem of integrating this group in their new places of residence. The final decision to resettle exiles in the young GDR was cemented by actions like signing the border treaty in Görlitz in 1950, the land reform granting new property to many expellees, and the pacification of the uprising of 17 June 1953, during which the issue of revision of the eastern border of Germany also had been raised (Urban 2009: 43).

12 | As already mentioned, the population of borderland districts on the Polish side for many years constituted only a fraction of what it had been, and this had a direct impact on infrastructure maintenance in the cities. For example, "about 3,500 people lived in Gubin in December 1945, 4,940 in March 1948, and just over 5,000 in August 1949 (one fifth of the city's capacity)" (Kochanowski 2008: 42-3).

population, either those still living in Poland or commuters from the other side of the border.[13] The restoration of normal life in the cities across the river became the main concern of the people, all the more that the border turned out to be penetrable. Although it was accoutred with signs of the new Polish authority, in itself it did not present an impassable barrier. It could be crossed without major problems. Germans seeking any kind of job benefited from this fact.[14] The consequence of overcrowding on the German side was a rapid growth of unemployment and the gradual impoverishment of the already afflicted German refugees, even raising the spectre of starvation. The main factor that contributed to the exchange of jobs and manpower, then, was asymmetry in the demographic situation, infrastructure, and food supply. The latter was significantly better on the Polish side. Shortage of workers on the Polish side and the relatively stable food supply were pulling factors for Germans. Many Germans, however, were still migrating to the west, which caused the Polish authorities to undertake an initial attempt of issuing administrative regulations in order to prevent professionals needed to maintain industry from leaving.[15]

Historical materials confirm that this was an important moment that initiated a new type of cooperation within border areas based on constant motion. The border had to be crossed on a daily basis, sometimes a few times a day so that both communities could function normally. The itinerant model of functioning in close proximity to the border necessitated the establishment of numerous inter-ethnic interactions. It should not be forgotten that this border line was different from what had been known and represented previously in the imagery of the common Polish-German heritage; the post-war reality was radically different. The entire situation was

---

13 | In early June 1945, it was officially proposed that qualified German workers settle in Zgorzelec (Kochanowski 2008f.).

14 | For example, as late as 1947, "half of the total number of over 1,000 of miners in the coal mine Turow would come from Germany every day" (Kochanowski 2008: 43).

15 | Of particular importance here was a decision "to keep or turn back, where it is possible, the number of circa 250 German experts necessary for the functioning of industrial plants." The Germans, however, were afraid to dwell on the Polish side, which at the beginning of July 1945, forced the Polish authorities of Zgorzelec to assist groups of workers on their daily commute over the border bridge to the plant (Kochanowski 2008: 42).

laden with strong mutual resentment, prejudice, and fear. As it turned out, however, this did not constitute a sufficiently strong barrier to socialization. On both sides, the communities were formed by exiles. The Polish exiles understand Germans who had to leave, as they too had been forced to leave and had nowhere else to go (Ibid.: 14). The period between 1945-49 is the first moment of establishing Polish-German cross-border relationships, both formal and informal, even though they were maintained out of convenience, not out of love.

In 1949 the German Democratic Republic was founded and encompassed the former Soviet Occupation Zone. The signing of border treaty with the GDR resulted the "dismantling" of this spontaneous borderland.

1950-1972: "Bridges of Friendship" and the Closing of the Border

From the 1950s the border was closed and the border rivers became natural barriers, constituting a "border wall" in the collective imagination. On the occasion of the state or party celebrations the contact was "artificially" restored. Because there was no agreement on local cross-border traffic, delegations of the local party, youth, or union organizations were forced to meet in the middle of the border bridges (Kochanowski 2008: 48).

The absence of the circulation and exchange of goods and services, as in the years 1945-1948/50, led to the collapse of the socio-economic infrastructure on the Polish side of the border. The image of overwhelming emptiness of these lands, contrasting with the problems of overcrowding in the central parts of the country was thoroughly documented[16] in the newspaper *Tygodnik Powszechny* in 1957. The authors, Malicki and Żychiewicz (1957), note that on the German side, the space had been systematically renewed so as to quickly rebuild or cover up the consequences of the war, whereas on the Polish side, there was no desire, no concept, and no motivation to take similar action. The post-war space of the Wild

---

16 | Here is how the Cracow reporters traversing the Western Lands in 1957 presented the situation: "Where there is work there is no housing. And where there is housing there is no work." [...].We have seen on the way a lot of empty, unoccupied houses. And we remember a hopeless crowd in the Cracow employment office" (Malicki and Żychiewicz 1957).

West still remained void. The state of constant instability and uncertainty regarding the future accompanied all the Polish newcomers to these lands from after the war until the mid-1970s, despite the state propaganda of the success of the unification of all the authentic "Polish Piast dynasty" lands within the People's Republic of Poland and a friendship with the new western neighbour, the GDR. This image was epitomized in the "bridges of friendship" across the border river, mentioned above. However, the image of friendship drawn in the official discourse was confronted by the reality disclosed in Malicki and Żychiewicz's reports. In their words:

Zgorzelec became famous for practicing Polish-German friendship [...].The central object in Zgorzelec [...] is this famous bridge over the Lusatian Neisse, honored so many times with the visits of all sorts of personages, from prime ministers to cyclists of the "Peace Race." The sight of the bridge completely surprised us. From the main street a very short, steep descent to the left and [...] that's it. We leave the car behind the corner and approach the border. Funny to admit – despite our identity cards and full legitimacy, we feel a little uncomfortable. "Taboo-ish" respect for the border zone, for years so carefully instilled, apparently has left its imprint. A WOP [Border Defence Army] soldier on duty stops us by raising his hand. We present him with our letter of identity and ask for permission to walk to the other side. When called, the second guard appears, a sergeant. He rigorously examines our documents, and then moves away to seek information in headquarters on the telephone before giving us the answer. We look at the opposite bank of the river. We see on the horizon a green city park, a wide panorama along the banks, the majestic cathedral dominates the city [...].Is the bridge sometimes used for unofficial purposes, such as tourism or family visits? No. Is it allowed to take pictures? No, of course, not. The sentinel puts us off with monosyllables to answer out questions. The German guard moves away from his end of the bridge and slowly, mechanically approaches us. At one third of the distance he returns, and just as slowly he recedes. The middle part of the bridge, here the "no man's land," is violated by a human foot only on the occasion of the official celebrations. What are Polish-German relations today? This question is in front of us, when we look at the border (Malicki/Żychiewicz 1957).

1972-1980: Navigating between Polish and Eastern German Planned Economies

In 1972, local border traffic on the basis of an ID card (i.e., visa-free and passport-free) was restored for the citizens of both neighboring republics. As a result, from 1972 to 1979 over 100 million citizens of the People's Republic of Poland and Eastern Germany engaged in tourist exchange. Most trips were undertaken in the border regions and towns of the neighboring country on short-term stays (Osękowski 2009: 148). For the first time since 1950, former German residents of these lands could meet Polish settlers and begin to establish a dialogue.[17] The possibility of private and purely personal relationships was, however, fraught with tensions and resentment.[18]

---

17 | As Opiłowska (2009: 167) writes, the opening of the border was a great opportunity for the borderland, as it opened up the possibility of direct contacts and breaking barriers. Also at this time the residents of the German borderland decided to make visits to their places of origin. Striking was that in all those years the residents of the Western Lands had apparently not settled them. Opiłowska's German respondents "highlighted that the Poles living in their homes were asking them each time with fear in their voice if they wanted to return. The houses were mostly unkempt, dirty, and – what surprised them most – unchanged for many years. Germans could find there not only the same furniture, but also cups standing in the same cupboard or reference books on the same shelves" (ibid.). The contacts, after initial uncertainty with regard to the motives of the Germans' visit, became friendly. The German respondents highlight Polish hospitality, often accompanied with excessive alcohol consumption (ibid.).

18 | In addition to Opiłowska's account, Osękowski writes that not only Poles were afraid of the previous inhabitants. He writes that also the Germans who travelled to the villages where their family homes and apartments had been were very bitter about what they saw. During these so-called sentimental journeys, they "visited the cemeteries where they buried their loved ones. What they saw, in most of them caused sorrow and bitterness. Their former homes were generally unkempt and largely devastated, and the cemeteries overgrown with bushes and weeds. This situation negatively affected the relationship between the Poles and Germans, and fostered new prejudices. During the mid-70s, the Polish authorities had decided to liquidate German cemeteries, which caused even greater resent-

The tourist border traffic of Germans engaging in what was referred to as "sentimental journeys" and Poles desiring to see the neighboring country very quickly turned into a project of purely economic nature, responding to demands created by specific shortages in local markets. The situation began to resemble that of the immediate post-war years: niche markets in the supply of goods and services were identified and resulted in a growing grassroots cross-border import and export. The socialist state obviously kept control over the systemic regulation of employment but failed to control the local cross-border trade and movement of goods. While travelling, the people were able to see and estimate the scale of the existing imbalances in the supply of goods. Through purchases people were complementing the deficiencies in the domestic market, but in so doing they were also introducing the new goods onto the market. The state did not have any control over the distribution and price of these goods. Since in the planned economy system, the quantity of goods in the market is supposedly shaped not by demand but rather by the calculation of technocrats, this meant that "tourist traffic" was clearly damaging neighboring markets. "Tourist traffic" exposed the failure of the socialist planned economy and showed the true extent of the consumption needs of the two neighboring communities.[19] This "shopping tourism" became then a kind of a manifestation of the market characterized by a relatively free play of supply and demand. The market mechanisms developed "spontaneously, and the price difference between the two outlets (the famous *przebitka*, an extra profit from selling the goods) was one of the main motives for crossing the border" (Mazurek 2010: 108-9).

The first and main beneficiaries of these new developments became the communities located closest to the border areas. This contributed to an increase in the attractiveness of the border and borderland towns and villages. There was an influx of highly qualified workers. Cultural life, the economy, housing, and above all tourism flourished (Osękowski 2009: 148f.). As Mazurek (2010: 109) concludes, the border regions witnessed not only an increase in exchange of goods; it saw also an interpenetration of consumption models.

---

ment among the outraged former citizens of the so-called recovered territories" (Osękowski 2009: 150).

19 | It is worth noting that in the years 1972-1974 about 900 business units started collaborating in the borderland (Osękowski 2009: 156).

Another corollary of these practices was a conflict of values, which manifested itself on several levels. First, a distribution conflict emerged, i.e. the conflict over the value attributed to goods on the markets, and this was directly attributed to the fact that the distribution of goods (always limited) was strictly regulated by the state. If we assume that borderland is not only a category of space but rather also a place of where cultural models and value systems confront each other, the question arises of how cross-border distribution conflicts were different from local distribution conflicts. As Mazurek notices, Poles and Germans derived different meanings from the experience of shortage. An experience of shortage was a consequence of the constant problem of competition for access to goods. The spontaneous "free market" emerging across the border, implied intervening in the planned economies of the two regions and deepening the shortages. This caused the conflict over distribution of *limited* supplies, which in turn resulted in increase of xenophobic attitudes (Mazurek 2010: 116-7). The avalanche of Poles penetrating the East German market brought an unanticipated effect of increased hostility between the neighbors.

Conclusion

We have briefly outlined some of the historical features of the Polish-German relations in the new border region. The specific characteristic of this border was that the people inhabiting the area on both sides had no experience of neighborhood with each other. There was a language barrier, there were no mixed marriages, and it seemed that the state project to designate a border line in order to separate and repel was successful. Moreover, people living on both sides of the border were displaced persons and shared the traumatic experience of expulsion from their homeland. We have tried to show that, despite these obstacles, neighborly relations were in fact established in different periods. Not always friendly, however, they contributed to making the border a space of transition rather than a barrier space.

We have attempted to show how the territorial expansion of a state was performed by settlers forming a specific, "tidal" frontier. The dynamics of a frontier of the pioneers advancing into the newly acquired lands had direct impact on the way the space was imagined. The newcomers had lived in constant uncertainty and fear that they might lose their new acquisitions. This, however, did not prevent them from negotiating the border and transcending post-war animosities in an attempt to establish a stable life in the divided cities in 1945-48. Only after this period, in 1950-72, when the border became closed completely, did the "frontier" became a "border" in Giddens' sense of the word. It divided two states understood as discrete, bounded, and completely sovereign entities. We have shown how in the later period, 1972-80, both states' economies, understood as discrete and bounded systems planned by their respective centers, were experiencing local intrusions in cross-border trade allowing for the (un-planned) circulation of goods between the two systems. These interpenetrations of different kinds have created a groundwork conducive to intercultural contact beyond the perimeters of the political control of the state. How these developments defined the qualities of the border and how they contributed to the current state of affairs is the topic of ongoing research.

REFERENCES

Barth, Frederik (Ed.) (1992 [1969]): Ethnic Groups and Boundaries: The Social Organization of Culture Difference, Illinois: Waveland Press Inc.

Barthel Franziska (2010): "Auswirkungen der Immigration polnischer Bürger auf den Landkreis Uecker-Randow am Beispiel von Löcknitz: im Fokus: Wohnungsmarkt, Siedlungsentwicklung sowie Bildungs- und Erziehungseinrichtungen", in: Schriftenreihe der Hochschule Neubrandenburg.

Berdahl, Daphne (1999): Where the World Ended: Re-Unification and Identity in the German Borderland, Berkeley: UC Press.

Buchowski, Mihał (2004): "Granica a uprawianie antropologii – uwagi wstępne", in: Janusz Kamocki/Kwaśniewicz Władisław/Spis, Anna (eds.), Polska-Niemcy. Pogranicze kulturowe i etniczne, Wrocław-Poznań: Wydawnictwo Poznańskie.

Cohen, Anthony P. (1985), The Symbolic Construction of Community, London: Tavistock.

Cohen, Anthony P. (Ed.) (1986): Symbolising Boundaries: Identity and Diversity in British Cultures, Manchester: Manchester UP.

Cole, J.W./Wolf, E. R. 1999 [1974]: The Hidden Frontier: Ecology and Ethnicity in an Alpine Valley, Berkeley: UC Press.

Donnan, Hastings (2001): "Anthropology of borders", in: Neil J. Smelser/ Paul Baltes (eds.), International Encyclopedia of the Social and Behavioral Sciences, vol 2, Amsterdam: Elsevier. pp. 1290-1293

Douglas, Mary (1966): Purity and danger, London: Routledge & Kegan Paul.

Eberhardt, Piotr (2010): Migracje polityczne na ziemiach polskich (1939-1950), Poznań: Instytut Zachodni.

Gennep, Aranold van, (1981 [1909]): Les rites de passage. Paris: Picard.

Giddens, Anthony (1987): The Nation-State and Violence, Berkeley: UC Press.

Górny, Konrad/Marczyk, Mirosław (2009): "Lubomierz – czy można odzyskać miasto niechciane?", in: Konrad Górny/Mirosław Marczyk (eds.), Antropologiczne badania zmiany kulturowej. Społeczno-kulturowe aspekty transformacji systemowej w Polsce, Wrocław: Wydawnictwo Bigi.

Gupta, Akhil/Ferguson James (1992): "Beyond "Culture": Space, Identity, and the Politics of Difference, in: Cultural Anthropology 7 (1), pp. 6-23.

Hann, Chris/Dunn, Elizabeth (eds.) (1996): Civil Society: Challenging Western Models, London: Routledge.

Kochanowski, Jerzy (2008): Zanim powstała NRD. Polska wobec radzieckiej strefy okupacyjnej Niemiec 1945-1949, Wrocław: Oficyna Wydawnicza Atut – Wrocławskie Wydawnictwo Oświatowe.

Kopytoff, Igor (1987): The African Frontier. The Reproduction of traditional African Societies. Bloomington: Indiana UP.

Kopytoff, Igor (1999): "The Internal African Frontier: Cultural Conservatism and Ethnic Innovation", in: Michael Rösler/Tobias Wendl (eds.), Frontiers and Borderlands: Anthropological Perspectives, Frankfurt a.M.: Peter Lang, pp. 31-44.

Lamar, Howard/Thompson, Leonard (eds.) (1981): The Frontier in History. North America and South Africa Compared. New Haven: Yale UP.

Ładykowski, Paweł (2011): "The Emerging Polish-German Borderland: The Past and the Present", in: Baltic Journal of European Studies 1 (2), pp. 167-191.

Malicki, Maciej/Żychiewicz, Tadeusz (1957), "Kraków – Zgorzelec – Szczecin. (Dziennik Podróży).", Tygodnik Powszechny, No. 23 (http://tygodnik.onet.pl/1547,1438590,dzial.html.)

Mazurek, Małgorzata (2010): Społeczeństwo kolejki. O doświadczeniach niedoboru 1945-1989. Warszawa: Wydawnictwo Trio.

Osękowski, Czesław (2009): "Sstosunki i pogranicze Polski z Niemiecką Republiką Demokratyczną latach siedemdziesiątych", in: Kerski, Basil/Andrzej Kotula/Krysztof Ruchniewicz/Kazimierz Wóycicki (eds.), Przyjaźń nakazana? Stosunki między NRD i Polską w latach 1949- 1990, Wrocław: Oficyna Wydawnicza Atut – Wrocławskie Wydawnictwo Oświatowe.

Opiłowska, Elżbieta (2009): "Stosunki między Polską a NRD w pamięci mieszkańców pogranicza", in: Kerski/Kotula/Ruchniewicz/Wóycicki (eds.), Przyjaźń nakazana?.

Pietrowicz, Aleksandra (2005): "Ziemia Odzyskana nie-obiecana (Sytuacja na Pomorzu Zachodnim w świetle raportu Sekcji Zachodniej Delegatury Rządu RP na Kraj)", in: Biuletyn IPN, No. 9-10.

Polak, Barbara (2005: "Polski Dziki Zachód. Ze Stanisławem Jankowskim. Czesławem Osękowskim i Włodzimierzem Sulelą rozmawia Barbara Polak", in: Biuletyn IPN, No. 9-10.

Roszko, Edyta (2011): Spirited Dialogues: Contestations over the Religious Landscape in Central Vietnam's Littoral Society, dissertation, Halle (Saale): Max-Planck Institute for Social Anthropology

Segeš Frelak, Justyna/Kriszan, Agnes (2012): "Charakterystyka pogranicza polsko-niemieckiego i społeczności loklanych objętych badaniem", in: Agnieszka Lady/Justyna Segeš Frelak (eds.), Znikająca granica. Nowa polska migracja do Niemiec – perspektywa lokalna, Warszawa: Instytut Spraw Publicznych, pp. 33-50.

Turner, Frederick Jackson (1994 [1893]): The Significance of the Frontier in American History and Other Essays. New Haven/London: Yale UP.

Turner, Victor (1967): The Forest of Symbols. Aspects of Ndebu Ritual, Ithaca, NY: Cornell UP.

Turner, Victor (1969): The Ritual Process. Structure and Anti-Structure, New York: Aldine.

Urban, Rudolf (2009), Życie i dzieło Güntera Särchena dla pojednania niemiecko-polskiego,Wrocław: Oficyna Wydawnicza Atut – Wrocławskie Wydawnictwo Oświatowe.

Wedel, Joachim von (2009): "Sytuacja na granicy polsko-niemieckiej jako symptom stanu projektu 'państwo narodowe'", in: Jarosław Jańczak/ Magdalena Musiał-Karg, M. (eds.), Pogranicze Polsko-Niemieckie po 2004 Roku: Nowa Jakość Sąsiedztwa?, Toruń: Adam Marszałek.

Wendl, Tobias/Rösler, Michael (1999): "Introduction: Frontiers and borderlands. The rise and relevance of an anthropological research genre", in: Rösler/Wendl (eds.), Frontiers and Borderlands.

Wilson, Thomas. M./Donnan, Hstings (1998): "Nation, state and identity at international borders", in: Thomas M. Wilson/Hasting Donnan (eds.), Border Identities: Nation and State at International Frontiers, Cambridge: Cambridge UP.

Wilson, Thomas M./Donnan, Hastings (2005), "Territory, identity and the places-in-between: Culture and power in European borderlands", in: Thomas M. Wilson/Hastings Donnan (eds.), Culture and Power at the Edges of the State: national Support and Subversion in European Border Regions, Münster: Lit.

The Dynamics of Unfamiliarity in the German-Polish Border Region in 1970s, 1980s, and 1990s

Bianca Szytniewski

Unfamiliarity indicates the feeling of strangeness that results from not having knowledge or experience of someone or something. The term "unfamiliarity," in a personal and spatial context, is best understood by looking at the interdependent relationship between two counterparts, such as the familiar and the unfamiliar, the insider and the outsider, us and them, or the acquaintance and the stranger. Something that is familiar to one person might be unfamiliar to another. Moreover, in one place the person might be regarded as an insider or observer, whereas in another, unfamiliar, setting, the same person becomes an outsider or stranger, a person being observed. Subsequently, unfamiliarity may be experienced and dealt with in different ways. Bauman (1995: 132-135) distinguishes for example between two possible effects of strangeness in modern city life. On the one hand, experiences of mutual strangeness may offer a feeling of pleasure and excitement, and are welcomed as a passing positive experience; while on the other hand, differences between the familiar and the unfamiliar could be emphasized to such an extent that people regard the stranger as a threat. Given the contextual usage of the term, unfamiliarity and strangeness will be used interchangeably in this paper.

Bauman's distinction was intended to apply to the modern city as a heterogeneous space with its distinct areas and different types of inhabitants and strangers. The experience of strangeness is therefore likely to occur in situations involving mobility, which contrasts with the immobility of the other as a result of ties and locality (Simmel 1950). In other words, strangeness appears when people move from one place to another, changing their status from insider or acquaintance familiar with their surroundings to one of outsider or stranger, new to and unfamiliar with the place of destination. Although strangeness is associated with mobility, it must be noted that in a state of immobility, feelings of unfamiliarity can also develop. In this case, there is no association or activity beyond the local space. The notion of unfamiliarity influences the mental image and may well become a factor of mobility.

Mobilities take place at different levels: for instance, at the local level, in a neighborhood, a city or between a city and a village, at the regional level, between two or more locations in different counties or provinces, or at the international level, between countries. Feelings of strangeness are especially intensified in cross-border regions as borders not only bring many different people together, but also "reflect our contending desires for sameness and difference, for a marker between 'us' and 'them'" (O'Dowd 2003: 14-15) as result of differences in cultures, histories, political ideologies, and economic and social systems.

In this contribution, I examine feelings of strangeness or unfamiliarity in relation to cross-border contacts and activities along the German-Polish border. Given the history of the German-Polish border, a high level of unfamiliarity among its inhabitants of the region is to be expected. Just after the Second World War, the allies agreed, under the pressure of the Soviet Union, to move the Polish territory westwards as a compensation for Poland's territorial losses to the Soviet Union. The Oder-Neisse border became a fact; however, the new border not only divided nations, it also divided cities built along the Oder and Neisse. As a result of forced migrations within Poland and across the border to Germany, towns along the redrawn border obtained completely new inhabitants with different national backgrounds. Most people had no local ties, let alone ties to the region and towns on the other side of the border. In addition, strict border regulations and policies prevented the new inhabitants from seeking cross-border contacts and becoming familiar with "the other side." The effects of the Oder-Neisse border are perhaps most visible in Frankfurt and Słubice, Guben and Gubin, and Görlitz and Zgorzelec, border cities and towns which were previously united within Germany (Buursink 2001).

Although East Germany and Poland were ideological partners of the Soviet Union for most of the period between 1945 and 1989, the German-Polish border was characterized as a closed border with little to no cross-border interaction except for a short period of cross-border (labor) mobility in the 1970s. From 1989 onward, the German-Polish border region opened up, creating opportunities for cross-border contacts and interaction. As a result of different border policies, some cross-border contacts and activities occurred while others did not; in addition, some situations may have encouraged familiarization in the cross-border region while others discouraged familiarization. At the same time, as previously mentioned, unfamiliarity, which could be both felt and/or imagined, may also be a source of attraction, giving people an incentive to explore the other side of the border and causing them to interpret a closed border as a barrier. Hence, the main objective of this paper is to go give further insight into these the dynamics of (un)familiarity by discussing the different elements of this concept and placing it in the context of the different historical periods characterizing the German-Polish cross-border region from the 1970s through the 1990s.

Unfamiliarity, Strangeness, and Otherness

Unfamiliarity, strangeness, and otherness are interrelated terms, which are occasionally used interchangeably or with a slightly different meaning, depending on the context. As previously mentioned, unfamiliarity indicates a feeling of strangeness that results from not having knowledge of or experience with for example a person, a place, or a situation. The difficulty in defining and placing strangeness and otherness is found in the different approaches to these terms. Stichweh (2004: 111) argues that a distinction needs to be made between the experience of strangeness and that of otherness. He regards otherness as a universal social experience that is a "precondition for my experiencing myself in contradistinction to the otherness of another human being." Strangeness, however, only occurs when the otherness of the other becomes irritating or disturbing. In other words, otherness leads to strangeness through the experience of annoyance or disturbance. Gurevitch (1988), on the other hand, sees the opposite relationship, stating that the experience of strangeness reduces assumptions of typicality and similarity, exposing the otherness of the other. In addition, otherness is triggered though a process of de-familiarization, of "making the other strange." This process of making the other strange is the result of an intentional cognitive action, an internal mental event, or an external change; it changes one's perception of and connection to the other and even displaces people from the surroundings with which they were previously associated (Gurevitch 1988: 1190). Making the other strange: this possibility illustrates that, to a large degree, unfamiliarity is individually constructed. As Bauman (1995: 146) puts forward, the understanding and placement of the other takes place as a result of remembering, selecting, and processing memories of past encounters, contacts, exchanges, and relations with the other. In addition, assumptions about the other play a crucial role in people's attitudes towards the other. According to Schütz (1962: 15) we assume that people are "guided by certain relevance structures, expressing themselves in a set of constant motives leading to a particular pattern of action and even co-determining [...] personality". Accordingly, these assumptions influence behavior and attitudes when people are confronted with the other.

Strangeness and otherness reflect upon a reciprocal social relationship between the familiar and unfamiliar, the insider and the outsider, or the here and there. Although a stranger is regarded as an outsider or an external actor, he still influences the group by bringing "qualities into it that are not, and cannot be, indigenous to it" (Simmel 1950). Moreover, people not only assume their own role as a result of meeting the other, but also experience and perceive the other in different ways as a result of their own unique biographical situation (Schütz 1962: 11, 19). These distinctions between one and the other, the here and there, may be regarded as mental borders (van Houtum 1999; van Houtum/Strüver 2002) which "are invisible to the human eye but [...] nevertheless impact strongly on our daily life practices" (Newman 2006: 172).

There are different ways to deal with strangeness. Mostly in modern societies, the strangeness of strangers is either reduced to a point where differences become irrelevant, or the differences and unfamiliarities are accepted to a certain extent and moved to the background in people's daily interaction (Bauman 1995; Stichweh 2004). However, strangeness continues to be a constant factor in daily encounters; it is a normal everyday occurrence, called by Stichweh (2004) the "universalization of the stranger." Even when people do not seek the experience of otherness, they may be confronted with it, influencing "the meanings we give to others and to ourselves" (Gurevitch 1988: 1196). Consequently, strangeness and otherness are clearly two interlinked terms, both of which give meaning to ourselves and expose the otherness of the other.

Unfamiliarity in Cross-border Regions

Cross-border regions have considerable levels of unfamiliarity as a result of political, economic, social and cultural differences between the two sides of a border. As such, borders function as symbols of identity (O'Dowd 2003: 27). Identity formation takes place at various levels, from local to national, differing from region to region and from time to time. Shields (1991) describes this as social spatialization where people organize themselves territorially, allowing regionalism to become a central part of their identities. Paasi (2009), however, turns this concept around and introduces the term spatial socialization. Instead of territoriality leading to identity formation, the socialization of actors in a territorially bounded spatial entity takes place by means of collective territorial identities, narratives, traditions, and images. A process of spatial belonging takes place whereby "people express and perform to belong, to create (and defend) their 'own space,' to separate, to differentiate, and to demarcate" (van Houtum/van der Velde 2004: 104). Furthermore, differences between people and places in cross-border regions may be stronger, as "borderlands, as front lines between states, are places of high sensitivity and self awareness, in which the sense of identity and belonging to a special place is heightened" (Amstrong 2003: 165).

The presence of differences in a cross-border region, which often lead to feelings of unfamiliarity, does not necessarily have a negative influence on the attitudes and activities of the locals. Both push and pull factors and keep and repel factors play a role in the degree of changes in mobility (Lundberg 1980; Timothy/Butler 1995; van Houtum/van der Velde 2004; Spierings/van der Velde 2008; van der Velde/van Naerssen 2010; Ernste 2010). Push and pull factors influence the decision to move, in this case, across the border. Whereas push factors involve reasons that cause people to want to escape daily situations that are perceived as less attractive than elsewhere, pull factors reflect the perceived opportunities and benefits on the other side of the border (Spierings/van der Velde 2008: 501). Factors that activate border crossing are job opportunities, easy access to and favorable prices for goods and services, recognizable social and cultural contacts, and curiosity about new places and people. Keep and repel factors are those that reinforce the decision to stay, leading to immobility. Keep factors imply the feeling of comfort and satisfaction, a feeling of "socio-spatial belonging" (van Houtum/van der Velde 2004). People are able to apply their skills and experiences professionally, have an acceptable standard of living, and are comfortable with cultural features like language and social norms in their daily lives. However, keep factors can also be strengthened as a result of external impositions such as the presence of a powerful nationalistic political ideology or strict border policies by one or the other country. Repel factors involve the attitude that "the other side" does not have anything additional to offer. In relation to cross-border mobilities, examples are to be found in the lack of opportunities and benefits as well as in strong political, economic, or cultural dissimilarities.

The level of familiarity and unfamiliarity between locals on either side of the border depends of several factors. These are identified as three core dimensions of unfamiliarity: personal attitudes, access to and selection of information, and experience.

First of all, *personal attitudes* affect feelings of (un)familiarity in the sense that a person might consider the other side of the border irrelevant as a result of indifference (Ernste 2010), indecision, unease, or lack of awareness. Feelings of comfort and satisfaction, i.e., a feeling of "socio-spatial belonging," also play a role (van Houtum/van der Velde 2004). However, people may also actively consider moving to the other side for functional reasons such as job opportunities or access to certain goods or cultural experiences; here, pull factors reflect the perceived opportunities and benefits at the other side of the border (Lundberg 1980; Timothy/Butler 1995; van Houtum/van der Velde 2004; Spierings/van der Velde 2008; van der Velde/van Naerssen 2010; Ernste 2010). Furthermore, people in a border region may be attracted by the desire to experience something new and unknown and thus regard the unfamiliar area as interesting and exciting (Bauman 1995; MacKay/Fesenmaier 1997).

Knowledge, in particular access to information, is identified as informational familiarity by Baloglu (2001) and Prentice (2004); it also influences the level of (un)familiarity. Facts and assumptions about the other side of the border are often based on both direct contacts and on indirect information from, for example, relatives, friends, and colleagues. Other sources are newspapers, television, schoolbooks, and official information. Depending on the openness of the border, the history of the border region and relations between neighboring countries, information flows may be interfered with by the government's use of propaganda to influence popular opinion.

The third, and last, dimension of unfamiliarity refers to *experiences*, meaning past experiences, taking into account that perceived images differ between first-time and repeat visits to a destination (Fakeye/Crompton 1991; Baloglu 2001; Lau/McKercher 2004; Prentice/Andersen 2007). In the context of a border region, experiences refer to active and passive contacts and experiences with people and places from across the border. These experiences can occur on either side and depend on the mobility of the individual or group. Furthermore, cross-border contacts could be discouraged or stimulated through previous experiences, border procedures, national policies, historical representations, and local memories.

Taking *personal attitudes, knowledge, and experiences* into account could yield new insight into people's (un)familiarity with people and places located across the border and their motives for crossing or not crossing the border. However, these dimensions are not definite; they are interrelated and influence one another. Furthermore, while familiarity may be high on one dimension, it may be low on another. For example, the daily cross-border commuter may work across the border but need not necessarily interact with the people there. Familiarization then becomes only partial and takes place at the workplace, but not with the locals or the town on the other side of the border. Hence, the decision to cross or not to cross a border also affects a person's (un)familiarity; over time it could change a person's attitudes, knowledge, and experience with regards to places and people located across the border.

Partitioned Cities at the German-Polish Border

As previously discussed, differences between people from different nation-states are intensified in border regions. The awareness of dissimilarities in policies, economic structures, traditions, and languages is likely to become part of everyday practices, especially for people living in the divided cities along the Oder and Neisse. From a historical perspective, cross-border contacts and practices will be discussed in the following paragraphs.

Discrepancies Between Two Neighboring Countries

Shortly after the Second World War, Polish policy makers implemented policies for nationalizing the Polish territories, in particular the former German territories in western Poland, to enhance Polish national identity and create a buffer against potential German aggression. Politicians and the media in Poland insisted on the integration of Poles into a cohesive and homogeneous society that represented a Polish national identity. As a result, the former German lands were referred to as "recovered territories" and part of "historical Poland," based on the fact that large numbers of Poles had lived under German rule, resisting German oppression while preserving their Polish identity (Kulczycki 2001: 205f.). In reality, the group of Poles that had lived under German rule was rather small. The largest group of inhabitants consisted of forced migrants from former eastern Poland, while other groups were Poles from central and southern Poland, Poles that had fled westwards during the Second World War, and (former) military personnel (Jajeśniak-Quast/Stokłosa 2000: 46ff.). At the same time, the Polish nationalization campaign included the expulsion of Germans. Subsequently, local communities on the German side of the border region not only had to adjust to a new state border but also had to cope with large migration flows of many expelled Germans. The demographic composition in the border regions on both sides of the border changed drastically.

As a result of the forced emigrations of Germans and the emphasis on the nationalization of Poles in these territories, differences between Germans and Poles were amplified, stressing the distinction between "us" and "them." Moreover, the use of the term "autochthon" or "native" for Polish inhabitants by Polish authorities to draw a contrast to the German inhabitants in the region led to a further division between the two nationalities. Germans subsequently were regarded as "alien intruders," not only in the border regions, but in the whole of Poland (Kulczycki 2001: 207).

Despite the territorial changes and national politics that followed the war period, the German Democratic Republic and Poland had both become part of the Soviet Union's sphere of influence, and this context dominated the two countries' political relations. By signing the Treaty of Görlitz on 6 June 1950, stating that "the current, determined border is the irrevocable border of peace and friendship that does not separate but rather unites both peoples," the German-Polish border was officially accepted. The signing of the treaty was followed by a period of propaganda to promote popular acceptance of the two socialist nations. In contrast to the period shortly after the war, images of the other, of those across the border, were promoted with the intention of uniting, not dividing. Newspapers and politicians spoke of 'brother nations," while street names in the border cities were named after German and Polish socialist heroes (Jajeśniak-Quast/Stokłosa 2000: 65f.).

For the most part, however, the physical border remained closed and cross-border activities did not develop at any other than a political level, with occasional festive meetings at the bridges in the border towns to celebrate for instance international Labor Day (Gazeta Zielonogórska/ Neuer Tag, 1967). As a result of this political context, direct and indirect cross-border experiences were limited, and knowledge and information flows about the other side of the border were often controlled by the government and therefore colored and selective.

Rapprochement and Estrangement Again

In the 1970s, inhabitants of the German-Polish border region experienced a period of open borders that had already started in 1956 when the Soviet Union handed over the control of the East German border to the East German government. Subsequently, many military and administrative restrictions were removed, contributing to a slow rapprochement between East Germany and Poland (Jajeśniak-Quast/Stokłosa 2000: 72). A period of increased cross-border activities followed in the 1970s, including the free exchange of goods, information, and people. Subsequently, common initiatives in sports, culture, and education were established between border cities like Frankfurt and Słubice, followed by cross-border labor mobility and the purchase of consumer goods. Furthermore, friendships were built across the border and the number of German-Polish intermarriages also increased (Chessa 2004: 81f.).

This first period of openness was characterized in particular by curiosity on both sides of the border. Previously, people could only see the river banks on the other side of the Oder or Neisse and imagine what the cities look like, but now they had the chance to experience the cities for themselves. This curiosity became an important pull factor to cross the border, mobilizing many people to visit the "unknown," "imagined," or "previously known" on other side of the border. As a result, cross-border tourism, and especially cross-border consumption, increased significantly. Whereas Germans were interested in foodstuffs, Poles mainly bought manufactured goods and textiles. The border cities were not prepared for the large flows of people who ventured across the border. In the case of Słubice, it became clear that shortages in hotels, restaurants, milk, bread, and butter existed or were eminent, and the only petrol station in the town could not meet the increase in demand. In addition, in Frankfurt, restrictions were put in place to prevent Poles from buying products made of leather and housekeeping tools made for export purposes. Consequently, when the German-Polish border closed again in 1980, some shopkeepers were relieved (Jajeśniak-Quast/Stokłosa 2000: 84, 88). It seems that at a certain moment, initial feelings of pleasure and excitement towards people and places across the border were taken over by feelings of annoyance. The novelty of the new border situation had passed and people realized that this was not a passing experience without lasting responsibilities but was rather becoming a permanent part of daily lives in the border cities.

As a result of the official recognition of the Solidarity movement by the Polish government, the East German government wanted to prevent a spill-over of anti-socialist ideas and decided to close the German-Polish border. In contrast to the 1970s, the last decade of socialist East Germany and Poland saw little cross-border cooperation and movement (Chessa 2004: 82).

Local Unity in a European Entity?

After the fall of communism, the road toward a transnational German-Polish border region seemed open again, especially in the context of EU enlargement. Germany was one of the main proponents of Poland's entry to the European Union. In the 1990s, the German-Polish Euroregion Pro Europe Viadrina came into being, and the two border cities, Guben and Gubin, signed an agreement of cooperation, announcing the establishment of the Euro city Guben/Gubin. The establishment of a German-Polish university subsequently took cross-border cooperation between Germany and Poland to a higher level. Established in 1993, and formalized in a governmental agreement between the German state of Brandenburg and the Polish national government in 2002, the cross-border university Collegium Polonicum is a joint venture of the European University Viadrina in Frankfurt and the Adam Mickiewicz University in Poznań. The Collegium Polonicum does not advocate homogenization and assimilation but emphasizes the "acceptance of diversity and its use as a potential for creativity" (Fichter-Wolf/Knorr-Siedow 2009: 15, 18).

Despite these isolated developments, the motivation to extend European integration to the German-Polish border region has had limited reach. For the most part, it could be argued that the road towards EU enlargement turned out to be mainly a political project, putting institutional and administrative structures into place without considering cross-border integration at the level of local everyday life (Dürrschmidt 2006: 259).

In the 1990s, both the former East Germany and Poland fell into different modes of economic transformation. The East German border region underwent extensive de-industrialization, resulting in the closing of many factories and a high unemployment rate. The Polish side, on the other hand, experienced a relatively stable transformation of its economic structures with a decline in industrial employment but an increase of jobs in the private sector generally (Krätke 1999: 633f.). Economic initiatives did not necessarily focus on common economic interests in the German-Polish cross-border region. For example, Germany's privatization policy included a strong orientation toward western Germany, ignoring the opportunities of low wages across the border. In general, only a small number of firms with foreign capital settled in the Polish border region (Krätke 1999: 634). Moreover, Matthiesen/Bürkner (2001: 45) perceive a "peripheralization of the immediate border zone," implying that German-Polish cooperation did not concentrate on the immediate border region but that new trade and service centers grew in nearby urban areas such as Berlin, Szczecin, Poznan, and Wroclaw. Immediate border cities seem to have been bypassed by regional cross-border initiatives, which may also have something to do with attitudes and practices of German and Polish locals in the cross-border region.

Although formal institutions and contacts at the level of policy-making were established across the border, local level social interactions and activities remained minor and generally dependent on particular individuals or organizations (Matthiesen/Bürkner 2001; Dürrschmidt 2002; Fichter-Wolf/Knorr-Siedow 2009). Much skepticism and localism was found among locals in the cross-border region. In Guben for instance, revitalized ethnicity, economic fears of competition, and an inward-looking mentality led to a strong tendency of in-grouping. While skeptical attitudes were also found in Gubin, Poles were at the same time curious and had a more positive attitude towards cross-border initiatives than the Germans in Guben (Matthiesen/Bürkner 2001: 46f.). Furthermore, both Germans and Poles were, and maybe still are, not entirely aware of the opportunities an integrated and open cross-border region could bring. Dürrschmidt (2006: 254f.) distinguishes two local developments. The first development involves the hyper-mobility of German locals, who started to take up temporary work elsewhere, for example in the Netherlands as bricklayers, without taking into account the opportunities on the other side of the border. In addition to the decrease of inhabitants in the German border cities, people became detached from the city and region, reducing further improvement of cross-border relations and practices. Secondly, strong feelings of belonging also played a role. Place became regarded as a closed system that does not extend beyond one's familiar setting. Moreover, past images and experiences were also important factors in the decision to move closer to or farther away from people and places across the border. A low level of trust between the inhabitants of the cross-border region also played a role in underlining perceived differences and increasing the felt social distance between the two nationalities (Krätke 1999; Matthiesen/ Bürkner 2001; Stryjakiewicz 2009).

In contrast to the 1970s, where the opening of the border led to interest in familiarization with people and places located across the border, the opening of the border in 1991 led to less mutual interest. Except for local socio-economic opportunities, both Germans and Poles were mainly looking westward, partly due to German unification and the prospective benefits associated with the European Union. As a result of socio-economic interests, a level of interdependency between Poles and Germans in the local trade and service sector emerged, bringing people on both sides of the border together. In the early 1990s, differences in price and quality of goods and services led to the rise of a bazaar economy in the small Polish towns just across the border (Gazeta Zielonogórska/Neuer Tag, 1990s). In addition to these interactions and exchanges on the bazaars, Poles were also familiarizing themselves with the German language and started looking for labor opportunities in Germany. Germans, however, continued to have only little interest in people and places across the border above and beyond their interest in obtaining cheap products and services on the Polish side. For the most part, German locals maintained an attitude of indifference, standing with their backs to the Polish borderland. On the one hand, people on the Polish side seem more interested in the opportunities available across the border, but on the other hand one could argue that the exchanges between people from both sides of the border occur mainly within the economic context alone. Subsequently, people's *personal attitudes, knowledge, and experiences* are framed largely within this context.

Conclusion

From an adjustment to a new and contested border, with open and closed periods of border crossings, towards an open border, the German-Polish border region has been in constant change. As mentioned in the introduction, historical developments in this particular cross-border region have indeed led to a high level of unfamiliarity between the inhabitants as a result of large migration flows. People were not familiar with one another or with each other's narratives, cultures, customs, and languages. Yet, they still had to live alongside each other. The physical border was closed for a long time, during which few cross-border contacts and exchanges were allowed. A latent interest in cross-border exchange, however, was demonstrated by the fact that the opening of the border in the 1970s led to immense numbers of border crossings, contacts, and exchanges. The second, and most likely permanent, border opening in the 1990s was experienced differently.

Coming back to Bauman's theory on strangeness, the border openings in the 1970s and the 1990s demonstrate interesting levels of unfamiliarity. During the first opening of the border, inhabitants of the border cities on both sides of the German-Polish border were curious about the neighboring city across the border. The earlier forced immobility that resulted from the closed borders heightened mutual unfamiliarity but actually increased people's interest in the other side of the border. After the opening of the border, people were able to familiarize themselves with the other side of the border through personal experience and through obtaining information from family, friends, and neighbors who had been across the border. As a result, people did not have to depend on information from the government or media. The initial excitement, however, was soon overcome by feelings of annoyance, especially on the German side of the border, resulting from over-consumption, which, with rise of cross-border exchanges, might also be regarded as over-familiarity.

Subsequently, with the opening of the borders in the 1990s, feelings of excitement and curiosity were only part of the picture. Whereas Poles continue to be interested in the other side of the border, where the unfamiliar, the new, and unknown, is regarded as attractive and has become integrated into daily routines, Germans are less inclined to look for opportunities in Poland. Perhaps the German unification led many inhabitants to seek opportunities in western Germany, or perhaps the de-industrialization of the region caused a German exodus, physically and mentally, from the border region. Assumptions of the other also play an important role, especially among the Germans who seem to hold negative attitudes towards the Poles. Feelings of belonging stress these assumptions, resulting in little incentive to cross the border. When the border is crossed, social contacts are not of interest; the focus is, rather, on obtaining goods and services.

This initial literature review demonstrated that unfamiliarity is likely to trigger interest, leading to actions, in this case border crossings, whereas familiarity, or partial familiarity, with the other side of a border seems to be associated with little interest and interaction. While in the 1990s, the opening of the borders opened many opportunities for cross-border cooperation, in particular in the context of EU enlargement, these opportunities may have been partly obscured by historical representations and mental images of the other. Differences are needed to evoke an interest in the other side of the border. However, becoming familiar or remaining unfamiliar is determined not only by circumstances and external factors, but also by the position of people living in the cross-border region. They are in charge of selecting and activating (un)familiarity and must decide how people and places located across the border are assessed and dealt with.

References

Amstrong, Warwick (2003): "Culture, Continuity and Identity in the Slovene-Italian Border Region", in: European Studies 19, pp. 145-169.
Baloglu, Seyhmus (2001): "Image Variations of Turkey by Familiarity Index", in: Tourism Management 22, pp. 127-133.
Bauman, Zygmunt (1995): The Stranger Revisited, and Revisiting. In Life in Fragments: Essays in Postmodern Morality, Oxford: Blackwell.

Buursink, Jan (2001): "The Bi-national Reality of Border-Crossing Cities", in: GeoJournal 54, pp. 7-19.

Chessa, Cecilia (2004): "State Subsidies, International Diffusion, and Transnational Civil Society: The Case of Frankfurt-Oder and Slubice", in: East European Politics and Societies 18, pp. 70-109.

Dürrschmidt, Jörg (2002): "'They're Worse off than Us': The Social Construction of European Space and Boundaries in the German/Polish Twin-City Guben-Gubin", Identities 9, pp. 123-150.

Dürrschmidt, Jörg (2006): "So near yet so far: Blocked Networks, Global Links and Multiple Exclusion in the German-Polish Borderlands", Global Networks 6, pp. 245-263.

Ernste, Huib (2010): "Bottom-up European Integration: How to cross the Treshold of Indifference?", in: Tijdschrift voor Economische en Sociale Geografie 101, pp. 228-235.

Fakeye, Paul C./Crompton, John L. (1991): "Image Differences between Prospective, First-time, and Repeat Visitors to the Lower Rio Grande Valley", in: Journal of Travel Research 30, pp. 10-16.

Fichter-Wolf, Heidi/Knorr-Siedow, Thomas (2009): "Border Experience and Knowledge Cultures: The Twin Cities of Frankfurt (Oder) and Słubice", in: disP 178, pp. 7-21.

Gurevitch, Z. D. (1988): "The Other Side of Dialogue: On Making the Other Strange and the Experience of Otherness", in: The American Journal of Sociology 93, pp. 1179-1199.

Jajeśniak-Quast, Dagmara/Stokłosa, Katarzyna (2000): Geteilte Städte an Oder und Neiße: Frankfurt (Oder)-Słubice, Guben-Gubin und Görlitz-Zgorzelec, 1945-1995. Berlin: Berlin Verlag.

Krätke, Stefan (1999): "Regional Integration or Fragmentation? The German-Polish Border Region in a New Europe", in: Regional Studies 33, pp. 631- 641.

Kulczycki, John J. (2001): "The National Identity of the 'Natives' of Poland's 'Recovered Lands'", in: National Identities 3, pp. 205-219.

Lau, Anita L. S./McKercher, Bob (2004): "Exploration Versus Acquisition: A Comparison of First-time and Repeat Visitors", in: Journal of Travel Research 42, pp. 279-285.

Lundberg, Donald E. (1980): The Tourist Business. Boston: Van Nostrand Reinhold Publishing.

MacKay, Kelly J./Fesenmaier, Daniel R. (1997): "Pictorial Element of Destination in Image Formation", in: Annals of Tourism Research 24, pp. 537-565.

Matthiesen, Ulf/Bürkner, Hans-Joachim (2001): "Antagonistic Structures in Border Areas: Local Milieus and Local Politics in the Polish-German Twin City Gubin/Guben", in: GeoJournal 54, pp. 43-50.

Newman, David (2006): "Borders and Bordering: Towards an Interdisciplinary Dialogue", in: European Journal of Social Theory 9, pp. 171-186.

O'Dowd, Liam (2003): "The Changing Significance of European Borders", in: James Anderson/Liam O'Dowd/Thomas M. Wilson (eds.), New Borders for a Changing Europe: Cross-border Cooperation and Governance, London: Frank Cass Publishers, pp. 13-36.

Paasi, Anssi (2009): "Bounded Spaces in a 'Borderless World': Border Studies, Power and the Anatomy of Territory", in: Journal of Power 2, pp. 213-234.

Prentice, Richard (2004): "Tourist Familiarity and Imaginary", in: Annals of Tourism Research 31, pp. 923-945.

Prentice, Richard/Andersen, Vivien (2007): "Interpreting Heritage Essentialisms: Familiarity and felt History", in: Tourism Management 28, pp. 661-676.

Schütz, Alfred (1962): Collected Papers I: The Problems of Social Reality. Edited by M. Natanson, The Hague: Nijhoff.

Shields, Rob (1991): Places on the Margin: Alternative Geographies of Modernity, London: Routledge.

Simmel, Georg (1950): "The Stranger", in: K.H. Wolf (Ed.), The Sociology of Georg Simmel, New York: The Free Press, pp. 402-408.

Spierings, B./van der Velde, M. (2008): "Shopping, Borders and Unfamiliarity: Consumer Mobility in Europe", in: Tijdschrift voor Economische en Sociale Geografie 99, pp. 497-505.

Stichweh, Rudolf (2004): "Strangers in World Society: Indifference and Minimal Sympathy", in: S. Iglhaut/T. Spring (eds.), Science and Fiction: Between Nanoworlds and Global Culture, Berlin: Jovis, pp. 111-123.

Stryjakiewicz, T. (2009): "Cross-Border Cooperation and governance: The Case of the Twin Cities of Frankfurt – upon – Oder and Słubice", in: Central European Journal of Spatial and Landscape Planning (Terra Spectra) 20, pp. 19-25.

Timothy, Dallen J./Butler, Richard W. (1995): "Cross-Border Shopping: A North American Perspective", in: Annals of Tourism Research 22, pp. 16-34.
van der Velde, Martin/van Naerssen, Ton (2010): "People, Borders, Trajectories: An Approach to Cross-border Mobility and Immobility in and to the European Union", in: Area, pp. 1-7.
van Houtum, Henk (1999): "Internationalisation and Mental Borders", in: Tijdschrift voor Economische en Sociale Geografie 90, pp. 329-335.
van Houtum, Henk/Strüver, Anke (2002): "Borders, Strangers, Doors and Bridges", in: Space and Polity 6, pp. 141-146.
van Houtum, Henk/van der Velde, Martin (2004): "The Power of Cross-Border Labour Market Mobility", in: Tijdschrift voor Economische en Sociale Geografie 95, pp. 100-107.

Historical Culture and Territoriality
Social Appropriation in the German-Polish Border Region in the 19th and 20th Centuries

Thomas Serrier

ENTANGLED HISTORICAL CULTURES AND APPROPRIATION OF A HYBRID TERRITORY

Border areas and regions characterized by their multicultural past, as exemplified by Germany's former eastern region and Poland's western region today, are experimental fields for changing "territorial regimes." This term refers to the individual and collective relationship to a politically structured territory, defined here as historical territory, i.e. as a geographical system of historically evolved relations. In the following, the changing forms of subjective identification of the territory situated in this area of tension between Germany and Poland are discussed.

The present contribution aims to clarify the changing modes of social appropriation of territories, especially border territories. In other words, it seeks to analyze the mutually dependent relationship of territoriality and historical culture.[1] Its focus is on German-Polish border areas. How did historical culture determine the geographical perception of this territory? To what extent did perception of the territory influence the historical culture(s) in the society on each side of the border? Obviously, significant changes emerged in the way people experienced this border region in the interplay with its political affiliations. Conversely, political constellations that resulted in territorial changes were also produced on a symbolic level (see Bourdieu 2001). It follows that analysis of the diverse constructions of

---

1 | For the term *historical culture*, see de Jong (1997: 282).

mental mapping[2] is a promising method for approaching the German-Polish border region.

It is critically important to recognize that the interwoven strands of "real history" are also reproduced on the terrain of recollections, cultural memories, and politics of history. The tense political and social relationship that characterized the region's multicultural existence is reflected in a correspondingly complex interplay and counterpoising of cultural memories and politics of history in which the actual demarcations or mental mapping of the territory fulfilled a key function.

METHODOLOGICAL REMARKS: SOURCES AND CASE STUDIES

We shall focus on four different cultural landscapes, moving from north to south: East Prussia with its strong mythical connotations (Kossert 2005); Danzig (Gdansk), which has stood as the outstanding example of a city on the border between Poland and Germany since the Middle Ages and which has a highly distinctive local identity (Loew 2003); the region of Greater Poland (*Wielkopolska*), which consisted of the Grand Duchy (later Province) of Posen in the Prussian and Prussian-German eras and which became the central setting for struggles over national identity before 1914 (Serrier 2002a, 2005); and finally, Silesia, which encompasses also Upper Silesia (Struve/Ther 2002; Struve 2003).

Of the three dimensions of historical culture defined by Jörn Rüsen – the cognitive, the aesthetic, and the political – we shall focus on the latter two, giving examples from travelogues, light fiction, and belles lettres as well as architecture and urban planning.

TERRITORIAL REGIMES: FROM SEALED TO OPEN TERRITORY?

If we now look specifically at the successive "territorial regimes" that governed the German-Polish border region over the last two centuries, we can draw a broad line through all the political and territorial upheavals from the 19th century to the post-1989 period and trace the transition from the desire for closure and mutual partitioning of the territory to recent

---

2 | For the term *mental map*, see Schenk (2002).

attempts to promote "open regionalism" (Robert Traba) or "postmodern regionalism" (Kazimierz Brakoniecki) by glorifying the diversity of the historical legacy, giving equal weight to each position.[3] In doing so, however, we have to be careful to avoid succumbing to a sentimental, idealized image of the present.[4]

This brings us to a point of principle. A disturbing effect of the tragic chapters in the history of 20th-century German-Polish relations is that the contemporary, and quite spectacular, attempts observable in Germany and Poland to establish identity in a "postmodern" sense, whether viable or not, are doomed to be backward projections of destroyed multiculturalism. It is impossible to understand the present vision of "remixing Europe"[5] without noting the bitter paradox that this imaginary process of remixing is actually flourishing against the backdrop of the radical schism that ultimately divided the Germans and the Poles geographically from each other during the war and the immediate postwar period.

Some pessimists offer arguments that cannot be contemplated within the bounds of political correctness: they argue that it was actually the ethnic-territorial homogenization of the Third Reich and the early People's Republic of Poland that created the necessary conditions for today's German-Polish dialogue. Proponents of this view include Stefan Chwin, whose novel *Hanemann* was published in 1995 (and appeared in English as *Death in Danzig* in 2004). Chwin's Gdansk novel established him as one of the first contemporary Polish authors to focus on the moment of expulsion of ethnic Germans from Poland as a central issue (Chwin 1999). Modern commentators like Chwin suggest provocatively that the Western Allies already mooted pacification of the German-Polish border as the result of the enforced resettlement of Germans east of the Oder and Neisse in the context of the Potsdam Treaty (Brandes 2001).

On the topic of expulsion, at this point we should mention the difference between two types of multiculturalism, a distinction that is fundamental for perception of the symbolic territory. There is a multiculturalism of togetherness or contiguity, or even mutual opposition, which is typical for the regions under consideration in the period of population shifts. This was counterpoised after 1945 or 1989 to a "multiculturalism"

---

3 | See the *Borussia* magazine series.
4 | For a polemic view of "reconciliation kitsch," see Bachmann (1994: 41f.).
5 | Borrowed from the term "unmixing Europe". See Schlögel (2001).

of successive existence, in which in one case the national homogeneous society of postwar Poland replaced the earlier multicultural society, but in many other cases it succeeded and replaced a different homogeneous society, namely German society. In this context, the careful use of quotation marks fulfils a precise purpose, because this "successive multiculturalism" involves the idea of the palimpsest that allows us to read the present and the lost past simultaneously on the historical parchment of a given space. In the space we commingle the periods.[6]

Chronological Overview

In the political context of the Prussian and Prussian-German state in the 19th century, the processes of mutual social exclusion based on categories of national identification were revealed in several stages. Around 1900 the dominant picture was of a mirrored dynamization of competing nationalisms.

The territorial conflict was expanded and intensified with terrible cruelty under the auspices of the "brutalization" of political morals after the First World War (Mosse 1990). The plans for mutual exclusion, intended at the time to achieve "healthy relations" [Esch 1998] in the central European mosaic of nationalities, were actually implemented in the wider context of the Second World War (1939-1948) by resettlement policies. The Germans began this during the Nazi occupation of Poland. Only a few years later, German inhabitants fled in the opposite direction to escape the advancing Red Army at the end of the war or and in the following months and years were forcibly resettled from their "adopted" homes in Silesia, Pomerania, and East Prussia by Poland's new communist rulers and by "repatriated persons" from the territory of "Kresy" in eastern Poland.[7] The current idea (at least in the context of the EU) of a territory that has become wide open again and of a shared historical legacy (Mazur 2003) blatantly contradicts the momentous exclusion of the mutual "other" from the national community's imagination. Despite the new type of reconciliation paradigm, this still partly persists today and was a major structural factor for the region until the collapse of the Iron Curtain.

---

6 | Paraphrasing Schlögel's title. See Schlögel (2003).
7 | For a general overview see Ther (2011).

Fluid Transitions: Posen in the 19th Century

The collective processes of differentiation typical of the whole nation in the 19th century were even more intense in the province of East Prussia, which was very mixed in terms of language, ethnicity, and culture in that period. For example, the eastern border regions of Prussia, or the German Reich after 1871, were populated by Germans, Poles, Lithuanians, Jews, and several Slavic-speaking minorities of unspecified national identity. From a transnational perspective the Reich appears as an empire of linguistic hybridity, particularly in the Prussian area of partitioned Poland (Serrier 2005).

The Prussian province of Posen around the year 1900 is a good example of the relation between historical culture and territoriality. The attempt by this border region with its Polish majority to identify itself with Germany was based on the creation of a "German" homeland conceived as a local metaphor for the whole nation (Cofino 1997). The invention of a German-encoded border province in the former Polish area of Greater Poland was largely achieved by trying to produce an adequate regional image. The representatives of the administration, and not least the assimilated Jews, played a bigger role in this than the weak regional elites on the German side (Serrier 2009).

Despite the exploitation of history in this province of eastern Prussia with its historically Polish character, the basically emotional relationship between "our own private little country" and the national fatherland implied by the term "homeland" *(Heimat)*, which was rooted in a person's self-identification with his or her surroundings (Petri 2001), proved extremely difficult to maintain. The Germans, confronted by the encroachment of the "Polish community in the Prussian state" (Bernhard 1907), were concerned about their self-image. The "Polish threat," sometimes extrapolated to the whole Slav people, was a common catchphrase (Renz 1905; Schlager 1902; Schirmacher 1908).

The centrality of the region in Polish memory contrasted with this. As a result, from the German standpoint, the territory was seen first as a region of fluid transitions, and second as an underdeveloped, still uncharted area – a typically colonialist view. "The east begins at the Silesian Railway Station in Berlin." This remark was made shortly before the First World War by a reporter from the *Frankfurter Zeitung* newspaper on his way to the so-called "Ostmark" ("Eastern March") (Frankfurter Zeitung

1911). His description clearly contradicted the propagandist speeches about the province's successful integration since its annexation by Prussia a century earlier.

The problematic situation described above gave rise to several simultaneous dilemmas for the Germans of Posen. Historical claims based on events that occurred before 1793 could sometimes prove extremely complicated, since the "German" epoch of medieval colonization of Eastern Europe was followed by the unambiguous "Polonization" of the modern era. The experience of historical characterization of the territory influenced the perception of the space and the regional relationship to history. The fashion for futuristic projections was enthusiastically welcomed, as was the trend for erecting historicizing buildings. A prime example of this was the Kaiserpfalz (Imperial Palace), dedicated in 1910. At the same time, inventing tradition went along with exhibiting innovation. The 1911 East German Exhibition *(Ostdeutsche Ausstellung)* in Posen served to elevate the province to a showcase of German modernity on the eastern border. Even if it had not been German in the past, so the argument went, Posen should at least be a flourishing area of Germany in the future.

The "toponymic waltz" (Serrier 2005: 262ff.) characteristic of the Posen region for the entire period of the partition of Poland offers a good introduction to the relationship between territoriality and historical culture. The historical watershed of the divisions of Poland raised the issue of a suitable name for former Greater Poland. The old name *Wielkopolska* seemed appropriate as a reminder of historical continuity. Even the Germans used the term "Greater Poland" *(Großpolen)* until 1848. In the second half of the 19th century there were three rival proposals for identification, which illustrates the mutual interaction of historical cultures as well as their mental positioning: "Wielkopolska," "Province of Posen," and "Ostmark." All these terms were used by various social groups around 1900; they express the historically nourished Polish resistance against the Prussian *tabula rasa*, or the current relations at that time (the term "province"), or the future projections typical of the German mode of mental appropriation of territory.

THE TROUBLED PAST:
DANZIG IN THE PRUSSIAN-GERMAN PERIOD

While a symbolic landscape first had to be created for the German side in Posen, the city of Danzig was a very different case. The tense relationship between the perspective of the local patriots and that of the Prussians, later Prussian-Germans, influenced the city's historical culture in the 19th century. Just as the Prussian takeover in 1793 led to inevitable confrontation between the old and new referential frameworks for the territory, some of the corresponding historical narratives proved incompatible. With the Prussianization of the geographical coordinates by the Prussian-state camp, those who saw themselves as city patriots recognized the oppositional potential of local history as an opportunity for identification beyond any state-endowed meaning. In relation to the affiliation of the symbolic territory over time, the historical interpretation models ultimately shifted towards a national interpretation. The project of re-establishing the nation as German resulted largely in anachronistic retrograde projections of emerging German-Polish antagonism onto the local past.

The degree of tension between local and national identities and the game played with history arising from this conflict are well illustrated by the literally "moving" fate of the statue of August III in the Artushof, as described by Peter Oliver Loew. The Artushof, along with the town hall and the imposing edifice of St. Mary's Church (the Marienkirche), was a major landmark in the city. A renowned emblem of the social and urban life of the Hanseatic city, it demonstrated the revived political self-confidence of Danzig's citizens to the outside world. Domestically it had always functioned as a special place of identification (Serrier 2002b).

Around the turn of the 18th-19th century, it became clear that nationalism was insidiously usurping the symbolism of the Artushof. Yet the identification was by no means wholly German nationalist. In fact, the Danzigers' pride resided in their enduring independence from the Teutonic Order-State and the German Reich during the centuries of unified rule by the Kingdom of Poland. The marble statue of the Polish king August III was dedicated in the Artushof in 1755. However, commemoration of the Polish king, who belonged to the Saxon dynasty, was not very welcome in Prussian Danzig. In 1831 the statue had to be removed from its place in the middle of the courtyard to an unobtrusive corner. The relegation caused inevitable uproar, resulting in August III being restored to his former place in 1857. In 1931, in the Free State of Danzig, then surrounded by Polish territory, the statue was finally retired to the city museum (Loew 2000).

Posen and Danzig both became Prussian at the same time, and both belonged to the larger German-Polish border region. Yet in some respects they present widely diverging pictures of historical politics and historical culture. This relates back to the different forms of territoriality in the two cities. The enforced concentration on local factors for pragmatic reasons posed a challenge to the 19th-century idea of the nation state and its desire for unity and homogeneity.

Upper Silesia and East Prussia as the "Bulwark" and "Postern" to the East in the Interwar Period

The experiences of the maximum expansion of the German eastern front during the First World War and the subsequent defeat of the German Empire and reconstitution of the Polish state, together with the restructuring of Europe decided in Versailles, profoundly changed the political and psychological framework of territorial perception in the German-Polish border region (Chu 2008). Hope of assimilation of the Polish population was not just destroyed. In fact, the resurrection of a Polish state confirmed the reality of the "Polish threat." Many Germans had already lost their homeland in Posen, West Prussia, and parts of Upper Silesia. In the course of this upheaval, a fundamental change also occurred in relation to the border area. It was no longer a matter of assimilating a territory of mixed nationalities under a German government, but of defending or recapturing a territory that would be seen as under threat from a German nationalist point of view, while the Poles were the new nation-state (Dyroff 2007). Every party in the Weimar republic shared the revisionist border policy on the Reich's eastern border with the sole exception of the German Communist Party (KPD). The denial of Poland's right to the former Prussian or German eastern regions fostered the revanchist propaganda of the anti-democratic right-wing in the Weimar parliament. It was only logical for Hitler to describe the Nazi military conquests in the Poland campaign of 1939 as reclaiming the seceded territories.

Nationalist resentment in Germany after 1918, after its great power ambitions had been quashed, opened the way for extremely rash imperial concepts of territory in Central Eastern and Eastern Europe. Meanwhile, the new German complex about the east (Koenen 2005), and the sense of wrongful injury to the organic integrity of the national corpus, inspired the exact opposite: obsessive fixation on border regions. It was not only the physical border, but also that the new acceptance of collective brutalization meant that a psychological threshold had been crossed. On the scale of possibilities for national dramatization, defense of the border *per se* replaced the image of a territory to be pacified.

This process is clearly illustrated by the transition from the turn-of-the-century Ostmark literature to the borderland literature of the interwar years, combined with a geographical shift from Posen to Upper Silesia or East Prussia. "Where was Germany?" was the question in *Die Geächteten* (*The Outlaws*, 1930), Ernst von Salomon's novel about the Freikorps. "Germany was the place that was being fought for [...] Germany was on the border." The answer is so surprising because, with harsh brevity, it elides the identity of the whole nation with the mystique of the border. Statements or notions of this kind were by no means isolated occurrences in the Weimar period.

The cover picture of Herybert Menzel's Nazi novel, *Umstrittene Erde* (*Disputed Soil*, 1930), shows shadowy Polish lancers emerging from the dark night and crossing a graphically demarcated border, the Reich border. Similarly, the entire perception of the German-Polish border, which is sometimes described as "bleeding," became more or less "militarized." By contrast, utopias of reconciliation, as in Viktor Kaluza's novel about Upper Silesia, *Das Buch vom Kumpel Janek* (1934), were a rarity. An extreme example of propagandist manipulation was a novel from 1932 that actually caused a diplomatic incident with Poland. Its title was deliberately aggressive: *Achtung! Ostmarkenrundfunk! Polnische Truppen haben heute Nacht die ostpreußische Grenze überschritten!* (*Attention! Ostmark Radio! Polish Troops Crossed the East Prussian Border Last Night!*) This unusually long title with its strident tone masqueraded as a genuine press report. To make it look like an authentic newspaper cutting, the advertising poster for the book omitted details about the author and publisher. A radio announcement triggered a panic reaction in East Prussia. The newspaper *Die Weltbühne* of 23 February 1932 explained Hitler's lead over Hindenburg in the 1932 presidential elections in some Masurian electoral districts with reference to the book's local impact. Its author, Hans Nitram, was later employed in Goebbels' propaganda ministry (Traba 2005a: 275.).

Remixing Memories:
From Divided Remembrances to a Common Memory?

Given the traumatic experience of "unmixing Europe" during the Nazi occupation and the early postwar period, it is evident that the perception of territory as a key cultural meeting-place between Germany and Poland was initially blocked. In the second half of the 20th century, independently of all the retrogressive steps conditioned by conjoining factors, there was a gradual development, picking up speed after 1989, from the destruction and burial of the "foreign" encoding of a symbolic territory to the discovery of (or search for) traces of the "other" past. As numerous local examples show, the past is not just a legacy that cannot be repressed; on the contrary, increasingly large groups from the second or third generation, descendants of more recent Polish settlers in the northwestern Polish regions, are consciously tracking it down and bringing it to light.

Looking at the interplay of territorial and historical consciousness, it is important to note that the moment of a mirror-inverted psychological blocking off of the "other" among the Polish and the Germans meant shutting out specific historical experiences and periods. German publications in expellee circles after the war sometimes gave the impression that the history of Danzig and Breslau had come to a standstill in 1945. Similarly, Polish attempts at establishing Polish neighborhoods by changing street names, deliberate "de-Germanizing actions" (Linek 1997) and Polish re-coding of existing places in Opole, Gdansk, Szczecin, or Wrocław,[8] were caught in the same need for homogenization.

In Poland, with the flourishing of free speech since the fall of the Iron Curtain, there has been a great increase in literary and scholarly works and a growth in regional cultural and historical associations discussing the topic of the pluricultural past of the northwest of Poland today. After 1945 the new political leadership in Warsaw created the image of a Poland that had been eternally homogeneous in order to stabilize the deep turmoil in the country and legitimize the Communist regime (Zaremba 2005). Although the myth of the "reclaimed" original Polish regions was

---

8 | To read how German Danzig turned into Polish Gdańsk see Loew (2003a); for Breslau/Wrocław see Thum (2011); about Breslau/Wrocław see also Davies/ Moorhouse (2002); for Stettin/Sczcecin see Musekamp (2010); for a general overview see Serrier (2007).

increasingly questioned over time, for a long period any doubts about this dogma were seen as a provocation, both domestically and geopolitically. Jan Józef Lipski's statement that the Poles are the "depositaries of German cultural heritage in Poland" was only accepted by the government and wide sections of society after 1989, and actually adopted as a new principle of action. More recently, the step from the cultural responsibility Lipski meant by the term "depositary" to the freedom of players to shape society together was taken by Robert Traba, the head of the Allenstein cultural association, *Borussia*, when he wrote in 2001, the 300th jubilee of the coronation of the first Prussian king, Frederick I:

We are no longer only depositaries; we are becoming intellectual co-inheritors of the Prussian cultural heritage. For the first time, this is happening not as a result of attempts at national appropriation, but because of the natural desire for emotional identification with the cultural landscape that has to be saved (Traba 2005b).

On the same note, after the Prussian jubilee year in 2001 Adam Krzemiński, editor-in-chief of the magazine *Polityka*, published an article with the still-provocative title, "Prussia, that's us!" (Krzemiński 2001). It has become quite common for Polish authors today to tackle controversial topics like the expulsion of the Germans from their cities, as Stefan Chwin did in his novel *Death in Danzig*, or Artur Daniel Liskowacki in his Szczecin trilogy. In this context we should mention the most spectacular and best-known process of historical revision: Polish scholarly historical studies and literary works on the expulsion of the Germans from Poland. The four-volume edition of the Polish records of this, produced by joint German-Polish cooperation, is a particularly important example here (Lemberg/Borodziej 2000-2004).

"Letting other people tell your story from their viewpoint" corresponds exactly to Paul Ricoeur's recent ideas on the topic of the mourning process and translation between cultures. A revived image of history and a new relationship to the concept of *"Heimat"* are inseparably linked here. In the northwestern regions of Poland, the former "German East," a new regional identity is taking root with a liberated approach to the history before 1945.

Writers such as Günter Grass, Horst Bienek, Siegfried Lenz and Arno Schmidt in West Germany, and Christa Wolf and Johannes Bobrowski in East Germany, alongside public figures like Countess Marion Dönhoff and, not least, the turn in West German policy towards East Germany associated with Willy Brandt, have made a significant contribution in this area. All these influential figures showed their willingness to tackle the past by critically challenging the overly emotional attitude to the concept of *Heimat* propagated by German expellee associations, or by dissociating themselves from the "anti-fascist" discourse of the former East German regime. Their approaches were welcomed particularly eagerly in oppositional circles in Poland. They served as a rebuttal of alleged "West German revanchism." Through this, the representatives of a "different" Germany paved the way to fundamentally question the legitimacy of the communist rulers in the People's Republic of Poland with their policy of suspicion towards Germany.

There is little doubt that the preparatory effect of that ideological criticism, particularly on the West German side, was essential for the "open regionalism" advocated by groups such as the Polish cultural society *Borussia* in Olsztyn, in former East Prussia. In the literary sphere this mutual rapprochement and recognition is reflected in works by authors such as Paweł Huelle, Olga Tokarczuk, Stefan Chwin, and Artur Daniel Liskowacki, who have become so important now and who are explicitly revaluating the intellectual heritage of the German past for their new home towns, Gdansk, Szczecin, and Wałbrzych. This paradigm change in the perception of the symbolic territory is also reflected on the symbolic level of the politics of history. For instance, in 2002 the city of Gdansk, to honour its "expelled son" Günter Grass, erected a statue of his fetish figure, Oskar Matzerath (Serrier forthcoming).

The essay "Bresław" by the writer Andrzej Zawada from Wrocław represents this trend, which tends towards hybridization, of combining the German past with the Polish present. The city of "Bresław" doesn't exist on any map. The name, a fictitious blend of Polish and German, suggests there could soon be intermingling of identity and not only in historians' fantasy or in writers' imagination (Zawada 1996). It may really be the case that the regime of national territoriality, which relies on demarcation, is in the process of dissolution (at least in some people's minds).

Conclusion

We could derive the following proposition on these current events in Poland's northwestern regions. Despite the discontinuity of players, the unity of place fulfils the decisive function in the configuration of "cultural memory," while the dividing moment is mainly preserved in "communicative memories," which remain unique. We still have to ask, how representative is the change in the territorial regime and in historical culture at the moment? Meanwhile, the shared retrospective view of this territory, which was once partitioned and partly disputed, testifies perhaps only to the constitution of a specific German-Polish "field" that is legitimated on both sides by maintaining political dialogue and by the sphere of cultural and scholarly collaboration, but that is far from being equivalent to the societies as a whole. Now and then, signs of return to a traditional victim discourse hit the headlines on both sides of the Oder.

Whatever the case, despite their fragmentary character, which can hardly be denied, the individual studies outlined in the present contribution have demonstrated that the *histoire croisée* approach based on historical relations can prove fertile for the specific field of research on collective memory. In fact, examining the interrelation of German and Polish collective memories from the aspect of their mutual interdependence is proving extremely productive, whether for analyzing the mutual delimitation of collective memories that characterized the regime of symbolic national territoriality, or for setting the present approaches of a German-Polish "memory transfer" against the historical backdrop with due caution and sobriety.

Translated from German by Karen Margolis

References

Bachmann, Klaus. (1994): "Versöhnungskitsch zwischen Deutschen und Polen", in: Transodra 8. September, pp. 41-43.

Bernhard, Ludwig (1907): Das polnische Gemeinwesen im preußischen Staate, Leipzig: Duncker & Humblot.

Bourdieu, Pierre (2001). Langage et pouvoir symbolique, Paris: Editions du Seuil.

Brandes, Detlev (2001): Der Weg zur Vertreibung. Pläne und Entscheidungen zum "Transfer" der Deutschen aus der Tschechoslowakei und aus Polen, Munich: Oldenbourg.

Chwin, Stefan (1999): "Das Geheimnis der Vertreibung", in: Die Welt, 21.8.

Confino, Alon (1997): The Nation as a Local Metapher. Württemberg, Imperial Germany and National Memory, 1871-1918, Chapel Hill: University of North Carolina Press.

Chu, Winson (2008): "The Geography of Germanness: Recentering German History in Interwar Poland", in : Bulletin of the German Historical Institute 42, Washington DC, Spring, pp. 95-104 (www.ghi-dc.org/files/publications/bulletin/bu042/095.pdf).

Davies, Norman/Moorhouse, Roger (2002): Microcosm. Portrait of a Central European City, London: Jonathan Cape.

de Jong, Henk (1997): "Historical Orientation: Jörn Rüsens Answer to Nietzsche and his Followers" in: History and Theory 36 (2), pp. 270-288.

Dyroff, Stefan (2007): Erinnerungskultur im deutsch-polnischen Kontaktbereich. Bromberg und der Nordosten der Provinz Posen (Wojewodschaft Poznań) 1871-1933, Osnabrück: fibre.

Esch, Michael (1998): "Gesunde Verhältnisse". Deutsche und polnische Bevölkerungspolitik in Ostmitteleuropa 1930-1950, Marburg: Herder-Institut.

Frankfurter Zeitung (Ed.) (1911): Das Problem des deutschen Ostens. Frankfurt a.M.: FZ.

Koenen, Gerd (2005): Der deutsche Russland-Komplex, Munich: C. H. Beck.

Kossert, Andreas (2005): Ostpreußen. Geschichte und Mythos, Munich: Siedler.

Krzemiński, Adam (2001): "Prusy – to my", in: Polityka 14.3.

Lemberg, Hans/Borodziej, Włodzimierz (eds.) (2000-2004): Unsere Heimat ist uns ein fremdes Land geworden..." Die Deutschen östlich von Oder und Neiße 1945-1950. Dokumente aus polnischen Archiven, Vol. 1-4, Marburg: Herder-Institut.

Linek, Bernard (1997): Odniemczanie" województwa śląskiego w latach 1945-1950, Opole: Wydawn. Inst. Śląnski.

Loew, Peter Oliver (2000): "Städtische Identität und nationales Bewusstsein: König August III. und sein Denkmal in der Danziger Erinnerung", in: Bernard Linek/Kai Struve (eds.), Nacjonalizm a tożsamość narodowa w Europie Środkowo-Wschodniej w XIX i XX w. Opole: PIN-Inst. Śląnski, pp. 13-36.

Loew, Peter Oliver (2003): Danzig und seine Vergangenheit 1793-1997. Die Geschichtskultur einer Stadt zwischen Deutschland und Polen, Osnabrück: fibre.

Mazur, Zbigniew (Ed.) (2003): Das deutsche Kulturerbe in den polnischen West- und Nordgebieten, Wiesbaden: Harrassowitz.

Mosse. George L. (1990): Fallen Soldiers. Reshaping the Memory of the Word Wars, Oxford: Oxford UP.

Musekamp, Jan (2010): Zwischen Stettin und Szczecin. Metamorphosen einer Stadt von 1945 bis 2005, Wiesbaden: Harrassowitz.

Petri, Rolf (2001) : "Deutsche Heimat 1850-1950", in: Komparativ 11 (1), pp.77-127.

Renz, B. [Hugo Behrens] (1905): Die polnische Gefahr und andere Novellen, Berlin: Kürschner.

Schenk, Frithjof Benjamin (2002): "Mental Maps. Die Konstruktion von geographischen Räumen on Europa seit der Aufklärung", in: Geschichte und Gesellschaft 28 (3), pp.493-514.

Schirmacher, Käthe (1908): Die östliche Gefahr. Lissa: Oskar Eulitz.

Schlager, Hans (1902): Die polnische Gefahr, Berlin : H. Schildberger.

Schlögel, Karl (2001): "Unmixing Europe oder Kosovo ist überall", in: Karl Schlögel, Promenade in Jalta und andere Städtebilder, Munich: Hanser, pp. 272-286.

Schlögel, Karl (2003). Im Raume lesen wir die Zeit. Über Zivilisationsgeschichte und Geopolitik, Munich: Hanser.

Serrier, Thomas (2002a): Entre Allemagne et Pologne. Nations et identités frontalières 1848-1914, Paris: Belin.

Serrier, Thomas (2002b): "Der Danziger Artushof im Wechsel der Zeiten: Kosmopolitismus als städtischer Erinnerungsort von der hansischen Blütezeit zur polnischen Gegenwart", in: Jacques Le Rider/Moritz Csáky/Monoka Sommer (eds.), Transnationale Gedächtnisorte in Zentraleuropa, Innsbruck et al.: Studien Verlag, pp.13-31.

Serrier, Thomas (2005): Provinz Posen, Ostmark, Wielkopolska. Eine Grenzregion zwischen Deutschen und Polen 1848-1914, Marburg: Herder-Institut.

Serrier, Thomas (Ed.) (2007): "Die Aneignung fremder Vergangenheiten in Nordosteuropa am Beispiel plurikultureller Städte (20. Jahrhundert)", in: Nordost-Archiv. Zeitschrift für Regionalgeschichte, Neue Folge XV/2006, Lüneburg, pp. 9-24.

Serrier, Thomas (2009): "Zwischen Inklusion und Exklusion: jüdische Erinnerungen im Spannungsfeld der deutschen und polnischen Nationsbildungen in der Provinz Posen", in: Martin Aust/Krzysztof Ruchniewicz/Stefen Troebst (eds.), Verflochtene Erinnerungen. Polen und seine Nachbarn im 19. und 20. Jahrhundert, Köln et al.: Böhlau, pp. 173-189.

Serrier, Thomas (forthcoming): "Günter Grass. Mit Blechtrommel und Nobelpreis in der Mitte des deutsch-polnischen Erinnerungsgeflechts", in : Hans Henning Hahn/Robert Traba/Górny Robert (eds.), Deutsch-polnische Erinnerungsorte, Vol 1., Paderborn: Ferdinand Schöningh.

Struve, Kai (Ed.) (2003): Oberschlesien nach dem Ersten Weltkrieg. Studien zu einem nationalen Konflikt und seiner Erinnerung, Marburg: Herder-Institut.

Struve, Kai/Ther, Philipp. (eds.) (2002): Die Grenzen der Nationen. Identitätenwandel in Oberschlesien in der Neuzeit, Marburg: Herder-Institut.

Ther, Philipp (2011): Die dunkle Seite der Nationalstaaten. "Ethnische Säuberungen" im modernen Europa, Göttingen. Vandenhoeck & Ruprecht.

Thum, Gregor (2011): Uprooted: How Breslau became Wroclaw during the Century of Expulsions, Princeton: Princeton UP.

Traba, Robert (2005a): Wschodniopruskośc". Tożsamość regionalna i narodowa w kulturze politycznej Niemiec, Poznań/Warszawa: Poznańskie Towarystwo Przyjacioł Nauk.

Traba, Robert (2005b): "Wo liegt Preußen?", in: Basil Kerski (Ed.), Preußen. Erbe und Erinnerung. Essays aus Polen und Deutschland, Postdam, pp.159-165

Zaremba, Marcin (2005): Komunizm, legitymizacja, nacjonalizm. Nacjonalistyczna legitymizacja władzy komunistycznej w Polsce, Warszawa: Wydawn. Trio.

Zawada, Andrzej (1996): Bresław. Eseje o miejscach, Wrocław: Okis.

The View of French Diplomacy on the German-Polish Border Shift, 1940-1950

Eloi Piet

Introduction

The Western territories gained back by Poland are Polish territories. Efforts to develop those territories made over the last eighteen months deserve all our attention. These regions have already lost their German character; the last remaining Germans will soon be gone. We, the French, consider the Polish borders – as established in Potsdam – to be totally legitimate, both historically speaking and from the perspective of the security of Poland and the other Slavonic nations (Roger Garreau)[1].

The demographic substitution that Poland meant to carry on along the Oder-Neisse border is baffling [...]. Modernity – as it is understood in the Western world – has receded toward the center of Europe in front of [the destitution in the ex-German territories colonized by Poland]. That may be one of the aspects of the Oder Neisse issue that is of interest not only for Germany but for the whole of occidental civilization, which is receding westward (Marc Popilet)[2].

---

1 | Statement made at the Polish news agency, on September 9, 1946 in Warsaw, by Roger Garreau, French ambassador in Poland. AMAE (*Archives du Ministère des Affaires étrangères*), Courneuve, Europe 1944-1970, Pologne, *minorités polonaises en Allemagne et question des frontières*, statement of Roger Garreau, French ambassador in Poland, September 9, 1946 in Warsaw, in a report of the French Intelligence Agency of the Minister of Foreign Affairs, l'*Ouest polonais et la nouvelle frontière polono-allemande*, p. 247.

2 | Introduction and conclusion of a report regarding the Polish colonization in ex-German territories pronounced by the French 'chargé d'affaire' in Poland, Marc

Here are two conflicting examples of the way French diplomacy interpreted change in the location of the German-Polish border from 1940 to 1950.³ Might a study of the way French diplomacy perceived the territorial shift, upon which it had a limited impact notably due to its declining influence in Europe, be of possible interest? At the outset of the research project whose results are reported in this contribution, the goal was only to study a description of Germans being expelled from Poland and how they were portrayed in French diplomatic archives in order to obtain a French viewpoint of the effect of *Flucht und Vertreibung* (escape and expulsion) of 15 million Germans from Central and Eastern Europe after the end of the Second World War. This research focused on the "Pologne" archives in Quai d'Orsay (the Foreign Affair offices) and on documents issued by French diplomatic centers in Poland reporting on changes in the location of the Oder-Neisse border. These other documents are located in the Warsaw Embassy and at the consulates in Wrocław, Szczecin, and Gdańsk. Even though it would have been hard to expect any commiseration for Germans expelled out of Poland on the part of French diplomats, their disinterest for this issue was nevertheless striking. To them, it was only a small element of a bigger and much more meaningful phenomenon: the German enemy had just lost over 100,000 square kilometers of territory that had been annexed and colonized by Poland. It therefore became necessary account for two other aspects of the border shift: the diplomatic fight, led by Poland, to obtain the Allies' full recognition of the Oder-Neisse line after Potsdam; and the Polish colonization of the *Recovered Territories* (*zemie odzyskanie*).

The Molotov-Ribbentrop Pact, signed on August 23, 1939, set up the conditions for the Nazi politics of extermination and exploitation from 1939 to 1944 and the Sovietization of the eastern border territories (*Kresy* in Polish) led by the USSR from September 1939 to August 1941. A total ethnic, political, and territorial transformation of the country then occurred during the post-war period (Borodziej/Lemberg 2004: 37ff.). The weakening of Polish society as a result of large-scale ethnic cleansing

---

Popilet on June 20, 1950. AMAE, Nantes, French Ambassy in Poland, folder no 25, *Terres de l'Ouest*, November 1945 – July 1948, report by Marc Popilet to the Foreign Ministry.

3 | We studied these two examples for our MA thesis at the Institute Pierre Renouvin, University Paris 1 Panthéon-Sorbonne with Professor Antoine Marès.

conducted by Moscow and Berlin and the liquidation of the Polish elite enabled Stalin to use Poland as a communist buffer state at Germany's expense. Moscow feared that the Allies would restore German industry and use it against the USSR (Soutou 2007: 121). The communist regime of Warsaw expelled about nine million Germans across the Oder-Neisse border between 1945 and 1947 and organized at the same time the settlement of 5 million Polish colonists to those territories. This ethnic and territorial displacement, held up as a compensation for the loss of the Polish boundaries annexed to the USSR, was one of the most significant in contemporary European history and was part of the larger phenomenon of displacement imposed upon 30 million Europeans between 1940 and 1970 period (Ther 2001: 44).

In the post war context, French diplomacy hardly could have any impact on such a major territorial shift. US assistance to rebuild France (Blum-Byrnes agreement, May 6, 1946) and the military alliance with Great Britain (Dunkirk treaty, March 4, 1946), and negotiations with Moscow for the disarmament of communist militias in France were the major issues for French diplomacy. In comparison, the German-Polish border shift was of little consequence. And yet, the Quai d'Orsay's view of the German-Polish border shift did touch on issues of major importance to liberated France, at least until 1947. Reinforced security against potential German aggression, access to coal reserves, and the apparently non-ideological union of Polish political parties were among these issues. French diplomacy consisted of a stream of information about the border shift, structured by the defense of French interests in Europe. Official positions were mixed with confidential analysis. This stream flowed on three levels. The first level is the French government, which made decisions regarding the official recognition of the Oder-Neisse border. The second level is the Quai d'Orsay, which prepared an alliance with Poland from 1946-47 before improving relations with what would become the Federal Republic of Germany (FRG) against Soviet wishes. The third level is represented by the French diplomats in Poland who reported on the colonization of former German territories. Instructions on how to represent the French view of a potential recognition of the Oder Neisse border and how to analyze the border shift came down from the first level. French observers in Poland, in turn, made suggestions about how France should position itself in this diplomatic border conflict pitting the USSR and Poland against the USA, Britain and occupied West Germany.

The study of French diplomacy regarding the Oder-Neisse border supposes an understanding of the imagery of French diplomacy. This imagery was a product of Paris observing the border shift through a perceptual system created by its strategic and ideological view of the international scene. From the 1945 German defeat to the beginning of the Korean war in 1950, both the border shift itself and the French perceptual system were transformed, resulting in a dramatic reversal of the French position.

The following analysis proceeds in three parts. The first part contains an analysis of diplomatic opinion on the shift during the war (1940-45). In 1942, French diplomats welcomed the annexation plans by the Polish government in London exile. Later, in the last months of 1944 they tightened their relations with the communist counterpart of the Polish Government in London exile, the Polish Committee for National Liberation (Pkwn), which was being supported by the Red Army in Warsaw. In both cases, the diplomatic gestures were intended help the allies encircle Germany, expected to be defeated soon. Part two contains an analysis of how French diplomats compared the river Oder – actual border of Poland – to the river Rhine that France wanted to make its eastern border at that time. France had been excluded from Potsdam but still had ways of controlling Germany's reconstruction, notably due to the seat on the Allied Control Council it was granted in September, 1945 (Bossuat 1997: 37ff.). At that point, the Cold War seemed unavoidable to the countries that defeated Germany. France had already chosen an alliance with America at the expense of an alliance with Poland and Czechoslovakia. Part three describes the reversal of the French diplomatic position on the new border, which then had been adopted by Warsaw. From 1948 to 1950, diplomats contrasted the failures of Polish colonization on the Oder to the modernization being achieved in France through the Marshall and Schuman plans and called attention to the fate of Germans who had stayed in Poland.

FRANCE AT WAR AND THE BEGINNINGS OF POLAND'S GESTURES TO THE WEST: SYMPATHY AND CAUTION (OCTOBER 1944 - AUGUST 1945)

The *Free French* (those who had decided to carry on fighting despite of the French defeat and to follow General de Gaulle after June 1940) gathered in London under de Gaulle's command, were able to meet the soldiers and the members of the Polish government of General Sikorski who had gone into exile. Remembering the sometimes difficult relationships with Poland during the inter-war period, the Free French viewed the first Polish projects of annexation of German territories that were presented in October 1940 suspiciously (Marès 1982). In 1941, the deadlock gradually dissolved: the common interest of Free France and the Polish government in cooperation, the commitment to the historical alliance between the two countries, and personal relationships established during the exile melted French reluctance. When in March 1942, Polish diplomats delivered a memorandum to the Foreign Office calling for the annexation of East Prussia, Upper Silesia, and Gdansk, the French were inclined to back it. In January 1942, de Gaulle gave his conditional consent. The head of the CNF (*Comité National Français*) had indeed ensured to Sikorski that France would support the Polish plan and that he was interested in reviving the historical alliance between the two countries. Besides the wish to benefit from a strong alliance within Europe, the French support fit into a wider scheme of efforts first launched by Clemenceau at the Paris Conference (January 1919- August 1920). France had then supported Polish claims on Upper Silesia, Gdansk, and Eastern Prussia against Germany, notably in the prospect of weakening this country to the advantage of a trustworthy ally.[4] The strategic weight of the German borders in Poland had urged France to sign a treaty of alliance with Warsaw in February 1921. Yet, de Gaulle demanded that the Polish cooperate with the Soviet Union. He admitted to Sikorski that he wished to deal carefully with the Moscow alliance and that France would not interfere in a conflict over Poland's eastern boundary. Free France avoided giving any guarantee regarding Poland's eastern borders. It offered support of Poland's plan to advance its western borders at Germany's expense, which in consequence would be beneficial to Paris.

An alliance with the Soviets was interesting for French diplomats who not only wished to revive the 1892 Franco-Russian alliance to dominate Germany permanently and also to counterbalance American influence after the victory (Laforêt 1999). The will to maintain a worldwide balance of power was closely linked to the goal of opposing its allies on Germany.

---

4 | "Security on the Vistula complemented security on the Rhine, and the more Germany was weakened in the east, the less menace she offered on the west" (Wandycz 1962: 29).

Paris suggested at that time that Germany should be divided, that the Ruhr and Rhineland should be economically united to France and that Saarland should be annexed to France outright. The Rhineland plan elaborated by the French Committee of National Liberation was intended to strengthen France's security and guarantee access to German coal, thought to be indispensable for rebuilding Europe (Bossuat 1997: 37ff.). These plans had been refused by London and Washington as early as the Yalta conference (February 4-11, 1945) but seemed to France to be backed by the USSR. Soviet diplomacy gave some hope to Paris. At that point, Stalin did not hide his goal of permanently annexing the Polish eastern border territories, which triggered a crisis in London. To France at war, it became obvious that the Polish government in London was doomed due to the progress of the Soviets towards the West and that it was necessary to keep it at a distance (Marès 1982: 325).

Initiatives had been taken by French diplomats in Moscow as early as 1943, showing the importance of rapprochement with Poland regarding the new borders of Germany. The ambassador in Moscow, Roger Garreau, went on to play a major role in the Franco-Soviet alliance treaty in December 1944. He thought that Soviet control over Poland, as inevitable as it was, would not prevent Poland from allying with France because it would lead to the weakening of Germany and accorded with Moscow's security requirements (Bariéty 2008: 210). Having been in contact with Polish communists since the end of 1943, Garreau managed to convince de Gaulle to tacitly recognise the PKWN, a rival of the government in London, so that Stalin's condition would be met when signing the December 1944 treaty. At first, this treaty was not a way to organize a Franco-Polish rapprochement at the expense of Germany's borders. De Gaulle was very reluctant to abandon his Polish friends in London and was disappointed by Stalin's ignoring France, which was not even invited to Yalta. Besides, reports written between January and March 1945 by Christian Fouchet, French diplomat in Poland and a friend of de Gaulle, gave a clear indication to de Gaulle that Poland, occupied by the Red Army, was becoming a vassal state where communism prevailed.[5]

Paradoxically, de Gaulle's foiled hopes did not prevent French diplomats from comparing Poland's recognized territorial claims on the Oder

---

5 | AMAE, Courneuve, Europe 1944-1970, Pologne, *Politique intérieure et reconstruction de l'État polonais*, pp. 129ff.

to the French claims on the Rhine. Garreau actively worked with the unofficial Polish foreign minister Zygmunt Modzelewski. In France, which was then governed by an alliance composed of socialist and communist resistance fighters as well as Christian democrats, the idea of a rapprochement with the PKWN (Laforêt 1999) – which claimed to be a national union as well – against Germany was developing. This rapprochement could have counterbalanced the creation of blocs in Europe, which would have been in keeping with de Gaulle's politics as head of the Provisional Government of the French Republic. The French ambassador in London, René Massigli's, was skeptical regarding the renewal of inter-war alliances with Central European countries now occupied by the Red Army, but the press and the parties in power subscribed to it (Soutou 1993).

The Potsdam Agreements (August 2, 1945) strengthened the rapprochement of France and Poland. France, who was not invited to the conference, learned that the "Big Three" had not accepted the division of Germany or the separation of the Rhineland. Yet, the former had confirmed to Paris it was an occupying power and had therefore the power to stop the constitution of a central administration in Germany. Thanks to its seat at the Allied Control Council and the Council of Foreign Ministers, Paris was able to stop the recovery of a democratic Germany that was ready to sign a permanent peace agreement with the Allies. This could only be a transitory situation. The PKWN worried that the British and the American had successfully insisted for recognition of the Oder-Neisse line only as a Polish *administrative border*. France was now aware of the importance of the territorial move in Eastern Germany and declared that was ready to recognize it in August 1945 under the condition that its plans for Rhineland (annexation of Saarland, internationalization of the Ruhr) would be added. As Warsaw and Paris developed relationships, France used de Gaulle's support for Polish annexations (which dated to January 1942) and related them to its claim. It does not seem that French diplomats thought thoroughly about the deportations of millions of Germans from Poland, as did their British counterpart (Frank 2007: 86ff.). France officially opposed the deportation of Germans from Central Europe to avoid a socio-economic imbalance but yet considering the same option – on a smaller scale – to secure possession of mining resources in Saarland (Soutou 1998: 170). The refusal to acknowledge the deportation of Germans from Poland that had started in June 1945 could be explained by the defense of French interests in Germany and was received by French diplomats who were enthusiastic about Polish colonization of the recovered territories.

The Rhine/Oder Comparison (September 1945 – November 1947)

From September 1945 to April 1947, France strongly disagreed with the reconstruction of a unified Germany, reclaiming at the same time its projects for Rhineland to be set up: the separation of the Ruhr and the Rhineland and the annexation of the Saarland[6]. During this period, the view French diplomacy cast on the German-Polish border shift appeared as a parallel between the rivers Rhine and Oder. In August 1945, French diplomacy declared that it agreed with the setting up of the Eastern border of Germany along the Oder-Neisse line, linking its official recognition to the French claims that the Western borders of Germany had to be modified[7]. Moreover, by renewing its alliance with Warsaw, Paris tried to escape from its isolation regarding this topic. The two countries worked on the re-launching of the 1921 treaty. The rapprochement with Poland may look surprising considering London's mistrust towards Warsaw and its allegiance to Moscow. To the French, this rapprochement did not act against the USSR security; on the contrary, it strengthened it. This presumptuous comparison between the river Rhine and the river Oder – in the eyes of the Quai d'Orsay, or at least of its people in favour of Moscow – was useful on three points: a reinforced security against Germany, the access to German coal and the rapprochement with a government supposedly of national unity, like in France. As for the German expelled out of Central Europe towards occupied areas in Germany, it was granted to Paris that out of the 6,5 million of German refugees from Central Europe that were planned to be resettled in Germany until July 1946, only 150.000 would go to and stay

---

[6] | In fact, it became in 1946 clear to the French diplomacy that the annexation of Saarland was quite impossible. However, it kept on demanding it officially until October 1956 in order to please French public opinion and to make the US accept a custom union between France and Saarland (Defrance/Pfeil 2012).

[7] | AMAE, Courneuve, Europe 1944-1970, Pologne, *Frontière germano-polonaise et politique polonaise à l'égard de l'Allemagne, 1945-1947*, note of August 7, 1945, unknown author, to Soviet, Britsh and Americain ambassadors in Paris, p.7.

in the French occupied zone (Soutou 1998: 171). The overpopulation of the US and British zones was consequently made worse but this rendered the situation easier for the French zone which was dependant on the American, notably for food. In the higher levels of French diplomacy, it was of utmost importance not to handle the issue of the deported Germans.

French diplomats in Warsaw, Szczecin, Wrocław and Gdańsk looked favourably at the Polish colonisation of recovered territories. During their diplomatic missions, diplomats lived in villas whose German owners had been dispossessed of them and did not hesitate to pilfer (*szaber* in Polish) to equip the houses[8]. In post-war Poland, the colonists and the administrators proved to be francophiles who were happy to help the French. Consequently, the opinion on Polish colonisation that can be read in the reports sent by the diplomats to Paris is clearly positive. Agreeing on the fact that 9 million Germans replaced by 5 million of Polish refugees did not make things easy, the French diplomats considered that the efforts made by the Polish would allow them to populate the former German territories and revive their economy. The French, who were happy with the work done by the administrators of the Polish Workers Party (PPR), considered the terror they had established on the East side of the river Oder as a way – brutal but suitable, according to them – to handle the instability of the area. Turning a blind eye to the political issues linked to colonisation, the French diplomats considered questions that were exclusively linked to France.

Consequently, on September 10, 1946, Garreau, since 1945 the French ambassador in Warsaw, harshly criticised what James F. Byrnes, US Secretary of state in Stuttgart said on September 6 when reminding that the Oder-Neisse line was to be a provisional border until the establishment of a global peace treaty with Germany. Garreau recognised, in the name of "the French" Poland's new border and briefly praised the Polish colonisation, specifying that the German democratic flaws would necessitate the setting up of Paris' plans of Rhineland[9]. Some French diplomats were

---

8 | AMAE, Courneuve, Europe 1944-1970, Pologne, *Silésie et territoires de l'ouest (Silesia and Western Territories)*, report of doctor-lieutenant Pauliac, transmitted by cabinet of general de Gaulle to sous-direction Europe centrale, August 25, 1945, p. 33.

9 | AMAE, Courneuve, Europe 1944-1970, *Pologne, Frontière germano-polonaise et politique polonaise à l'égard de l'Allemagne*, 1945-1947, pp. 236ff.

more careful, underlining that all the Polish people worked together for their nation's greatness rather than staying divided by their ideological beliefs. The appearing political pluralism that the communist administration of the recovered territories and its minister Władysław Gomułka claimed to be representative of, attracted the French diplomats whose country had been reconstructed by an alliance ranging from the Christian Democrats to the Communist Party (until March 1947). The Quai d'Orsay also thought that the Poles could in the future free themselves from the Soviet hold by using German industries and coal mines as an impulse towards reconstruction. This reminded of France being obsessed by the fear of being dependent on the US and on their loans given to reconstruct (Soutou 2007: 148).

French diplomats were indifferent to the Germans who had stayed or to the conditions of their deportations towards the occupied zones. They only mentioned those points when the British government raised them, criticising what Warsaw had done to the Germans in the Polish territories. In this Anglo-Polish argument, the French were in favour of the Poles, stating that the British remonstrance was groundless. Yet they did not check the veracity of those, not going in person to check the conditions of deportations. The accounts made by the French diplomats regarding the relationships that they had with the Germans who had stayed on the East side of the Oder river are telling in this respect. The Wrocław consul evicted 22 Germans out of the villa chosen as a consulate and would underline the arrogance of the Germans who had stayed in Breslau[10]. These nationalist *a priori* assumptions against the Germans were to be found in other circles. During a stay in Gdańsk in May 1945, Madeleine Pauliac, doctor-lieutenant in the French Red Cross, talked to a German lady which complained about the fate of her counterparts who had been raped in great number by Soviets and Poles. Pauliac answered back mentioning the concentration camps[11]. In her report to de Gaulle's Cabinet, she described the situation of the Polish civilians in Gdańsk but only addressed very

---

10 | AMAE, Courneuve, Europe 1944-1970, Pologne, *Silésie et territoires de l'ouest*, report of the French consul in Lower-Silesia, Charles Birckel on Wrocław city, December, 1945, pp. 67-73.

11 | AMAE, Courneuve, Europe 1944-1970, Pologne, *Silésie et territoires de l'ouest*, report of doctor-lieutenant Pauliac, transmitted by cabinet of general de Gaulle to sous-direction Europe centrale, August 25, 1945, p. 33.

briefly the lot of the deported German, evoking the French press mocking the German expelled from Alsace in 1918. This hostile indifference for the German on the part of the French diplomats and relief workers contrasts with the opinion of their British counterparts in Poland. The French position can be explained by the sufferings of the German occupation in France, and by the sympathy for the Poles. The strengthening of the Soviet and communist oppression on Poland ordered by Stalin during the Szklarska Poręba conference (September 22-27, 1947) led the French diplomats to watch powerlessly a friend-country being submitted to *sovietisation* and Stalinism.

THE SHIFT OF THE FRENCH DIPLOMATIC VIEW ON THE ODER-NEISSE LINE (NOVEMBER 1947 – JULY 1950)

The shift of the French diplomatic perception on the new German-Polish border started in the last months of 1947, characterised by the end of the four-party government in Germany and the beginning of the Cold War. Paris then realised that its attempts to make the most of the conflict between the Anglo Americans and the Soviets was starting to be too dangerous. The French government – scared by the Soviet aggressiveness – managed to rally the side of London and Washington under one condition: a custom union and the unification of Saarland to France. France also obtained 2.4 billions of dollars, out of 13 billion that had been given to Europe through the Marshall plan in June 1947. Paris had chosen its side. The USSR urged the powerful French Communist Party to counteract and in December 1947 strikes were set up and the government – boycotted by the communists since March – had to call for 80.000 reservists. Close the USA, the Quai d'Orsay was backed on parliamentary and governmental levels by the non-communist parties and their electorship who were shocked by the Prague coup in 1948 much more than by the Berlin blockade in June. In an old democratic European country, a well-structured communist party – with the help of Moscow – had taken the power in the absence of the Red Army.

A strong US military presence enabled by the Brussels treaty (March 1948) in return, Paris had to give its support to the setting up of something that it had always dreaded: the setting up of a Western German state with an important industrial potential. France had become a *cold warrior* ready to defend the river Elbe when signing the North Atlantic Treaty in April 1949. On the other side of this river, serving as a border for Europe and for Germany between West and East, Warsaw had taken the same way, but in an opposite direction. Despite strong cultural, economic and sometimes diplomatic exchanges until 1947, France and Poland stopped trying to maintain their friendship and started a *little cold war* in 1949 (Jarosz/Pasztor 2005: 120ff.). The Polish government sued French diplomats arrested in Poland, accusing them of being spies. And Paris responded by police retaliations on the Poles of France close to the Polish United Workers Party (PZPR).

Contrarily to how it stood in 1945, Polish propaganda praised the German Democratic Republic (GDR) and its *good Germans* in order to oppose them to France, accused of being the slave of American imperialism. Poland's flatorous words to the GDR were rewarded by the Görlitz/Zgorzelec treaty signed on July 6, 1950. Through this treaty, the GDR recognised the Oder-Neisse line as Germany's Eastern border. Imposed by Moscow, this position on the part of the GDR was immediately criticised by Bonn, Washington and London which considered as a violation of the Potsdam agreement all territorial shifts impacting on Germany's sovereignty that were made without the consent of the Potsdam signatories. From 1945 to April 1947, Paris supported unofficially the Oder-Neisse line in order to defend its interests in Germany. On July 1950, France declared that it only recognized the FRG as the legitimate German state and its right to represent this country in its 1937 borders (Laurent 1974/75: 122ff.). This statement showed a modification in France's way of considering the border shift between Germany and Poland but according to us, this position can better be explained by a realist continuity of the French position rather than by an idealist break that would have benefited to German people. Between 1945 and 1947, three criteria had conditioned the creation of a parallel made by the French between the rivers Rhine and Oder: the security against Germany, the access to its coal and a projection on Poland of a political project that was wished by the French opinion. This diplomatic shift was to be found amongst the French diplomats in Poland who expressed different, although closely related reasons (the political project was in 1949 reconciliation with the Germans).

Some observers of the Polish colonisation noted that the *sovietisation* of the economy in the recovered territories created in 1947 had dreadful economic consequences. Added to this point was the critique of political

Stalinism imposed on Poland as early as 1948 with Gomułka being evicted in favour of Bolesław Bierut. Through the description of the fear of the colonists subjected to political pressures that ceaselessly grew stronger, French diplomats draw a panorama pervaded by the image of the Quai d'Orsay's close relationship with the USA. For instance, the gathering of Soviet troops in Western Poland and the weight of local politics were described as the persistence of late Prussia, which symbolised for the French the totalitarianism which was a characteristic of the Third Reich and German militarism[12]. Similarly, experts at the Quai d'Orsay gave no credit to the declarations of friendship and cooperation of the GDR and Poland. Economic necessity rather than reconciliation, bloc perspective rather that spontaneity of the peoples: the French diplomats could have brought close the German-Polish cooperation on the Oder line and the Franco-German reconciliation that was beginning with the European Coal and Steel Community. But the French experts chose to oppose the colons' hatred for the Germans and the nationalist propaganda of the PZPR against the European and international opening-up of France. The freedom of movement of goods and people that was occurring in Western Europe undeniably contrasted with the situation experienced by the Germans who had stayed in Poland where they were often exploited. In 1950, Poland had extended the status of germanised Poles to almost all the Germans that had not been expelled[13]. Officially, this was to enable families who could prove that they had ties with Poland to stay, unofficially, this aimed at keeping workers and minds that were necessary to the reconstruction of the recovered territories. The French made no mistake about it, considering that these Germans played a key role against the economic failures of decolonisation. Consequently, they paid attention to their plights that they had ignored in 1945 and 1946. This new idealist empathy relied on a realist critique of the Poland's politico-economic evolution.

This new interest had a consequence on Paris's position regarding the conflict opposing the British occupying authorities and Warsaw in March 1950. Following talks between these two parties, it had been planned that

---

12 | AMAE, Nantes, Ambassy in Warsaw, carton n° 25, *Terres de l'ouest*, report of French consul in Wrocław Guy Monge on an exhibition on the Recovered Territories in the city, June 2, 1948.

13 | Atlas Zwangsumsiedlung, Flucht und Vertreibung, Ostmitteleuropa, 1939-1959, Warsaw: Demart 2009, p. 202.

at that moment, thousands of Germans who had stayed in Poland could join their families in Western Germany. And yet Poland kept the Germans who were useful for its economy or enabled them to join the GDR and with the latter, they screened the "unproductive people" letting them move to the FRG. London and Washington immediately expressed their opposition, denouncing on the one hand the violation of the agreements and on the other the damage done to the people deported and their family. Humanitarian arguments were taken over by the French ambassador in Warsaw adding some weight to France's view on these Anglo Saxon critiques against Poland[14]. These very same critiques had seemed groundless a few years ago for the French diplomats. It would be too hasty to conclude that France's position was only fed by an idealist concern to help the refugees' families of the FRG. The High Commission of the French Republic in Germany compared Warsaw's attitude towards the German repatriates to the harsh recruitment by this capital city of Polish minors in the North of France to cover the German minors of Silesia[15]. This commitment towards the FRG in March 1950 was nurtured by French resentments against Poland due to the competition that had been on since 1946 for labour force.

Conclusion

The reversal in the way French diplomacy regarded the German-Polish border shift from 1940 to 1950 can largely be explained by the Cold War, which was a turning point for Europe. Its impact can be observed at the three levels. In 1945, the French government unofficially backed the Oder-Neisse line, hoping to create an alliance with Poland with the consent of the USSR. A condoned Polish alliance would have granted France reinforced security against Germany and access to coal. In 1950, the French government, absent the communists, who had left it in March

---

14 | AMAE, Nantes, Ambassy in Warsaw, carton n° 20, *Transferts de populations*, note of Jean Baelen ambassador in Poland to Polish foreign ministry, March 9, 1950.

15 | AMAE, Nantes, Ambassy in Warsaw, carton n° 28, *OTC in organisation de l'Allemagne, 1950-1952*, note of François Seydoux, chief of the direction Europe, to French embassy in Warsaw, April 4, 1950.

1947, acknowledged the 1937 German-Polish border after having signed two months earlier a treaty of alliance with the FRG. The USA as an occupying force of West Germany, guaranteed coal and security to France. In 1945, part of the Quai d'Orsay tried to revive the inter-war alliances with Central Europe to encircle Germany and stop the bloc partition in Europe. In 1950, the French Foreign ministry agreed with the FRG to guard against a potential Soviet expansion over the Elbe line. In 1945, diplomats in the recovered territories, referring to issues related to France, described in positive terms the Polish colonization, considering deportation to be but a minor detail. This way of considering the situation lasted until 1950 and represented the Oder-Neisse line as a foil to the plans of Marshall and Schuman.

In spite of that turning point, it must be underscored that the continuity characteristic of French diplomacy and its relationships with Warsaw played a key role in the reversal of its view on the Polish shift. A concurrence on immigration between Paris and Warsaw, and diplomatic relations that were actually more complex than implied by their mutual declarations of friendship, worsened the Franco-Polish friendship. Moreover, a structural weaknesses in the two countries urged them to call for help from outside Europe. Tensions between the Polish and French governments must be taken into account if one wants to understand the rift between the two countries. Yet both countries treated this new conflict as an accidental break in their historical friendship, and in 1953, after Stalin's death, they took the initiative to resume contact (Jarosz/Pasztor 2005). Finally, the reversal of French opinion on Poland's border from 1940 to 1950 can also be explained by the evolution of the concept of border within French diplomacy. In 1945, borders were used as a diplomatic tool to create new German boundaries in order to check German power. A parallel between the rivers Rhine and Oder was drawn, for instance. But by 1950, from the viewpoint of Paris, the contestation of the borders had become an obstacle to the constitution of a strong and peaceful Europe, and France had begun opening up its own borders, notably with Germany. Yet French diplomats in Poland still insisted that Poland was tightening its borders with its neighbors and with Western Europe as well as strengthening the military and police takeover of the western voivodeships. This stands in stark contrast to the opening up of France's borders within Western Europe that was then underway.

Over the long term, France was to abandon its negative view of the Oder-Neisse line and insisted that the FRG recognize it as Germany's eastern border. In March 1959, de Gaulle, who was recently back in power, required the recognition of the Oder-Neisse line by the FRG as the prerequisite for any future German reunification. Thirty years later, François Mitterrand obtained from the FRG the definite recognition of the Potsdam line as one of the preconditions for receiving French support for German reunification. France was aware of the perils linked to territorial resentment between Poland and Germany and thus worked to normalize east-west relations and to put an end to the Oder-Neisse disagreement.

Translated from French by Charlotte Faucher

References

Bariéty, Jacques (2008): "La délégation diplomatique et la mission militaire de la France libre en Union soviétique, juin 1941-décembre 1944", in: Georges-Henri Soutou/Emilia Robin Hivert (eds.), L'URSS et l'Europe de 1941 à 1957, Paris: PUPS, pp. 185-214.

Borodziej, Włodzimierz/Lemberg, Hans (2004): Die Deutschen östlich von Oder und Neisse, 1945-1950, Marburg: Herder-Institut.

Bossuat, Gérard (1997): L'Europe des Français, Paris: Publications de la Sorbonne.

Defrance, Corinne/Pfeil, Ulrich (2012): Entre Guerre Froide et intégration européenne: reconstruction et rapprochement, 1945-1963, Villeneuve-d'Ascq: Presses universitaires du Septentrion.

Frank, Matthew (2007): Expelling the Germans: British opinion and post-1945 population transfer in context, Oxford: Oxford UP.

Jarosz, Dariusz/Pasztor, Maria (2005): Conflits brûlants de la Guerre Froide, les relations franco-polonaises de 1945 à 1954, Lavauzelle: Panazol.

Laforêt, Christophe (1999): "Arrière-pensées et illusions: les tentatives de renouvellement de l'alliance franco-polonaise, 1945-1947", in: Revue des études slaves 71 (2), pp. 263-278.

Laurent, Suzanne (1974/75): Les relations franco-polonaises concernant les nouvelles frontières de la Pologne de 1943 à 1948, à travers la presse et les documents français, MA-Paper, Paris: Université Paris I.

Marès, Antoine (1982): "La France libre et l'Europe centrale et orientale (1940-1944)", in: Revue des études slaves 54 (3), pp. 306-336.

Soutou, Georges-Henri (1993): "Georges Bidault et la construction européenne, 1944-1954", in: Serge Berstein/Jean-Marie Mayeur/Pierre Milza (eds.), Le MRP et la construction européenne, Paris: Complexe, pp. 197-230.

Soutou, Georges-Henri (1998): "La France et le problème des réfugiés et expulsés allemands après 1945", in: Guido Müller (ed.), Deutschland und der Westen: Internationale Beziehungen im 20. Jahrhundert, Stuttgart: Steiner, pp. 166-173.

Soutou, Georges-Henri (2007): La guerre de cinquante ans, Les relations Est-Ouest 1943-1990, Paris: Fayard.

Ther, Philipp (2001): "A century of forced migration: the origins and consequences of ethnic cleansing", in: Philipp Ther/Ana Siljak (eds.), Redrawing nations in East-Central Europe, 1944-1948, Lanham, Maeyland: Rowman & Littlefield.

Wandycz, Piotr (1962): France and her Eastern Allies, Minneapolis: University of Minnesota Press.

Cross-Border Interaction in Europe's Neighbourhood

Borders, De Facto Borders and Mobility Policies in Conflict Transformation
The Cases of Abkhazia and South Ossetia

Giulia Prelz Oltramonti

INTRODUCTION

The two separatist conflicts that led to the establishment of de facto independences from Georgia in South Ossetia and Abkhazia in the early 1990s[1] created a status quo regarding territorial boundaries that lasted until the Russo-Georgian conflict of August 2008. However, far from being immutable, the dividing lines between the separatist territories and the rest of Georgia were subject to processes of "hardening and softening," influenced both by state and non-state actors, throughout the stalemates that characterized most of the 1990s and 2000s.

This contribution looks at the influence of regional and local actors on the evolution of external and internal boundaries, borders, and de facto borders of Abkhazia and South Ossetia between the ceasefire agreements of the early 1990s and the Russo-Georgian war of 2008. Although a range of variables can affect the transformation of boundaries and borders concurrently, the main focus of the following analysis is on mobility policies – policies aimed at enhancing or reduce the movement of goods and people. As argued below, these have proven to be a key factor framing the social and economic boundaries and borders in the case of Georgia and its separatist territories.

The analysis begins by distinguishing between borders, ceasefire lines, and de facto borders in order to clarify the specific nature of the dividing

---

[1] | For an overview of de facto states in the former Soviet Union, see Lynch (2004).

lines that separate Abkhazia and South Ossetia from the rest of Georgia. It then provides a review of mobility policies in conflict situations, which are traditionally confined to trade sanctions and trade incentives. Analytically, there is a need to expand upon a narrow approach to mobility policies to include both formal and informal policies promoted by state and non-state actors. A wider understanding of mobility policies is therefore proposed before approaching the empirical cases.

Borders, Ceasefire Lines, and De Facto Borders

Although the words "boundary" and "border" are terms used in everyday language, clarity requires some brief defining remarks. If boundaries are the dividing lines at which something changes, separating areas of certain rules of behavior (Migdal 2004), borders can be defined as "fixed, legal, geopolitical entities" (Goodhand 2008). In cases of conflict, borders' very permanence and legality may be tested, for example by a change in the interpretation of international law, by differences in the way key parties interpret the law, by a change in international law itself, or in the constellation of geopolitical factors. As expressed by Jackson, "[borders] are not a permanence but merely a staged claim to permanence" (Jackson 2008: 269). Moreover, the permanence and the legality of borders may fail to coincide.

Not all the boundaries containing Abkhazia and South Ossetia fall under the category of "border." While the lines dividing the Russian Federation from Abkhazia and South Ossetia were, during the timeframe under scrutiny, internationally recognized borders between Georgia and the Russian Federation, the status of the lines separating these two de facto states and Georgia is less clear. The ceasefire lines of Abkhazia and South Ossetia remained fixed dividing lines, patrolled respectively by a Commonwealth of Independent States (CIS) peacekeeping force stationed under the observation of a small United Nations Military Observer Mission since 1993, and a peacekeeping force of Ossetians, Russians, and Georgians, monitored by a mission of the Organisation for Security and Cooperation in Europe, since 1992.

However, the term "ceasefire line" does not capture the multifaceted dynamics that shape relations between two neighbors in any areas other than security and the cessation of hostilities. Ceasefire agreements usually lead either to peace accords or to the resumption of conflict. In some cases, however, ceasefire agreements linger on as the status quo for prolonged periods of time. Ceasefire lines can therefore evolve into demilitarized and highly securitized zones, such as in the cases of Korea and Nagarno-Karabakh, or into semi-permeable boundaries with low levels of violence, such as in the case of Transdniestria. During prolonged stalemates, ceasefire lines take on the traits of borders, with the exception of legal recognition under international law. Parallel to the denomination of Abkhazia and South Ossetia as "de facto states", we will thus refer to their borders as "de facto borders."

THE POLITICAL ECONOMIES OF BORDERS AND BORDERLANDS

Boundaries can be hardened or softened to suit various interests, a process defined as "boundary activation" (Tilly 2003). Borders can undergo similar processes. Inquiries into what happens when a border is activated, especially on the impact of the porosity of borders on stakeholders of border systems, centered initially on anthropological issues of identity (Donnan/Wilson 1999; Flynn 1997; Long/Villarreal 1999). However, a better understanding of political-economic agendas in civil wars (Berdal/Malone 2000) has led scholars to pay greater attention to war economies in their regional contexts (Pugh/Cooper 2004), including also the transitional locations between state and region and, accordingly, borders and surrounding borderlands (Goodhand 2008).

Conventional liberal wisdom is that when boundaries harden, opportunities are lost. However, studies have shown that reality is multifaceted, with winners and losers arising from border activation. Jackson points out that borderlands in fact generally create "energies and opportunities arising from the contrasts and discontinuities that they both create and then police" (Jackson 2008: 266).

In order to understand the mechanisms behind such processes, we should first elucidate the role of borders in political economies. Borders are first and foremost "sites and symbols of power" (Donnan/Wilson 1999: 1) As such, borders are key locations where the state asserts its authority by erecting border and customs posts and by limiting the flows of people and goods eligible for transit. Because of the costs of transit authorities can impose, an incentive to cross the border is created: the service of moving goods (and people) across the regulated boundary can bring profits. As Donnan and Wilson assert, "[the] existence [of borders] as barriers to movement can simultaneously create reasons to cross them" (Donnan/Wilson 1999: 87). To illustrate, let us point out that for the residents of the borderlands commerce across dividing lines often represents one of the few ways to make a living. For the private sector, borders represent a hurdle (in terms of logistics and finances) but also an opportunity to increase profits from additional services. For administrations and law enforcement agencies, borders are the line along which taxation can be extracted, whether officially through duties or unofficially through bribes. Stakeholders of border systems are therefore numerous and diverse.

Mobility across borders is a priced asset that influences the livelihoods and the economies of the regions surrounding them. Hence, elucidating what sort of influence various stakeholders have in determining the porosity and permeability of conflict borders leads to a new understanding of the dynamics that underpin conflicts in borderlands.

Mobility Policies in Conflict Settings

Because borders are never static, mobility policies affect the evolution of borders and boundaries (Newman/Paasi 1998). States and non-state actors can harden or soften borders according to their particular interests and can draw on a multiplicity of methods for doing so. Within this framework, mobility policies should be examined carefully in cases of conflict because of the unusual nature of the political economy of borderlands.

For cases of conflict, mobility policies traditionally have been analyzed in terms of formal arrangements that regulate the flow of goods. The two most scrutinized options are trade sanctions and trade incentives of various kinds.[2] A combination of the two can also be implemented, a method that has been hailed as the most effective (Amini 1997). Since the early 1990s, support for all-encompassing economic sanctions weakened because they were generally deemed ineffective in bringing about major changes in policy (Hufbauer et al. 1990: 94). Their negative impact on civilian livelihoods and their fostering of criminal behavior were also put forward as reasons for discontinuing or avoiding embargos (Ballen-

---

2 | For an analysis of power relations in sanctions see Baldwin (1971).

tine 2003: 279). While it is extremely difficult to quantify the results of sanctions, their effectiveness depends "on what goals they are measured against" (Dowty 1994: 192). Relevant goals have been classified into three main categories: behavioral change, containment, and regime change (O'Sullivan 2003).

In some cases, all-encompassing sanctions proved not only ineffective, but also counterproductive, generating a "rally 'round the flag" effect (Cortright 2007b: 392). In the Abkhaz case, they reinforced a siege mentality (Matveeva 2002: 419); the impact of trade restrictions on South Ossetia in 2004, discussed below, is similar in this sense. On the other hand, however, sanctions can at times support the creation of internal opposition, as has happened in the case of Transdniestria in 2006. Different reactions to commercial restrictions depend on the varying nature, implementation, and framework of changes in customs regulation.

A general preference for incentives versus negative sanctions has increased in the last decade (Newham 2000: 8). In both cases, however, the effectiveness of inducement strategies depends on the sender's objectives, the nature of the recipient regime, the political dynamics between sender and recipient and, crucially, the presence or absence of exogenous incentives (Cortright 1997a: 272-290; Rock 2000). Two more factors affect the effectiveness of both sanctions and incentives. First, receivers may perceive economic pressure differently than intended by senders. Secondly, the ability of countries to implement sanctions and incentives varies, as does their ability to monitor financial and commercial flows regionally. These factors partly depend on the state capacity of senders; the role of the neighboring countries and of regional powers is also crucial in the implementation of national strategies for dealing with separatist entities. However, the failure to implement sanctions consistently alters their effectiveness while undermining the legitimacy of the sender (Pugh/Cooper 2004: 227).

The sanctions/incentives approach, however, reflects the actions of a very limited pool of actors, namely governments and international bodies, and fails to take into consideration the micro-dimension of boundary dynamics. The need arises then to expand our understanding of mobility policies in order to encompass the large variety of actors, both formal and informal, and methods that affect the de facto borders under scrutiny. In the framework of this contribution, mobility policies are thus understood to include formal policies aimed at allowing or limiting the movement of people and goods, planning of infrastructure that facilitates or hampers the movement of people and goods, and commercial policies between de facto states and other regional actors. They also involve unofficial policies, such as facilitating or impeding unsanctioned trade, influencing peacekeeping operations, and promoting or reining in non-state violence in the borderlands.

This approach expands the understanding of the scope of mobility policies, which traditionally included only sanctions and incentives, to a wider concurrence of factors behind the hardening and softening of borders. An analysis of such mobility policies shows clearly which actors sought to harden and which actors sought to soften borders and boundaries, asking also why and how.

Georgia's and Russia's Mobility Policies: Implementing and Undermining Sanctions and Incentives

The two actors that had a decisive impact on the borders, whether de facto or de jure, of Abkhazia and South Ossetia are Georgia and the Russian Federation, being the only two countries that share a border with the de facto states. South Ossetia is in fact landlocked by its two larger neighbors, while Abkhazia has an extensive coastline along the Black Sea.

Georgia lost control over most of the territory of the two separatist regions after the 1991-1992 conflict with South Ossetia and the 1992-1994 conflict with Abkhazia. Although ceasefire agreements held, with some resumption of violence, until 2008, no peace agreement was reached. Georgia never recognized the independence of the de facto states; its stated goal remains to reintegrate the two regions within the Georgian state, following the principles of territorial integrity and national sovereignty. The Georgian authorities decisively rejected the status quo and attempted to craft their mobility policies accordingly. In the case of Russia, however, the implementation of mobility policies with regard to Abkhazia and South Ossetia must be seen in the context of its policy regarding its neighbor countries and, more generally, of its foreign policy. While there is no straightforward interpretation of Russia's policy towards its closest neighbors or the South Caucasus, especially in the 1990s, the key factor underlying it was the attempt to maintain a strong influence over bordering countries and to secure its own borderlands.[3]

In the case of Abkhazia, the CIS-imposed embargo banned official contacts for all CIS members, restricted economic co-operation, and prohibited trade of most goods without licenses from the Georgian central government with the exception of food and medical supplies (Soviet Bezopasnosti SNG 1996: 377ff.). Notwithstanding the trade restrictions, Georgia and Russia remained the two main trading partners of Abkhazia. Adding barriers and burdensome bureaucratic procedures to any movement of goods, the restrictions contributed to the creation of a grey economy (Closson 2007: 168; Chkhartishvili et al. 2004: 134). Although officially upheld by all parties, they were increasingly ignored since the late 1990s. Obstacles to crossing are circumvented by illegal trading along the Inguri and Psou Rivers and through the Abkhaz seaports, as well as by bribing low-wage state officials at checkpoints on the ceasefire line (Closson 2007: 168).

Commercial dynamics along the Psou River, marking the de jure border between Russia and Georgia, and the de facto border between Russia and Abkhazia, largely reflected political shifts in the relationship between Russia and Georgia. In 1999, the Russian President Vladimir Putin abrogated by decree the Russian commitment to uphold the embargo, canceling most restrictions on crossing the Psou River. While repeatedly claiming to uphold the blockade, Putin expressed in 2004 the belief that this commitment did not include curtailment of commercial activities or private investments.

On the Abkhaz-Georgian ceasefire line, on the contrary, the embargo was always officially upheld, and repeated efforts were made to curtail smuggling (Kukhianidze et al. 2004: 55). However, under the presidency of Eduard Shevardnadze, pervasive corruption at all levels of the security forces and state institutions made the ceasefire line highly permeable to smugglers (Closson 2007: 170). Commodities smuggled through the ceasefire line included petroleum products, scrap metal, stolen cars, and timber. These goods entered the Georgian market or were re-exported through the ports of Batumi and Poti (Kukhianidze et al. 2004: 15; Kukhianidze et al. 2007: 77).

---

3 | For an analysis of Russia's foreign policy and Russia's policies in the Caucasus, see Lynch (2005), Baev (1997).

In 2004, the Georgian government attempted to limit the various actors who participated in trade across the ceasefire line and to limit the overall volume of trade. These policies were born out of the necessity to augment the Georgian budget and the belief that Abkhazia could be forced to negotiate if its sources of revenue dried up. The Georgian president Mikhail Saakashvili insisted on the implementation of trade sanctions with other regional governments, repressed paramilitary groups and corrupted bureaucrats involved in smuggling, and attempted to reduce sea-borne trade (Lynch 2006: 41; Sepashvili 2004c). Nevertheless, smuggling increased slightly as a consequence of the shift of trading routes after the closure of the Ergneti market in South Ossetia (Kupatadze 2005: 70). In 2008, Tbilisi made the first attempts at initiating a dialogue on some forms of economic cooperation, such as a customs-free zone and investments; the conflict in August choked off these initial belated steps.[4]

On the South Ossetian front, the movement of people and goods was practically unrestricted until December of 2003, when the newly elected Georgian leadership started anti-smuggling operations along the ceasefire line and then proceeded to close the Ergneti market in May and June 2004. A de facto economic blockade was imposed, as forces of the interior ministry controlled access roads and villages in the southern part of the region, and some roads used for contraband were destroyed.[5] The logic behind this move was the belief that that the de facto regime would collapse if deprived of revenue (Khutsidze 2004). It is noteworthy that the anti-smuggling operation entailed an increased presence of Georgian security forces, which in turn was perceived as a build-up for military aggression (ICG 2004: 11f.). At the same time, the Georgian government repeatedly declared that it would differentiate between the regime and the civilian population, offering a range of incentives (Lynch 2006: 42; Sepashvili 2004a, 2004b). However, armed conflict flared up again in August 2004, when the Georgian military and police retreated, sustaining seventeen casualties.

Tbilisi's policy backfired as it antagonized both the South Ossetian elite and large segments of the South Ossetian population. Expectedly,

---

4 | Interview with Gia Jandieri, a founder and the vice-president of the New Economic School of Georgia, July 2008.
5 | 'Governor Blows up By-Roads to Prevent Smuggling', Civil Georgia, 23 December 2003.

the regime denounced Tbilisi's humanitarian initiatives as "a destabilization attempt" and suspended relations with Tbilisi.[6] The civilian population did not respond positively and did not contribute to destabilizing the regime of the de facto president, Eduard Kokoity. On the contrary, the blockade had a boomerang effect, strengthening Kokoity's popularity (ICG 2004: 13) and significantly reducing the possibility of employment in trade and the accessibility of Tbilisi's markets for small producers (Freese 2004). Incentives were in poor relation to needs. The restoration of the railway to Tsinkhvali and the support to farmers through the provision of fertilizers could have proven effective in the long-term; more immediate actions, such as a medical mission that distributed medicines in Tskhinvali, had little reach into the South Ossetian population.[7] Finally, aid was seen with suspicion and, as its delivery was not coordinated with Tskhinvali, the local police barred intended recipients from accepting it.

Trading did not stop outright, but it was considerably curtailed by the closure of the Ergneti market and the enforcement of trade regulations at roadblocks. It was initially diverted to the only legal border crossing between Russia and Georgia, the Zemo Larsi checkpoint (Freese 2004). This new route bypassed South Ossetia, depriving its inhabitants of trade revenues; moreover, the trade of some commodities was abandoned, as it was no longer profitable after the imposition of customs duties. In 2006, this route was also suppressed, as Russia closed the checkpoint indefinitely for maintenance.[8] This not only paralyzed traffic between the two states but severely affected the region as a whole and, in particular, Armenia and North Ossetia.[9] In retaliation, Georgia closed the checkpoint at Ergneti, which had allowed the transit of people between 2004 and 2006.[10] Still a soft border in 2003, the de facto border between Georgia and South Osse-

---

6 | 'Tskhinvali Cuts Links with Tbilisi, Demands Compensation', Civil Georgia, 12 June 2004.

7 | Georgian Healthcare Minister Visits Tskhinvali, Delivers Aid', Civil Georgia, 8 June 2004.

8 | 'Russia Closes Border Checkpoint with Georgia', Civil Georgia, 8 July 2006.

9 | 'Armenia for Reopening of Russo-Georgian Border Checkpoint', Civil Georgia, 11 July 2006; ICG (2004: 25); Alieva (2005).

10 | 'Tbilisi Denies Entry to Passengers Coming via Roki Tunnel', Civil Georgia, 10 July 2006.

tia had hardened considerably by 2006; after the 2008 conflict, that same border became sealed altogether.

A Wider Understanding of Mobility Policies: The Role of Abkhazia, South Ossetia, and Local Stakeholders

From within Abkhazia and South Ossetia, variations in the state of their external de facto borders was linked to aspirations for state-building harbored by the leadership of both de facto states. But it was also linked to opportunities for profit that the leaders of the de facto states and of the neighboring regions crafted through boundary activation. Therefore, the approach to the management of dividing lines greatly differed between Abkhazia and South Ossetia not only because of their history, demographics, geographical situation, and economic viability, but also because of the stakeholders' interests.

In the case of Abkhazia, the destruction caused by the war and the blockade imposed by the CIS in 1996 led to a dramatic decline in social and economic conditions (Closson 2007: 165). Damaged and looted infrastructure, both public and private, remained unreconstructed (UNDP 1998). Both agriculture and tourism, the two main pillars of the pre-war Abkhaz economy, suffered from war destruction, the subsequent isolation of Abkhazia, and underinvestment (Gotsiridze 2002). Railways, which traditionally played the main role in heavy-cargo transportation, fell into despair during the conflict. The role of the state-run Russian Railway Company in rebuilding the railway in 2004 was crucial and, for many, an intentional provocation (Lynch 2006: 49; Sepashvili 2004c). The Abkhaz leadership greatly encouraged the restoration of infrastructure between Abkhazia and the Russian Federation, linking its hopes for economic viability of their de facto state to its northern neighbor.

The restoration of the railway and other forms of infrastructure linking Abkhazia and Georgia was seen as a national security problem (Rimple 2005). Abkhaz authorities neither sealed the de facto border nor did they facilitate transit. While Russian peacekeeping forces patrolled the ceasefire line, Abkhaz authorities left the adjacent borderland, which was traditionally mainly inhabited by ethnic Georgians, to the control of militia. Abkhaz militia turned the Gali region borderland into an opportunity zone, activating the security/insecurity boundary, and creating opportunities for profit making. In the second half of the 1990s and early 2000s, they carried out periodic sweeps through the Gali region, contributing to the movement of internally displaced persons back and forth across the Inguri River (Billingsley 2001).

However, actors other than the Abkhaz militias and authorities benefited from this boundary activation. Along the security zone straddling the Inguri River, stakeholders in large smuggling networks included security services (Russian, Abkhaz, and Georgian), militias (Abkhaz and Georgian), officials (Abkhaz and Georgian), as well as peacekeeping forces, suppliers, and distributors of various nationalities (Closson 2007: 170). In addition, residents of the adjacent areas, often returnees to the Gali region or IDPs from the Gali region living in Sagramelo, carried out small-scale smuggling (Kukhianidze et al. 2004: 6). It allowed them to make a living, given the state of economic despair of the Gali region and the serious problem with landmines in fields previously used for agriculture (Kukhianidze et al. 2007: 84). Also, smuggling allowed residents of Abkhazia to have some access to consumer goods in spite of the embargo.

Along the ceasefire line, the involvement of Georgian security forces and bureaucracy was crucial for smuggling networks until 2004. Low-waged Georgian officials, earning as little as 7 USD per month, demanded bribes to supplement their income (Korsaia et al. 2002). Local departments of law enforcement agencies and influential actors in the Sagramelo region controlled large-scale smuggling, in particular of petroleum products (Closson 2007: 168, 172f.). The Abkhaz Government in Exile, the Georgian Tax Department and MPs from Sagramelo owning petrol stations were identified as having providing support to groups involved in smuggling (Closson 2007: 173f.). Officials within the Ministry of Interior had stakes in drug and weapons smuggling, kidnapping, and extortion;[11] senior officers of anti-drug departments were involved in trade of narcotics (Cornell 2003: 33).

South Ossetia opted for the opposite approach to security/insecurity boundary activation in the borderlands straddling the ceasefire line. Until 2004, the South Ossetian authorities guaranteed secure passage to goods crossing the de facto state line and maintained a policy of permeable de

---

11 | Interview with G. Baramidze, Saakashvili's new Minister of the Interior, reported in K. Stier (2003).

facto borders from within South Ossetia. These did not represent mechanisms of legal trade along the Transcaucasian highway (TransCam) (ICG 2004: 25). Goods usually bypassed Russian customs fees and bureaucratic procedures through customary payments of bribes; at the same time, they were not subjected to Georgian customs, as Tbilisi was unable to establish border posts at the Roki tunnel. The Georgian central government refrained from setting up customs posts along the ceasefire line between Georgia and South Ossetia, being adamant that the ceasefire line should be treated as an internal administrative boundary (Kukhianidze et al. 2007). The circulation of goods between Tskhinvali, the market village of Ergneti, located on the border, and Tbilisi, although unsanctioned, proceeded fluidly, relying on the support of corrupted Georgian officials. Access to and from the Ergneti market was highly profitable, as protection was provided for a price (Closson 2007: 181).

In the early 2000s, the European Commission proposed the establishment of a joint customs regime; as an act of compensation, it would have contributed to the overhaul of the TransCam itself. The South Ossetian government rejected it, on the grounds that it would have curtailed its sovereignty; more realistically, such an agreement would have curtailed the scope of smuggling and future profits (OCHA Georgia 2003: 2).

In fact, the stakeholders' analysis of the South Ossetian stalemate revolves around the TransCam trade and the evolution of trade regimes. A trans-territorial network composed of Russians, South Ossetians and Georgians orchestrated the trade; the stakeholders of this network were members of the elite, bureaucracy, business groups, and consumers (Closson 2007: 180). IDPs, refugees, and residents of the conflict areas conducted mainly small-scale trade. Although control over TransCam smuggling was gradually concentrated into the hands of a few well-connected businessmen and members of the elite, the trade continued to provide a living to residents of South Ossetia and adjacent areas in Georgia. It created jobs and contributed to keeping prices of basic goods low, being as they were virtually duty-free (ICG 2004: 10).

Conclusion and Future Research

The medium- and long-term consequences of the hardening and softening of boundaries in the interwar period were numerous and had economic, social, and political impacts both on the borderlands examined here and on the wider region. Indeed, the resurgence of full-scale violence in South Ossetia in 2004 shows that mobility policies had effects that were not limited to the transit of people and goods. While this aspect deserves a separate study, a few repercussions can already be discerned in terms of the diplomatic relations between the major actors at stake, processes of conflict resolution and confidence building between Georgia and the de facto states, the viability of the de facto states, and the livelihoods of borderland populations. Such analysis, however, should build on an awareness of the long-term dynamics and short-term consequences of the hardening and softening of boundaries during the interwar period.

Russia's mobility policies were consistent with its policy of maintaining a presence in the South Caucasus. The increasing permeability of the international border between the Russian Federation and the two de facto states led to a northward orientation of the two separatist regions in terms of trade and economic reliance. However, Russia's refusal to acknowledge Abkhazia's and South Ossetia's independence until 2008 shows that, instead of an institutional approach, it opted for a more practical and informal strategy in pursuit of its foreign policy goals.

Georgia's mobility policies, on the other hand, were at times in opposition to its overarching goal of the reintegration of Abkhazia and South Ossetia. Its insistence on the implementation of the CIS embargo in Abkhazia and the lack of initiative in establishing commercial and transport links across the de facto border led to a further widening of the cleavage between Abkhazia and the motherland. Its more pragmatic approach in South Ossetia contributed to peaceful relations and reduced animosity until early 2004, when the decision to curtail the commercial flow on the TransCam precipitated conflict. In addition, limitations on the movement of goods and people across the de facto borders (whether explicit or implicitly generated by a lack of legal framework and infrastructure) severely impacted the livelihoods of borderland populations and of the residents of the de facto states, creating a siege mentality and failing to foster respect for Georgian sovereignty. At the same time, as this study showed, a multiplicity of actors were involved, including non-state actors who profited through boundary activation. In the case of Abkhazia, and in South Ossetia before 2004, the maintenance of a de facto border, respectively semi-permeable and permeable, suited the interests of key stakeholders of borderland economies.

A similar variety of actors and interests characterized the drive for boundary activation and deactivation within the de facto states, which in turn affected economic viability and aspirations for state building. Inevitably, local actors reacted to the policies implemented by their larger neighbors, accommodating themselves to Georgian and Russian policies that sustained the process of hardening and softening of the boundaries. They nevertheless contributed to boundary dynamics within the territories under their control, whether by acquiescing to violence as a method for boundary activation in the Gali region, or by regulating trade and increasing security on the TransCam.

A new scenario has emerged for the post-2008 observer. South Ossetia's de facto border is sealed; regional residents, IDPs, and international organizations are prevented from crossing it. Along the line dividing Georgia and Abkhazia, it is business as usual for the most part, with a stronger military presence. It seems that Abkhazia and South Ossetia's mobility policies have taken different trajectories, under strong pressures from their Russian ally. At the same time, Georgia is seeking to soften the de facto borders through its 2010 State Strategy on Occupied Territories. Its proposal, so far, has gone unanswered.

REFERENCES

Alieva, Ramila (2005): Georgia: Smuggling Crackdown Hurts Azeris, IWPR, 17 February.
Amini, G. (1007): A Larger Role for Positive Sanctions in Cases of Compellence? Los Angeles: Center for International Relations Working Paper No. 12, University of California.
Baev, P. (1997): Russia's Policies in the Caucasus, London: Royal Institute of International Affairs.
Baldwin, David A. (1971): "The Power of Positive Sanctions", in: World Politics 24 (1), pp. 19-38.
Ballentine, K. (2003): "Beyond Greed and Grievance: Reconsidering the Economic Dynamics of Armed Conflict", in: K. Ballentine/J. Sherman (Eds), The Political Economy of Armed Conflict: Beyond Greed and Grievance, London: Lynne Rienner.
Berdal, Mats/Malone, David. (2000): Greed and grievance: Economic agendas in civil wars, Boulder, CO: Lynne Rienner.

Billingsley, Dodge (2001): "Security Deteriorates Along the Abkhazia-Georgia Ceasefire Line", in: Jane's Intelligence Review, 6 September.

Chkhartishvili, David/Gotsiridze, Roman/Kitsmarishvili, Bessarion (2004): "Georgia: Conflict Regions and Economies", in: Phil Champlain/Diana Klein/Natalia Mirimanov (eds.), From War Economies to Peace Economies in the South Caucasus, London: International Alert.

Closson, Stacy R. (2007): State Weakness in Perspective: Trans-territorial Energy Networks in Georgia, 1993-2003, Unpublished PhD thesis, London: LSE.

Cornell, Svante E. (2003): "A Growing Threat to Transnational Organised Crime", in: Dov Lynch (Ed.), The South Caucasus: A Challenge for the EU, Chaillot Papers No. 65, Paris: ISS.

Cortright, David (2007a): The Price of Peace: Incentives and International Conflict Prevention, Lanham: Rowman and Littlefield.

Cortright, David (2007b): "The Economic Tools of Peacemaking", in: William Zartman (Ed.), Peacemaking in International Conflict, Methods and Techniques, Washington, DC: US Institute of Peace Press.

Donnan, Hastings/Wilson, Thomas (1999): Borders: Frontiers of identity, nation and state, Oxford: Berg.

Dowty, Alan (1994): "Sanctioning Iraq: The Limits of the New World Order", in: The Washington Quarterly 17 (3), pp. 179-198.

Dzhikaev, Vakhtang/Parastaev, Alan (2004): "Economy and Conflict in South Ossetia", in: Champlain/Klein/Mirimanov (eds.), From War Economies to Peace Economies.

Flynn, Donna K.(1997): "'We are the border': identity, exchange, and the state along the Bénin-Nigeria border" in: American Ethnologist 24 (2), pp. 311-330.

Freese, Theresa (2004): "With All Roads to Tsinkhvali Closed, Zone of Conflict Residents Pray for Saakashvili and for Peace", in: Central Asia-Caucasus Institute Analyst, 30 June.

Goodhand, Jonathan (2008): "War, peace and the places in between: Why borderlands are central", in: Michael Pugh/Neil Cooper/Mandy Turner (eds.), Whose peace? Critical perspectives on the political economy of peacebuilding. London: Palgrave, pp. 225-244.

Gotsiridze, Roman (2002): "The Economic Situation in Blockaded Abkhazia", in: Central Asia and the Caucasus 6 (18), pp. 176-184.

Hufbauer, Gary Clyde/Scott, Jeffrey/Elliott, Kimberly Ann (1990): Economic Sanctions Reconsidered: History and Current Policy, Washington, DC: Institute for International Economics.

ICG (International Crisis Group) (2004): Georgia: Avoiding War in South Ossetia, Europe Report, No.159, Tbilisi and Brussels: ICG.

Jackson, Stephen (2008): "Potential Difference: Internal Borderlands in Africa", in: Pugh/Cooper/Turner (eds.), Whose peace?

Khutsidze, Nino (2004): Ajara Boosts Government's Financial Hopes, Civil Georgia Report, 8 May.

Korsaia, Svetlana/Kuparadze, Mamuka/Mirziashvili, Mikheil (2002): Hoping for Peace, Georgia: NGO Conciliation Resources.

Kukhianidze, Alexandre/Kupatadze, Alexandre/Gotsiridze, Roman (2004): Smuggling through Abkhazia and Tskhinvali Region in Georgia, Tbilisi: TraCCC.

Kukhianidze, Alexandre/Kupatadze, Alexandre/Gotsiridze, Roman (2007): "Smuggling in Abkhazia and the Tskhinvali region in 2003-2004", in: Louise Shelley et al. (eds.), Organized Crime and Corruption in Georgia, London: Routledge.

Kupatadze, Alexander (2005): "The Impact of the Rose Revolution on Smuggling through Abkhazia and South Ossetia", in: Insight Turkey 7 (4).

Lynch, Dov (2004): Engaging Eurasia's separatist states: unresolved conflicts and de facto states, Washington, DC: US Institute of Peace Press.

Lynch, Dov (2005): What Russia Sees, Chaillot Paper No.74, Paris: ISS

Lynch, Dov (2006): Why Georgia Matters, Chaillot Paper No.86, Paris: ISS.

Long, Norman/Villarreal, Magdalena (1999): "Small Product, Big Issues: Value Contestations and Cultural Identities in Cross-border Commodity Networks", in: Birgit Meyer/Peter Geschiere (eds.), Globalization and Identity: Dialectics of flow and closure, Oxford: Blackwell.

Matveeva, Anna (2002): "Georgia: Peace Remains Elusive in Ethnic Patchwork", in: Paul van Tongeren/Hans van de Ween/Juliette Verhoeven (eds.): Searching for Peace in Europe and Eurasia, London: Lynne Rienner.

Migdal, Joel S. (2004): Boundaries and belonging: states and societies in the struggle to shape identities and local practices, Cambridge: Cambridge UP.

Newham, Randall E. (2000): "More Flies with Honey: Positive Economic Linkages in German *Ostpolitik* from Bismark to Kohl", in: International Studies Quarterly 44 (1), pp. 73-96.

Newman, David/Paasi, Anssi (1998): "Fences and Neighbours in the Post Modern World: Boundary Narratives in Political Geography", in: Progress in Human Geography 22 (2), pp. 186-207.

OCHA (Office for the Coordination of Human Affairs) Georgia (2003): South Ossetia Briefing Note, Tbilisi: UN.

O'Sullivan, Meghan L. (2003): Shrewed Sanctions: Statecraft and State Sponsors of Terrorism, Washington, DC: Brookings Institution Press.

Pugh, Michael/Cooper, Neil (2004): War Economies in a Regional Context: Challenges of Transformation, London: Lynne Rienner.

Rimple, Paul (2005): "Abkhazia and Georgia: Ready to Ride on the Peace Train?", in: Eurasianet, 4 August.

Rock, Stephen R. (2000): Appeasement in International Politics, Lexington: University of Kentucky Press.

Sepashvili, Giorgi (2004a): 'Experts Suggest to Focus on Economic Projects in Conflict Resolution', Civil Georgia Report, 13 January.

Sepashvili, Giorgi (2004b): 'Saakashvili Sends Reconciliatory Signs to South Ossetia', Civil Georgia Report, 1 June.

Sepashvili, Giorgi (2004c): 'CIS Summit Reveals Rift in Russian/Georgian Relations', Civil Georgia Report, 17 September.

Soviet Bezopasnosti SNG (1996): "Reshenie Soveta Glav Gosudarstv SNG o Merax po Uregulirovaniyu Konflikta v Abxazii, Gruziya, Dokument No. 258", in: M.A. Volxonski'i/B.A. Zaxarov/N.Yu. Cilaev (eds.), Konfliktyi v Abxazii i Yuzhno'I Osetii, Dokumentyi 1989-2006, Moscow: MGIMO.

Stier, Ken (2003): "Behind a Desk, Georgian Official Promises War on Corruption", in: Eurasianet, 19 December.

Tilly, Charles (2003): The Politics of Collective Violence, Cambridge: Cambridge UP.

UNDP (1998): United Nations Needs Assessment Mission to Abkhazia, UN.

"Good fences make..."
The Separation Fence in Israel and its Influence on Society

Simon Falke

INTRODUCTION

Twenty years after the collapse of the Berlin Wall, the question is still asked in many places whether "good fences make good neighbors." This is a quote from Robert Frost's poem *Mending Wall* (Frost 1914). In a recently published book, the former SED-Generals Heinz Kessler and Fritz Streletz (2011) praise the benefits of the Berlin Wall. Without it, there would have been war, they argue, although the public seems to have made a different judgment. For many, walls and fences belong to a long-obsolete world of conflict between nation-states, and the end of a bipolar world order was seen as the beginning of a so called "borderless world" (Ohmae 1995). But in fact, after the worldwide euphoria over the demolition of the Berlin Wall, border conflicts actually expanded in the globalized 21st century. The future of border conflicts continues to be discussed intensely. In a recent contribution to these debates, Michael Gehler and Andreas Pudlat (2009) put out an edited volume entitled *Borders in Europe,* whose contributors draw a multifaceted picture of the history and social importance of Europe's borders. The European Union is certainly a special case. The Schengen Agreement regulates the free movement of goods and people within the EU, but the boundaries of member states certainly have not lost importance, as shown by intensified border controls in Denmark, Italy, and France last year.

All these developments have stimulated interest in international "border research." In clear contradiction to the "borderless world" prognostication, border conflicts have increased during the last 20 years. New walls and new fences are thus often playing new and important roles in social conflict. This time around, scholars take boundaries to mean not only the lines between nation-states, although these certainly remain significant because of their external effects. Current scholarship from various institutions is based on a much more differentiated concept of borders, as seen in the work of John Agnew, G.H. Blake, David Newman, or Anssi Paasi. The new approach aims "to understand the boundary phenomenon as it takes place within different social and spatial dimensions" (Newman 2003). These authors argue that the construction of new fences and walls has long-term repercussions on both sides of the border they create. Although they often do serve protective functions, at least for a short time, artificial boundaries can become a catalyst for intra-societal conflicts and conflictual constellations. However, the study of long-term interactive effects of borders and the societies they encompass is a large enterprise, and this contribution focuses on more direct effects of fences and walls.

GENERAL ASPECTS OF BORDERS AND THE ISRAELI SITUATION

During the last few years, the erection of walls became an issue of debate in North America along the US-Mexico line and in Greece along its mainland border with Turkey. Saudi Arabia, too, is considering the option of fencing itself off completely from Iraq and Israel. Above all, however, the cordoning off of the West Bank, which for Israel also includes Judea and Samaria, has received great attention and much criticism globally. The Israeli policy marked a temporary climax to the discussion about borders and walls, but even the European Union has had to deal with conflicts over border fences since the accession of Cyprus and the failure of the Annan-Plan to be ratified by referendum in 2004.

The actual significance of physical demarcation for the development of amicable relations with neighboring states and peoples remains unclear. In this context, the conference "Fences, Walls and Borders: State of Insecurity?" held in 2011 in Montreal, raised the question of whether we have entered a new phase of fixed borders after the fall of the Berlin Wall. Contrary to the expectations of many after the end of the Cold War, the 21st century has seen a new boom of security along national borders. The question is whether the return to border fences and walls as a political tool is symptomatic for a new era of international relations. State actors pursue different legal, economic, and demographic strategies when they tighten border security by erecting walls and fences. However, different national motivations for the physical demarcations and the respective geographic circumstances make it difficult to see any overall pattern internationally.

The separation fence[1] in Israel is a prominent example of such a demarcation. It is not an international symbol like the Berlin Wall was. However, it is an important within the Middle East conflict, which regularly sends global shock waves. From the Israeli point of view, the separation fence is a response to the violence that erupted during the course of the Second Intifada. Viewed in isolation from the international context, border issues in Israel and Palestine offer the possibility of examining the meaning of borders for society and society's influence on the geography of the state.

During Benjamin Netanjahu's visit in Washington D.C. in 2011, President Barack Obama tried to contribute new impulses to the discussion of a peace solution in the Middle East. His demand that Israel return to a modified version of its 1967 borders failed to generate popular support in Israel. According to a *Dahaf* survey from the same year, 77 percent of Israelis reject a return to these borders (Hoffmann 2011). Recent clashes between Syrian and Palestinian demonstrators and Israeli soldiers along the border on the Golan have transformed this area, where a cease-fire agreement had held for years, into a combat zone again. The border fence between Israel and Egypt will be completed in 2012. This barrier should prevent illegal immigration of Africans to Israel. The representative of the Knesset Ya'acov Katz recently pointed out that every year about 7000 people immigrate illegally over this border to Israel, commenting that if "infiltrators continue to enter at this rate, there will be 50,000 by the end of 2012, 40,000 in Tel Aviv [...] It pains me that ten percent of Tel Aviv's residents will be infiltrators" (Harkov 2011). Israel seems to have problems on every border. However, the boundaries in the north and south of the country are different from the demarcation of the West Bank on a decisive point: the separation fence along the West Bank is not a national border.

---

1 | Depending on one's point of view, the fence is called different things: separation fence, security barrier, apartheid wall etc. In this contribution, the term "separation fence," which underscores its function of separating societies, is used.

Let us now examine the West Bank as a materialized territorial demarcation and turn the focus inwards onto the residents of the state of Israel. The interactions between boundaries and people's lives can be understood using material indicators, although this is a very complex undertaking. Newman points out that "the linkage between territorial demarcation and the formation of ethnic and/or national identity is a "chicken and egg," mutually enforcing, relationship" (Newman 2004). Israel's very heterogeneous society is certainly a large field for social experimentation. The following discussion thus focuses on the political elite at the time of construction of the separation fence; social reactions are examined using monthly "Peace index"[2] surveys by Ephraim Yaar and Tamar Hermann.

FENCES, WALLS AND THE SETTLEMENTS

In the Middle East, the perception of boundaries plays a central role in conflicts of nation building, territory, and resources. In Israel and Palestine, for both sides the concept of the border "is a vague, elusive and problematic term, after they have lived more than one hundred years without clear boundaries, but lived with constant, mutual attacks" (Grossmann 2003). The drawing of political borders generally fails because of the fact that internationally accepted borders may serve to separate something from something else but they only work if the people they separate recognize them as legitimate (Wokart 1995). The conflict in the Middle East shows that a national border can encourage mutual recognition of national sovereignty. Since the peace agreement with Egypt in 1979 and with Jordan in 1994, the boundaries between Israel and these two Arab neighbors have been set. The borders with Lebanon, Syria, and the Palestinians have yet to be settled, however. The absence of immovable national boundaries is the driving force behind today's political and social discussions in Israel.

Under the administration of Ariel Sharon, Israel began with the construction of the separation fence along the West Bank in June of 2002. According to government sources, it does not signify a political and diplomatic separation from the Palestinians (Landau 2004; Tirza 2006). The fence is ostensibly intended to fulfill only security functions for the citi-

---

2 | Yaar, Ephraim; Hermann, Tamar: Peace Index, available online: www.tau.ac.il/peace/(08.02.2012).

zens of Israel (Rabinowitz 2001). For the former UN ambassador and negotiator in the peace process with the Palestinians, Dore Gold, the fence is a purely military barrier (Gold 2003). Ariel Sharon's government insisted that this arrangement does not reflect a new political border between Israel and Palestine (Tirza 2006). Since its founding, the concept of border is of central importance for Israel, and its boundaries have been subject to constant changes since 1948. The unilateral construction of the separation fence could be seen as defining a new horizon for relations between Israeli and Palestinian societies. It is doubtful that the eastern border, in the form of an impenetrable wall, will ever guarantee security for the state of Israel. As a consequence, a basic question arises. Will the fence function as a border between both societies at all, and if so, how?

One example of the problems associated with the wall as a means of improving security lies in the fact that Israeli settlements were established beyond the Six Day War armistice line of 1949. Their position clearly complicates the regulation of a state border along the West Bank. A large number of settlements are located beyond the bounded territory. The presence of settlers, whose properties expressly belong to the state of Israel, precludes any possible claim that the wall is intended to mark a political border. Eva Horn argues that settlers are not on this or that side of the border. Rather, their political significance derives from the fact that they themselves represent the border (Horn 2004). The settlements therefore mark a different argumentative level in the Israeli-Palestinian border conflict. Characteristically, Eyal Weizman has employed the term "elastic borders" (Weizman 2009). For this reason, a political significance can hardly be ascribed to the separation fence. According to Georg Simmel, a political border should symbolize the consciousness that power and right do not extend to the other side (Simmel 1983). So far, however, settlements in the occupied territories have prevented the creation of a politically binding, mutually recognized border between Israeli and Palestinian society. "At no stage has the state of Israel defined its own borders – optimal, official, secured – or acted to constitute these borders and win international recognition for them" (Zertal 2005). In the Middle East, national borders are judged necessary for the production of identity, peace, and security (Rabinowitz 2001). The lack of such borders, argues Tom Segev (2007), means that the citizens of Israel live in uncertainty and tentativeness, which hinders their search for their own identity.

Impact on Society

Quite concrete demands arise from this approach for the constitution of the Israeli society. The unilateral initiative of Palestinian President Mahmoud Abbas to seek recognition of a Palestinian state made national borders an even more urgent issue on the political agenda. Territorial borders are anything but obsolete. Especially in Israel and Palestine, their importance will increase. The state of Israel is facing a development that will determine its future. The final definition of its state borders forms the central component of the Middle East peace process because borders are not only a place of differentiation and demarcation, but also of transition, convergence, and mixture. As Stephane Hessel (2011) said in an interview with *Die Zeit*, "I can cross the border separating me from my neighbor, but I cannot cross all borders. Still, if there were no borders, we would feel no need to cross them." Through the construction of the separation fence, the isolation of society takes place from inside and outside by defining "Palestinian" as an exclusion criterion. Therefore, the separation fence functions as a social demarcation. This perception is of great importance because the majority supports the idea of separation within the Israeli society. The search for societal limits lies behind the objective of differentiating oneself from the Palestinians, but it could also indicate a process taking place in space within the society. In this way the separation fence might be seen as an element of social cohesion. "Society is characterized by the fact that the space of its existence is enclosed by clearly deliberate borders and internally belongs together" (Simmel 1983). The separation fence could be an expression of the direction society is taking. Indeed, Barry Rubin describes the focus on political security, apparent since the outbreak of the Second Intifada, as a new paradigm for Israeli society (Rubin 2006).

The border-society mindset is related to social motivations for the construction of the separation fence. Boundaries are the result of social relations within a society (Simmel 1983). Or, as Newman puts it, the "existence of lines and territorial compartments in the form of states creates a territorial frame within which the social construction of national identity has an important territorial dimension" (Newman 2004). The constitution of the Jewish population was particularly strongly influenced by the experience and trauma of the years 1939-1945 and 1973, according to Moshe Zimmermann (1996) and Tom Segev (1995). The border situation and threats from the outside have always been a central part of the history of the state of Israel (Primor 2010). "This unique border situation is assumed to influence the individual, his comprehension and conceptualization of reality, and the interrelationship between individual and collective processes" (Shalit 1987). Georg Simmel describes the security function of the border as a framework that has meaning, much like a work of art, for the social group (Simmel 1983). With the help of such a "work of art," the Israeli society has been trying to create a buffer from the world and to enclose itself since the foundation of the state. From this viewpoint, the construction of the separation fence becomes a metaphoric mirror of the society. Approval or disapproval of this fence reveals one's attitude about the social order. Danny Tirza called the separation fence, therefore, a "political seismograph" (Weizman 2009).

Acceptance among the Israeli population of the construction of the separation fence was very high at the outset; surveys by Ephraim Yaar and Tamar Hermann (2003) showed an agreement of 57 percent among Israelis in June, 2002. The majority desired social separation at that time (Primor 2010; Witzthum 2004). Palestinians, too, desired separation (Arian 2002). The demand and search for security, according to Moshe Zimmermann, has moved people to vote for a separation of both populations (Zimmermann 1996). A vast majority of the Israeli population supports the demarcation along the West Bank and is therefore against the idea of soft borders in the Middle East. From this perspective, the separation fence can stimulate the images of danger, self-protection, and defense. As terror and violence spiraled upward, a large majority of public opinion (71 percent) supported Sharon's national unity government and its policies to achieve peace and security in 2003 (Arian 2002). Interesting to note is the increased participation of the "undecided population" during the last elections. The political divisions of right and left have lost their social bases (Primor 2003). Ten years after the beginning of construction, the separation fence is there for all to see along the West Bank. It separates the conflicting parties. And for the first time most Israelis now can clearly visualize where a possible future border would be. Although these boundaries are not necessarily permanent because they also create new realities and affect people's lives (Newman 2004), the social protests in Israel during the past summer can be understood as a consequence of the inner dynamics set in motion by the placement of these artificial boundaries.

Conclusion

The demarcation has become a guiding theme of policies supported by the majority (Elizur 2003).[3] An epochal political transformation is being caused by the construction of the separation fence and in the consolidation of left and right positions on the issue (Baskin 2002; Witzthum 2004). Ariel Sharon succeeded, by constructing the separation fence, in taking up an original idea of the Israeli left and in reconstructing it with his own territorial vision (Lagerquist 2004). Neither Zionist revisionism nor complete separation had been able to prevail within Israeli society, but the realization of a physical and social demarcation has generated a new sense of national unity (Lagerquist 2004). David Grossman argues, significantly, that the Israeli enthusiasm for the construction of the separation fence is more a psychological need than a well-considered diplomatic and military policy (Grossmann 2003). "Israelis and Palestinians will eventually have to sit down together to solve their problems. Since such negotiations are unlikely for the time being, however, a properly constructed fence could serve as an interim measure" (Makovsky 2004). According to this view, the separation fence acts as a preliminary stage for peace negotiations in the Middle East. It can contribute to overcome the emotionality stoked by the demands to a return to the 1967 borders, a line that has become the "default boundary" (Newman 2004) for all political negotiations between Israel and the Palestinian Authority.

Where borders are drawn, power is exercised. In this respect the border discourse is at the same time a national discourse. The separation fence became a mirror of the Israeli society. Do good fences make good neighbors? Within the state of Israel, the separation fence seems to be making the majority adjust to necessary changes. In this context, Robert Frost's famous question could be reversed: Do good fences make good inhabitants? Territory plays a significant role in the way in which their identity is expressed. This perspective should be considered, although border walls and fences are sometimes negatively connoted. The "social protesters" in Israel have yet to express their views on this topic, but at least the European media are reporting on internal political and social

---

3 | According to Peace Index, approval of the politics of the "unilateral dissolution" was at 60 percent of the Israeli population in 2012 (Yaar, Ephraim; Hermann, Tamar: Peace Index, available online: www.tau.ac.il/peace/(08.02.2012).

conflicts in Israel in detail for the first time. This I regard as a positive development. Israeli society defines itself no longer through the distinction to the Palestinians or the "Arab world." They look with increasing scrutiny at their own social groups. Similar to the German border discourse in the 1920s, the West Bank borderland will have to be re-understood as a common cultural space (see Kreienbrock 2010). Geography still serves the art of war in the Middle East, but it can become part of the art of change if there is an overarching counterstrategy. The emotionally charged borders of 1967 urgently need a new accentuation. Israel is situated at the transition from imperial to national borders. The separation fence stands as a symbol for the security needs of Israel. As a security border it has taken on an integral role in everyday life. The separation fence is thereby becoming a cultural institution and serves by discursive practices to break the recurring argument of the "non-defensible borders of 1967" (Gold 2003; Landau 2004; Sharon 2005; Tirza 2006)[4]. A good fence does not make equally good neighbours and inhabitants, but a secure fence along the West Bank can help to give the necessary stability, the stability of a national border, that the Israeli society needs in order to find a way to peace in the Middle East. Even if it means that the settlers in the West Bank who live beyond the fence will be separated and thus become the losers of this intra-societal process.

References

Arian, Asher (2002): Israeli Public Opinion on National Security 2002, in: Jaffee Center for Strategic Studies (Ed.), JCSS Memorandum 60, Tel Aviv: JCSS.

Baskin, Gershon (2002): "Proposals for Walls and Fences, and their Consequences", in: Palestine-Israel Journal 9 (3) (www.pij.org/detailp.php?id=119).

Elizur, Yuval, 2003: "Israel Banks on a Fence", in: Foreign Affairs 82 (2), pp 106-119.

---

4 | See also Benjamin Netanyahu, quoted by Natasha Mozgovaya: "Netanyahu to AIPAC: Israel cannot return to ‚indefensible' 1967 lines", in: Haaretz 24.05.2011.

Fischel, Angela (2008): "Editorial", in: Horst Bredekamp et al. (eds.): Grenzbilder. Bildwelten des Wissens. Kunsthistorisches Jahrbuch für Bildkritik, vol. 6,2, Berlin: Akademie Verlag, pp. 7-8.

Frost, Robert 1917: "Mending Wall", in: Alice Corbin Henderson/Harriet Monroe (eds.): The new poetry, New York: McMillan, p. 110.

Gehler, Michael/Pudlat, Andreas (eds.) (2009): Grenzen in Europa. Historische Europastudien in Erfahrung, Gegenwart und Zukunft, vol. 2, Hildesheim: Olms.

Gold, Dore (2003): "Defensible Borders for Israel", in: Jerusalem Letter, 15.July, Jerusalem Center for Public Affgairs (www.jcpa.org/jl/vp500.htm).

Grossmann, David (2003): Diesen Krieg kann keiner gewinnen. Chronik eines angekündigten Friedens, München: Carl Hanser.

Harkov, Lahav/Katz Yaakov (2011): "10 % of Tel Aviv to be infiltrators in 2012", in: Jerusalem Post, 13. June (www.jpost.com/NationalNews/Article.aspx?id=224807).

Hessel, Stephane (in conversation with Richard David Precht) (2011): "Wir brauchen einen neuen Aufbruch", in: Die Zeit, 1.June, pp. 57-58.

Hoffman, Gil (2011): "Poll: 77 % of Israelis oppose going back to pre-'67 lines", in: Jerusalem Post Online, 9. June (www.jpost.com/DiplomacyAndPolitics/Article.aspx?id=223951).

Jaspers, Karl, 1932: Existenzerhellung, Philosphie, vol. 2., Berlin: Springer.

Jeggle, Utz (1997): "Trennen und Verbinden. Warum ist es am Grunde des Rheins so schön?", in: Utz Jeggle/Freddy Raphael: D'une rive à l'autre – kleiner Grenzverkehr, Paris: Ed. de la Maison des Sciences de l'Homme, pp. 75-91.

Kessler, Heinz/Streletz, Fritz (2011): Ohne die Mauer hätte es Krieg gegeben, Berlin: edition ost.

Kreienbrock, Jörg (2010): "Von Linien, Säumen und Räumen. Konzeptualisierungen der Grenze zwischen Jacob Grimm, Friedrich Ratzel und Carl Schmitt", in: Eva Geulen/Stefan Kraft (eds.): Zeitschrift für deutsche Philologie 129, pp. 33-50.

Lagerquist, Peter (2004): "Fencing the Last Sky: Excavating Palestine after Israel's 'Separation Wall'", in: Journal of Palestine Studies 33 (2), pp. 5-35.

Landau, Uzi (2004): "The Security Fence: An Imperative for Israel", in: Jerusalem Issue Brief 3 (15) (www.jcpa.org/brief/brief3-15.htm).

Makovsky, David (2004): "How to Build a Fence", in: Foreign Affairs 83 (2), pp. 50-64.
Newman, David, 2003: "Boundaries", in: John Agnew/Katharyne, Mitchell/Gerard Toal: A Companion to Political Geography, Oxford: Blackwell, pp. 123-137.
Ohmae, Kenichi (1995): The End of the Nation-State. The Rise of Regional Economies, New York: Simon and Schuster.
Primor, Avi/Korff, Christiane von (2010): An allem sind die Juden und die Radfahrer schuld. Deutsch-jüdische Missverständnisse, München: Piper
Primor, Avi (2003): Terror als Vorwand. Die Sprache der Gewalt, Düsseldorf: Droste.
Rabinowitz, Dan (2001): "Borderline Collective Consciousness", in: Palestine-Israel Journal 8 (4) (www.pij.org/details.php?id=792).
Rubin, Barry (2006): "Israel's New Strategy", in: Foreign Affairs 85 (4), pp. 111-125.
Segev, Tom, (1995): Die siebte Million. Der Holocaust und Israels Politik der Erinnerung, Reinbek: Rowohlt.
Segev, Tom (2007): 1967. Israels zweite Geburt, Bonn: Bundeszentrale für politische Bildung.
Sharon, Ariel, 2005: Prime Minister Ariel Sharon' Speech at the United Nations Assembly, 15. September, New York: UN (www.un.org/webcast/summit2005/statements15/isro50915eng.pdf).
Shalit, Erel (1987): "Within Borders and without. The Interaction between Geopolitical and Personal Boundaries in Israel", in: Political Psychology 8 (3), pp. 365-378.
Simmel, Georg (1983): "Soziologie des Raumes", in: Heinz-Jürgen Dahme/ Otthein Rammstedt (eds.), Georg Simmel. Schriften zur Soziologie, Frankfurt a.M.: Suhrkamp, pp. 221-242.
Tirza, Danny (2006): "The Strategic Logic of Israel's Security Barrier", in: Jerusalem Issue Brief 5 (18) (www.jcpa.org/brief/briefoo5-18.htm).
Weizman, Eyal, 2009: Sperrzonen. Israels Architektur der Besatzung, Hamburg: Edition Nautilus.
Witzthum, David (2004): "Die israelisch-palästinensische Konfrontation und ihre Widerspiegelung in der öffentlichen Meinung Israels", in: Aus Politik und Zeitgeschichte B 20, 10 May, pp. 29-37.
Wokart, Norbert (1995): "Differenzierung im Begriff "Grenze". Zur Vielfalt eines scheinbar einfachen Begriffs", in: Richard Faber/Barbara

Naumann (eds.): Literatur der Grenze – Theorie der Grenze, Würzburg: Königshausen und Neumann.

Zertal, Idith (2005): Israel's Holocaust and the Politics of Nationhood, Cambridge: Cambridge UP.

Zimmermann, Moshe (1996): Wende in Israel, Zwischen Nation und Religion, Berlin: ATB.

Authors

Barbara A. Despiney Zochowska, Dr. habil.
Studied economics in Wrocław and European Studies in Nancy, received her doctor degree in economics at the University of Paris 1 (Pantheon-Sorbonne); works currently as a research fellow at the C.N.R.S. – Centre d'Economie de la Sorbonne.

Sabrina Ellebrecht, M.A.
Graduated with an MA in Social Sciences from the Albert-Ludwigs-University Freiburg and the University of KwaZulu Natal, Durban; currently doctoral student at the Institute of Sociology at Freiburg University.

Simon Falke, M.A.
Studied political science, geography and history at University of Bonn, where he is currently teaching and working on his doctor dissertation.

Jaqueline Flack, M.A.
Graduated in sociology, German and comparative literature at Eberhard Karls University Tübingen; currently research assistant at the International Centre for Ethics in the Sciences and Humanities (IZEW) in Tübingen and doctoral student at European University Viadrina Frankfurt (Oder).

Agata Ładykowska, M.A.
Studied ethnology and cultural anthropology at the University of Warsaw; currently PhD candidate at the Max Planck Institute for Social Anthropology in Halle (Saale) and researcher at the University of Warsaw.

Paweł Ładykowski, Dr.
Studied ethnology and cultural anthropology and received his doctor degree from the University of Warsaw; currently assistant professor at the Institute of Archaeology and Ethnology, Polish Academy of Sciences.

Eloi Piet, M.A.
Doctoral student in history at the University of Paris 1 (Pantheon-Sorbonne).

Giulia Prelz Oltramonti, M.A.
Studied social and political science at University College London and war studies at King's College London; currently PhD candidate in political science and teaching assistant at the Université Libre de Bruxelles.

Roswitha Ruidisch, Dipl.-Geogr.
Studied geography at the Catholic University Eichstätt-Ingolstadt and the University of Bayreuth; currently doctoral student at the Institute of Geography and Regional Studies at Klagenfurt University.

Antje Schönwald, Dr. phil.
Studied European ethnology and cultural studies in Marburg and received her doctor degree in anthropogeography from Saarland University, where she is currently working at the chair for sustainable development.

Bastian Sendhardt, Dipl.-Pol.
Studied political science and philosophy in Erlangen, Bielefeld and Cracow, currently PhD candidate at Bundeswehr University Munich and research assistant at the Warsaw office of the Friedrich Ebert Foundation.

Thomas Serrier, Dr. phil.
Studied German and Polish philology at the Ecole Normale Supérieure and the Institut des Langues O', Paris; received his doctor degree in German philology and historical science from University of Paris VIII –Saint Denis; currently maître de conferences at the Institute for European Studies at UP VIII and visiting professor at European University Viadrina, Frankfurt (Oder).

Angela Siebold, Dr. des.
Studied history and political science and received her PhD from Ruprecht Karls University Heidelberg, where she is currently teaching and working as a researcher at the Chair for Contemporary History and head of the carrier service of the Historical Seminar.

Bianca Szytniewski, M.A.
Studied International Relations at the Uinersity of Utrecht and European Union Studies at the University of Leiden; currently PhD candidate at Radboud University Nijmegen.

Editors

Arnaud Lechevalier, Dr. habil.
Graduated in economics and political sciences, doctor degree and habilitation at the University of Paris 1 (Pantheon-Sorbonne); since 1996 maître de Conferences at UP 1 and since 2007 researcher at Centre Marc Bloch – German-French Social Science Research Center, Berlin; since 2008 visiting professor at European University Viadrina Frankfurt (Oder).

Jan Wielgohs, Dr. phil.
Studied philosophy and social sciences and received his doctor degree from Humboldt University Berlin; researcher at the Institute of Sociology and Social Policy at the Academy of Sciences of the GDR and at the Max Planck Research Unit "Transformation in the New German *Länder*" in Berlin; since 2001 lecturer at European University Viadrina Frankfurt (Oder) and academic coordinator of the Frankfurt Institute for Transformation Studies.

Angela Siebold, Dr. des.
Studied history and political science and received her PhD from Ruprecht Karls University Heidelberg, where she is currently teaching and working as a researcher at the Chair for Contemporary History and head of the carrier service of the Historical Seminar.

Bianca Szytniewski, M.A.
Studied International Relations at the Uinersity of Utrecht and European Union Studies at the University of Leiden; currently PhD candidate at Radboud University Nijmegen.

Editors

Arnaud Lechevalier, Dr. habil.
Graduated in economics and political sciences, doctor degree and habilitation at the University of Paris 1 (Pantheon-Sorbonne); since 1996 maître de Conferences at UP 1 and since 2007 researcher at Centre Marc Bloch – German-French Social Science Research Center, Berlin; since 2008 visiting professor at European University Viadrina Frankfurt (Oder).

Jan Wielgohs, Dr. phil.
Studied philosophy and social sciences and received his doctor degree from Humboldt University Berlin; researcher at the Institute of Sociology and Social Policy at the Academy of Sciences of the GDR and at the Max Planck Research Unit "Transformation in the New German *Länder*" in Berlin; since 2001 lecturer at European University Viadrina Frankfurt (Oder) and academic coordinator of the Frankfurt Institute for Transformation Studies.